I Saw the Light...
But HE Saw Me First

A Story of Faith, Hope and Love

Victims Survive – Victors Thrive

Peg Yarbrough Rhone

Copyright © 2017 Peg Yarbrough Rhone

All rights reserved. No part of this publication may be reproduced, in whole or in part, stored into a retrieval system, or transmitted in any form, or by any means (electronic, mechanical, photocopying, or otherwise), without prior written permission by the copyright owner and publisher of this book.

The experiences of the author are true throughout this book, however some identifying details such as names have been changed to protect the privacy of others.

ISBN 978-1-54-327437-0

DEDICATION

I dedicate this book to my heavenly Father,

and His son, Jesus Christ.

To my hubby, Chris, my partner in love and in life.

And to the other Chris, Chris Johnson Steele (Chris J),

who showed me the Light

EPIGRAPH

I wandered so aimless, life filled with sin

I wouldn't let my dear savior in,

Then Jesus came like a stranger in the night

Praise the Lord I saw the light

—*"I Saw the Light" Hank Williams*

It is possible to live through hell, and get better, not bitter

Contents

Preface: *Would You Believe…*   vii

Part I: Descent Into Madness

1. Fasten Your Seat Belt Kids, It's Gonna' Be a Bumpy Ride!   1
2. Safety   15
3. From Demons to Drink   24
4. Tilt-A Whirl   30
5. You Can Run, But You Can't Hide   41
6. I Want Answers!   51
7. A Bridge Too Far   55
8. High Anxiety and Low Expectations   65
9. The Agony of Defeat   77
10. There's Ghouls in Them Thar' Hills!   89
11. On a Warm San Francisco Night   96

Part II: The Restoration

12. Running On Empty   105
13. And Then it Happened!   118
14. From Victim to Victor   133
15. Love Will Find A Way   146
16. The Triumph and the Tragedy   164
17. Life, the Final Frontier!   171
18. Clear Shining After Rain   176
19. God Things Happen to Those Who Wait   190
20. Jesus IS Just Alright With Me   221
21. God and Greta Garbo   245
22. He Restoreth My Soul   265
23. Reach Out in the Darkness and You May Find a Friend   308

CONTENTS

24. A *Living* Sacrifice Can Burn With *Life*!	323
25. Don't Quit!	338
26. I Saw the Light… But He Saw Me First	347
Epilogue: I Will Fear No Evil!	371

Appendix

1 – Angels and Demons	383
2 – Inner Healing	403
3 – How to Get Help	413
Additional Resources	414
Acknowledgements	415

PREFACE

Would You Believe...

I wrote this book to give hope to the walking wounded.

These pages are my true story of heartbreak and hope, fear and faith, and victim to victor. This is my story of walking out of bondage and into the light of God's deliverance.

In today's world where 'bad' means good, and selfishness abounds, I recall a simpler time when our houses were never locked, neighbors knew each other by name and we helped one another out, just because we could.

But even in those halcyon days of the fabulous fifties, darkness slithered in and out of my life like a cold black snake and for many years I did not understand where the evil was coming from—but now I do. Back then I did not know that no matter how good things might appear on the surface, evil never sleeps.

I would have remained a prisoner of my own broken past but for the mercy of the living God, and His Son, Jesus. I am an unashamed follower of Christ, he is my hero. He pulled me up from the cesspool of life, washed me clean, and set my feet on solid ground.

Some of the things you read in this book will seem fantastical, bizarre, miraculous, or beyond belief; and yet they ALL actually happened to me. And something deep inside my heart tells me that there are going to be a lot of you who will read these pages and say, "Oh, my goodness. Something like that happened to me, too, but I thought I was crazy!"

Preface

Or, perhaps you have never told anyone else about your own experiences for fear of being ridiculed. You are the one for whom I am writing this book. Those of you who feel that no one has ever really *heard* your story; or think no one would believe it if you told it.

A lot of things that happen in this life are inexplicable; they are 'out of the box.' And, for those of you who cannot believe my story, that's okay, this book is simply not for you.

In the following pages I will share with you my own experience, strength, and hope. Although I must say, I feel like Lady Godiva, parading my nakedness down the street for all to see. After all, this is *my* life we're talking about here, warts and all; and I must admit that it does take a modicum of courage to put one's self out there for public consumption.

I would describe writing this book as skydiving for the soul; it feels both scary and hopeful at the same time. Scary to put my life out there for all to see, but hopeful that people will read this book and see that they too, can be set free from a painful past, and self-destructive thoughts and emotions that have plagued them their whole lives.

One thing I have learned in my sixty-some years here on this earth is that truth is stranger than fiction. There is more to life than what we can know with our five senses. Even for the layman, there are too many unexplained things that happen *not* to believe that there is another realm, an invisible realm, a spirit realm, which causes things to happen for which there are no logical explanations. Spiritually, there is the Kingdom of God, and the kingdom of darkness, and they both affect our lives. God's

Preface

Kingdom issues peace, love and healing, but the latter foments chaos, misery, and death. Those are the realms we will be delving into.

Be forewarned, the first half of the book is my descent into the darkness, but hang in there because the darker the night, the brighter the light. My goal is to showcase the depth of deliverance that took place in my own life in the hope that it will inspire others to reach out for help. If I can make it, you can too. There is a loving God, just waiting to give you a leg up.

I have not written this book to convince anyone of my particular belief system, but if reading my story brings some clarity to your own heart and life, then I have done my job.

If this book helps even one fellow traveler find hope, and some measure of peace, then that will be the greatest satisfaction I could derive from it.

Let the healing begin!

Part I

Descent Into Madness

*Guard your heart with all diligence;
for out of it are the issues of life.*

Proverbs 4:23

Chapter 1

Fasten Your Seat Belt Kids, It's Gonna' Be a Bumpy Ride!

Guard your heart with all diligence; for out of it are the issues of life.
Proverbs 4:23

There I was, in our big old chicken house with the dirt floor, it was almost empty, save myself, my mom, and the intruder. He was salivating and wielding a machete. He wasn't after me, he was chasing my mom, and I felt totally helpless to save her. Soon, he was right on top of her, chopping both legs off above the knees! She is running on bloody stumps towards me with her arms outstretched crying for me to help her, and we are both trying to get away from the madman... and then I wake up, covered in sweat.

Why did I have such a horrific recurring nightmare as a child? Because by age five or six I was already messed up. My heart, my psyche was on overload, and it would take me a long time to get better.

The gospel of Luke says that God sent His Son "to seek and to save that which was lost." That was me, little girl lost.

This is a story of lost and found. This is my story of overcoming life's misery through Christ.

Life is hard. People who say it is *not* are simply lying to you. I was an all-American honor student who was an alcoholic by the age of fourteen. That's not something I am proud of, I'm just reporting facts.

In my case, the trick was to stay alive long enough to figure out that as bad as life could get, things *could* get better if I just hung in there. And for me, they have. My challenge is the same as yours: when times are darkest, do not give up hope!

Like every baby, I came into this world as a beautiful package of pure innocence; relinquishing the safety of my mother's womb for a shocking and hostile environment called Life. And like every child that is born into this world, from the most primitive village in the bush, to the ritziest palace on earth, the cry of my heart was universal, "LOVE ME! Care about me. Keep me safe."

Then... reality hits. Life is hard, challenging, and sometimes brutal. Life is a contact sport!

The great healer Louise Hay said, "If your mother did not know how to love herself, or your father did not know how to love himself, then it would be impossible for them to teach you to love yourself. They were doing the best they could with what they had been taught as children." One can only give what one has.

I believe that my parents raised me the best they could, but they had their own heartache and emotional damage they were acting out. That's why, in even the most well-meaning families, things can happen that communicate to our baby brains, "You are *not* the center of the universe." "*Your* needs are *not* all that important." And given enough negative stimuli we begin to embrace the belief, **"I don't really matter!"**

This brings us to the whole nature versus nurture debate, and I fall more heavily on the side of nurture. I believe that how we were treated by others as children is the biggest component in shaping our self-esteem. Nature, and our DNA, certainly plays a huge part in developing the innate talents and abilities we have inherited genetically, but how we were treated by the people around us has an even greater impact on molding us into the kind of person we will become as an adult, and the attitudes about life and self that we develop. The image that we carry of ourselves, deep down in our hearts, will affect how we deal with everything that happens to us for the rest of our lives.

We all want to be happy, accepted, healthy and productive, but let's face it, that's a tall order.

The Bible says to "Guard your heart with all diligence, for out of it issues life." The problem is, when you're a toddler, you don't know how to guard your heart yet, you are relying on the adults who care for you to do that. And this becomes a problem if you aren't surrounded by adults who *want* to protect your heart; some might even want to harm you; hurting your heart instead of guarding it, thereby devaluing your self-image, starting in childhood.

From a psychological standpoint, I understand that the human personality is basically formed by the time we reach five or six. By then we have passed the 'age of plasticity,' and deep inner change is harder to come by (but not impossible). Therefore many events that I was too young to fully recall also molded my self-image, my self-esteem, and my own inability to see myself as both worthy and important.

Fasten Your Seat Belt Kids, It's Gonna' Be a Bumpy Ride!

If you think you missed out on this kind of negative reinforcement while growing up, you might want to rethink that assessment. None of us do. I'd have say if you don't think so; you are in deep denial, because none of us comes through childhood unscathed. If the damage wasn't from your parents, then it was by some other authority figure, or even a really nasty 'friend.'

I think every birth certificate should come with a "WARNING" label that reads: "Fasten Your Seat Belt Kids, It's Gonna' Be a Bumpy Ride!" And some rides are bumpier than others.

The true story of everybody's childhood is, "Oops. This is going to leave a mark!" The only variations are in how big and how deep your marks are.

So much of our identity as adults is based on the 'naming and shaming' put upon us when we were children. But, thank God, we can overcome that with the Lord's help.

Every child begins to shape his or her identity by the events and people around them. Was your childhood dominated with approbations and "atta' boys," or was it mainly criticism, and barrages on your self-worth? We all have some of both while growing up, but many of us get hammered more on the negative end of things than the positive.

With that said, I can't think of anything more degrading than impressing upon a child that they must endure the pain and humiliation of sexual molestation for some grown-up's sick gratification. That's a heavy, heavy bruise to the soul. And that's what happened to me.

Fasten Your Seat Belt Kids, It's Gonna' Be a Bumpy Ride!

But, hey, I didn't know at five or six years old how screwed up my life was, I had no point of comparison. It would be many years later when I began to see the light, and start the healing process of my own broken self-image, that the pieces began to fit together. So let's begin at the beginning.

I was born in the small town of Rome, Georgia, named for the Eternal City in Italy, because our Rome was also surrounded by seven hills. In front of our City Auditorium was a huge statue of a she-wolf, and crouched underneath her, faces upturned, trying to feed off her teats, were two human toddlers, desperate for nourishment. They were Romulus and Remus, the mythical founders of ancient Rome. As a child, that statue always scared the dickens out of me. It must have hit a raw nerve.

Was that statue a metaphor for my own childhood? Raised by wolves? Trying to survive my freaky youth? Trying to find nourishment for my soul?

Unlike Rome in Italy, Rome, Georgia is a rather slow-paced picturesque town, a gossipy place, nestled in the foothills of the Blue Ridge Mountains. But the bucolic setting was no indication for the insidious deeds which were taking place in my childhood home.

I was called Peggy, which is short for Margaret Anne, a good Catholic name. I came clambering into this world with all the same wishes and dreams as every other child: feed me, protect me, and show me I matter; preferably to human beings, and not just to a she-wolf.

"Little Peggy" came from good Irish Catholic stock (with some fanatically neat German, and a little Cherokee Indian thrown in for good measure). Our family dutifully went to church every Sunday, like all good Catholics should. To all appearances, we lived a "Leave It to Beaver" lifestyle at home, at least that's how it looked on the surface; nice home, good looking well-respected parents, a mama who dressed all her four kids to match. What could go wrong with this picture? Our family looked like 1950's heaven.

But, what was happening inside might have caused a parish priest to blush.

I believe that Mama and Daddy did their best to raise us right, but I was still totally damaged goods by the time I was six or seven. By then I was already a nervous wreck.

You see, my grandfather, Noah, whom we called Pa, was a pedophile. A tall, thin man, he was known for being an impeccable dresser. He always wore crisp, white, starched shirts, a gorgeous necktie with a gold tie clasp, beautifully pressed gabardine slacks, spotless shoes, and his solid gold Mason ring with the diamond in it. German to the core in his outward cleanliness, that was just a veneer for all the evil he had brewing on the inside. Pa came from generations of well to do farmers. When he moved his family to Cedartown, GA, in the 1920's he owned several stores on main street. He stood over six feet tall, ramrod straight, with glacier blue eyes that made one think, "Don't mess with me, or you'll regret it!" Perhaps he could have been a handsome man if not for the cruel set of his eyes and mouth.

Pa, and my Granny, Etta, (whom I loved with all my heart), moved in with us after he lost his fortune, when I was about three, and my life was never the same.

The molestation started on East Eleventh Street. When I think back on that kitchen with its faded yellow walls, I still get queasy. There was a big porcelain sink, about four feet wide, that had a dish-draining section molded to one side. It formed a table of sorts. Just right for Pa to get the job done. He would take me to the sink, ostensibly to 'bathe me,' and then do things to me that should not be done to any child, or for that matter, to any non-consenting adult; and as a tiny three-year-old girl, I certainly was not at the age of consent. The molestation continued, at various locations in our house, or his car, or other places for years.

Pa told me that what he was doing to me was 'good' and a sign of love—yeah, right.

As a result of this abuse I would wake up many mornings feeling confused, dirty, and ashamed. I couldn't shake the ever present sensation that something just felt wrong.

Even though I was physically neat and clean, I constantly felt dirty inside, and no amount of soap and water could wash it away. My subconscious was trying to block out what was happening to me, but still, I felt the violation and the shame like a dark python of sorrow, choking the joy out of my soul. This molestation started a long cycle of fear in my life. I lived on pins and needles, waiting for the other shoe to drop, waiting for it to happen again. It was like living in straitjacket of anxiety, and no one was cutting me loose.

Fasten Your Seat Belt Kids, It's Gonna' Be a Bumpy Ride!

I went back to look at that house on East Eleventh recently, and even though the rest of the houses on the block have been smartly refurbished by the yuppies, that one still remains hollow, even sinister looking. In most of my trips home, it is the only house in that nice neighborhood that is vacant. I wonder why? It's like the house itself took on the darkness of the events that took place there, and just can't let it go.

In those darkened rooms, my childhood innocence was stolen; and I never again felt safe or happy—at least not for a long, long time.

In my current profession as a counselor, I am floored by how many children, girls especially, are molested by family members and trusted grown-ups in positions of authority. It is epidemic. The numbers are staggering.

I look at child-abuse, whether sexual or emotional, as a form of 'soul murder' because this most accurately describes what happens to an innocent child's heart—a form of emotional death, where the child just shuts down, or goes numb. Childhood abuse causes death to trust, death to self-worth, death to innocence, and death to any illusion of safety in this world. Instead, these children grow up feeling full of shame: dirty, damaged and defeated; all through no fault of their own.

Even as a child I knew that what was happening to me was wrong, but I was coerced into not telling anyone the dirty things that were being done to me by my own grandfather. He should have loved me and kept me safe, guarded my heart. Instead, he selfishly violated my most personal inner sanctum, and 'murdered' my ability to trust people. My grandpa left me filled with fear, shame, and torment. I mean, if I couldn't trust my own grandfather, who the heck could I trust? Total strangers? I don't think so.

One morning, when I was about eight, Pa's brother, Uncle Jim, came to visit us. He cornered me in the hallway and pushed me behind a door. His calloused hands went up my shirt and twisted my undeveloped breasts until they hurt. He had such a look of lust and greed on his face it was sickening. Thank God, I had the presence of mind to shout out at the top of my voice, "Granny!" Jim jumped back like a scalded cat, but gave me the same look as Pa did: "You tell anyone and I'm *really* going to hurt you." Both brothers pedophiles, along with one of Pa's sons. It ran in the family. How sad.

Satan is an equal opportunity destroyer, and he loves nothing better than to pass along twisted behavior from one generation to the next.

For years I had a recurring nightmare that a man was hurting me really badly, and I was unable to scream. No matter how hard I tried, no sound would come out of my mouth. I would wake up, covered in sweat, with my throat hurting from the nightmare all because of what Pa and Uncle Jim had done to me. Soul murder.

Pa's father was even worse than him. A vile, evil man, who according to Pa, once killed a man, just because he could. These were the awful stories that Pa told me instead of fairy tales. Grim to say the least.

As a kid, I couldn't process what was going on. I couldn't guard my heart, I wasn't mature enough yet. My mind was not yet equipped with *how* to deal with this kind of betrayal. And since the perpetrators were trusted family members, I was left with the lie based thinking, "What did I do to cause this to happen? Why do *I* feel so violated? What is wrong with *me*?"

Of course nothing was wrong with me. I felt violated because—**I WAS violated!**

But a child is not emotionally equipped to process this kind of madness.

And so I began the vicious cycle of lie based thinking, that is, carrying a self-image based on lies: toxic thoughts buried deep in my psyche like, "**I am** worthless" or "This was all *my* fault," when nothing could have been further from the truth. The more heinous the lie, the deeper and more long-term the psychological damage.

There was no one there to guard my heart, so my grandpa went in and wreaked havoc on both my body and my soul.

When our heart, our subconscious, is deeply damaged, all of life will be distorted. We begin to see life through a very twisted lens.

The lies planted in my heart ruled my world and destroyed my confidence until the day I changed how I saw myself, but that day was still a long way off.

When I was about thirty-four years old, I went on a movie date to see Eddie Murphy in "The Golden Child." Near the beginning of the film a very young girl is brutally murdered, and the man who murdered her confessed that he was paid "... some Chinese take-out, and a carton of cigarettes" to kill her. I almost threw up in my seat. I leapt to my feet and rushed out of the crowded theater; I had to get some fresh air because that line triggered such a deep wound in my soul, children are worthless—*ergo*, YOU are worthless. In that movie the life of an innocent girl was worth some Chinese take-out, and a carton of cigarettes. That one line triggered my fight-or-flight response so deeply, that I took off like a scalded cat.

Perhaps you've had moments like that in your own life. Something you couldn't fully explain, but to which you had a dramatic overreaction. There's always a reason for that reaction buried deep inside your soul.

Some thirty years after my abuse, that movie still triggered the emotional damage that had been embedded in my psyche. It triggered the lie from my childhood that I was deemed 'expendable,' and 'worthless,' a 'thing' to be used by Pa for his perverted pleasure, and that I was only on earth for one reason, for someone else's sick gratification. That one line from a movie ripped the scab off and opened that deep childhood wound, and "Little Peggy" was back in Pa's hands again, feeling all the pain and humiliation.

Rushing out of the packed theatre was not a way to make great impression on a first date, but that's how deep these wounds run until we deal with them. (By the way, the man who took me to see the picture is now my husband, so it all worked out okay.)

Now we move on to part two of my crazy childhood. As it turns out, the molestation was not the worst part. It simply opened the door to even more egregious horrors in my life.

Fasten Your Seat Belt Kids, It's Gonna' Be a Bumpy Ride!

As the old saying goes, "Truth is stranger than fiction," and my story fits that to a 'T.' By the time I was six or seven, something even worse was happening that blew out all my circuits.

We had moved from East Eleventh to 1200 Dean Avenue, a nicer and bigger home. It is so strange that both my sister and I have a hard time remembering where we slept as children, and we lived in that house on Dean Avenue for over fifteen years. But, I vividly remember a period-of-time when I slept on a twin bed, in a green bedroom that was right next to mom and dad's room.

During that period-of-time, dark, human shaped apparitions began to wake me up in the middle of the night. They would always be the same, dark shadowy figures, just standing there, 'staring' at me. I could *feel* them looking down at me from the foot of my bed. I would stare back, wide-eyed, frozen in terror, heart pounding in my throat, and covered in sweat. I could sense the pure malevolence only a few feet away. Adrenaline would shoot through my skinny little body. Quaking with fear I would pray, "Hail Mary full of grace..." "Hail Mary full of grace..." "Hail Mary full of grace..." I whispered over and over, as fast as I could, hoping that would make 'the thing' go away.

There are no words to describe the abject panic that flooded my soul at the sight of these wraiths: one resembled the outline of a Roman soldier, with large plumes on his helmet, and the other one resembled a 'witchy woman,' it felt mean and twisted. Although the soldier seemed a bit more benign of the two, they both struck mind-numbing terror into my heart.

They never spoke, they just emitted a cold sinister *feeling*; staring, watching, and waiting. They were, of course, supernatural malevolent spirit beings—they were demons. In hindsight, considering Pa's personality, this shouldn't have been surprising.

I would instinctively pull the covers up and tug them tight around my neck. I felt like I had to cover my neck. I would never watch any vampire movies with the other kids, because vampires went for the neck. The truth is, I didn't watch any kind of horror movies because I was living a real life horror movie in my own house.

Even on hot Georgia summer nights I would sleep with a blanket over me because I wanted the weight, the protection, of the blanket as an added barrier between me and the evil ones.

Thankfully, these apparitions did not appear every night, but it happened often enough that I had a tremendous fear of going to sleep. All day long I was a nervous wreck, wondering if 'they' would appear again, or would Pa come in and try to touch me? That's a lot to worry about at any age, but especially as a defenseless child.

I told a few family members about the things that appeared in my room, but they just laughed it off, and told me I was being a baby, and imagining stuff. They said, "There is no such thing as the Boogeyman." Oh, how wrong they were.

And when I wasn't demon plagued, I would have horrific nightmares, like the one about my mom, having her legs cut off. Years later I understood that my 'mom' in the dream was actually me, crying out for help, feeling 'cut off at the knees' not able to deal with life, relegated to the 'chicken house.' It was my subconscious trying to work out the feelings of fear and inadequacy that I wrestled with on a constant basis, and how I felt in my own real life situation... Somebody *please* help me!

I dreaded nighttime with a passion. NOTHING good happened at night. My sister told me how hard it was to wake me up in the mornings when we were kids, which of course, was caused by sleep deprivation. By the first grade, I had dark purple rings under my eyes, bit my finger nails down to a bloody quick, and licked my lips raw from anxiety. In short, I was a nervous wreck. I would go through my whole day with a sense of dread and nervous exhaustion, knowing that night always followed day, and there was nothing I could do to escape it.

It is a debilitating thing for anyone to live in such a constant state of anxiety.

During the day, I tried to talk, play, run, and climb trees, anything that exerted lots and lots of energy in an effort to get myself so completely and utterly exhausted that I might collapse into bed, comatose; so worn out that *nothing* could wake me up.

I also used humor as a distraction. I did comedy routines at my parent's parties where I would mimic their favorite performers from the Ed Sullivan show. The adults thought I was riot, and oh, soooo adorable. But that only further amplified the dichotomy of my life. I thought, "If only they *knew*..."

Despite all of this, I tried to be an optimist, a 'glass half full' kind of kid. Early on I came to the sobering realization that no one was going to save me, so I had better save myself. And I knew I'd better fasten my seat belt, because I was in for one heck of a bumpy ride.

Chapter 2

Safety

"Get thee behind me, Satan."
Matthew 16:23

Safety is something every child should feel, and count on. It's a tragic thing to grow up never feeling safe in your own home.

My story is not about a poverty stricken waif who escaped the mean streets of Philly, or the absurd insanity of a life of hedonistic wealth; I am the product of a 'normal' middle class, cookie-cutter family from the 1950's. My life looked average in every way. We looked happy and wholesome on the outside, but insidious things were happening on the inside, which makes my tale even more of a wake-up call to all the 'normal' people out there who can't understand why they are full of rage, or guilt, or low self-esteem.

There was nothing 'normal' or safe about my childhood. Parts of it were destructive, appalling and abusive. But, my story is really every one's story, because we have all been damaged to one degree or another. I wonder, how many other adults continue to suffer lives of quiet desperation because they have never dealt with the demons of their past?

In AA they have a saying, "You are only as sick as your darkest secret." The Bible's answer to that is to share your faults and your hurt, with one another, so that **you may be healed**. The healing comes in dealing with the pain, not by burying it. Talk to a trusted friend (heavy emphasis on the 'trusted') or even better, to

Safety

a good Spirit-filled counselor. Holding all the pain inside will just cause it to fester.

As a child, if I tried to tell my mom about my sexual abuse, but she just gave me a deer in the headlights look, so I thought, "What's the point?" Like all good dysfunctional families, everyone ignored our dystopian life. We buried it. My parents were damaged goods because they never got the help they needed, so they were ill-equipped to help anyone else, even their own children. We kept our mouths shut, and acted like nothing was happening. We repressed our feelings, and turned a blind eye, while the insanity continued.

I find it remarkable that kids can go to school, have lots of friends, and even act fairly normal, while terrible abuse is taking place in the home—but we can. The human mind is an amazing thing. We are geared for survival.

Because of the abuse I never felt safe in my house, even in broad daylight. The family dynamic was such that I was also the scapegoat for everyone's frustrations; probably because I was already subconsciously trained to think I was supposed to be the whipping girl. So I attracted even more abuse to myself. The Bible says, "As a man thinks in his heart, so is he." Or, we attract into our lives what we believe about ourselves, in our hearts. Today, the Law of Attraction is fairly common knowledge, but not so much back in the 50's. I was being programmed from a very early age to be hurt by others, so I attracted pain like a moth to the light.

My brother often used me as his personal punching bag. I remember my Granny telling my mama, "that young un's gonna' kill Peggy, one of these days." But, the beatings went on for years,

Safety

until one day my dad, Papa Joe, came home unexpectedly and saw what my brother was doing to me. He yanked him off of me, and knocked him across the room. (Thank God my brother never touched me again.) Of course, we never talked about *that* incident either. The pattern was set: shut-up, cover up, and buck up, act like nothing has happened.

With all of this abuse piling up inside, and no way to release it, I was a walking toxic dump of negative emotions, queuing up for a meltdown.

Satan delights in taking away a child's innocence. If he can get a child on a negative glide path of self-loathing and low expectations at a young age, he is halfway home to producing one more very messed up adult.

There are four core traumatic beliefs the devil likes to sow: victim hood, powerlessness, worthlessness, and loss. By around eight years old, I had an abundance of all four.

But before I go any further, I want to bring up two saving graces in my childhood. One was a person, and the other was a place.

The person was my Granny, Etta Folsom Mercer, who lived with us, and was (unfortunately for her) married to Pa. My mom worked during the day, and so Granny raised me. She was a pure-hearted country girl from South Georgia, and was the most Christ-like person I have ever met to this day. She had suffered a cruel and hard life herself at the hands of Pa, and yet she was still tender and loving. She had the kind of compassion that most Christians only wish they had. She had a genuine heart of love. She was my first living example that you can go through hell, and come out better and not bitter. She showed me by example that **love is a choice**.

I know it must have torn Granny's heart out to watch my suffering, doing what she could, but unable to change anything. God, how I loved that little 4' 10" woman. And back then she was the only person whom I believed loved me unconditionally; the only one I believed would never take advantage of me. Her love was a pure *agape* love, God's love, and she is still my role model.

Granny tried to love me and care for me the best she could, but her pleas to my parents fell on deaf ears. Why they chose not to respond to her, I'll never know.

And with so much torment taking place inside my home, I desperately needed a place to escape. Thankfully, God gave me one. The only place I ever felt any sense of peace and safety was high up in a beautiful maple tree in our side yard, whose branches reached up into the heavens, almost like arms outstretched in worship.

I must admit, we did live on a beautiful piece of property. Our house was ivory stucco, with dark green trim, and a huge wrap-around front porch. Ironically, it was very well cared for, and always neat as a pin. A master horticulturalist had lived there before us, and all across the front of the house bordering our porch were fabulous rose bushes parallel to the boxwoods. They gave forth every color of the most vibrant roses you could ever dream of: white, deep blood red, and yellow with pink tips. They were huge, fragrant roses. Along the outer edges of the property were rows of purple and blue irises. The ample back yard was surrounded by ten foot high hedges that enclosed apple trees, mimosa trees, tulip trees, and maple trees. The outdoors was my sanctuary, my true place of worship.

On one side of the house there was a tall maple tree, whose loving branches I would climb up into. My perch was high above the roof of our house, where no one could see me or *touch* me. There was a comfortable limb that I would lay back on like a hammock. I would nestle myself in there and have long, long talks with God. Peering up through the green leaves into the blue sky above, I felt like He was right there next to me, my best friend.

Like it or not, I heard about God every morning for one hour in catechism class at Saint Mary's Parochial school. But I didn't believe most of what I heard. The Dominican nuns taught us that God was an angry Father, full of wrath and ready to send me to Hell at a moment's notice. They taught a message, not of love, but of fire and brimstone. They told me I'd better be perfect because all of mankind lived with one foot in Hell and the other one on a banana peel, and that it would not take much for me to slip up. Then God would surely send me to Hell, where I would fry for eternity. Not very comforting stuff to tell a child.

For some reason I instinctively scoffed at this ridiculous notion. Plus, I knew that their concept of Hell was only myth; I knew that Hell was right here, right now. Hell was at 1200 Dean Avenue, and I was living in it! And the devil was my grandpa, Noah, and the apparitions that showed up in my bed room at night and scared the living daylights out of me. The wraiths were not God's good angels who always said to people, "Fear not," they were demonic. I reckoned that if those nuns could see through my eyes for just a few days, they could have had a ringside view of Hell for themselves.

Apparently I knew something the nuns didn't know, God is good. This was a truth that came from my Granny, and from my inner being. I rejected the distorted views of the Bible that the nuns taught. I refused to believe that God was the source of the pain in my life. My God made the blue skies, robin's nests, fleecy white clouds, Lake Altoona, tree houses, and fast bicycles. My God made all *good* things. Something else was responsible for the bad things; namely the devil. Pa's evil temperament and his lasciviousness was his own choice: the devil didn't *make* him do those horrible things to me, but I'm sure the devil had a big hand in leading him down that path.

It would still take me a few years before I learned that: *all* good things come from God, and all bad things come from the devil. But that's the truth.

I've often heard people say, "Well, if there's a good God, why do bad things happen to good people?" That's kind of like saying, "Well, if there are good dentists on earth, why do people have rotten teeth?" Uh, because some people decide *not* to go to the dentist and get their teeth fixed. Just like some people choose to ignore God's love, and be as mean as a snake.

God is good, He's a 'white hat,' but a lot of folks just don't want to listen to Him, and live life the way He prescribes it: in love. They don't want to embrace His love, kindness, and mercy. They willfully ignore God to their own detriment, and to the detriment of those who are affected by their evil deeds. And, like decayed teeth, their actions are rotten to the core.

Safety

Bad things happen because human beings *decide* to DO bad things. Even as a child, I could understand that much. This is not rocket science. It's called free will.

There is a character named Kaiser Soze in the film *'The Usual Suspects'* who said, "The greatest trick the Devil ever pulled was convincing the world he didn't exist." Oh, how right Kaiser was. Satan loves to blame the true God for the evil deeds that Satan's own minions do, and the madness they inspire in the hearts of men.

Despite all the crap that was going on in my life, I knew in my heart of hearts, that the God and Father of my Lord, Jesus Christ, was *not* the one making my life miserable. I just didn't know how to get un-miserable yet.

Thankfully, God led me to that beautiful maple tree. It was my 'church,' my place of worship, and peace, and solace; and the only spot where I felt truly safe and untouchable. It was there that my soul felt nourished and loved, not by a person, but by the presence of the living God. And that was where I poured out my troubles. Granny and God were my two saving graces.

I would sit up in that lovely tree and wonder if Michael the archangel would ever deem to fight my battles for me. I would ask the God, who made such beauty in nature, why people blamed Him for their own evil hearts and deeds? I somehow understood that God wasn't my problem, people were the problem.

In that lovely maple tree I spent hours at a time talking to God: and I worried and I wondered, I wondered and I worried. I worried about kids who did not have enough to eat each day. I worried if other kids were being abused like me. I worried about kids who were being picked on at school. I worried if the demons would appear in my bedroom again that night. I worried if I would get molested that day. I worried if I would ever get released from my torment.

And I wondered. I wondered how people could be so mean to each other. I wondered how on God's green earth molesting a child could make a person feel good when it was so wrong. I wondered if I would live through the hell called "Peggy's childhood" and make it to adulthood. I wondered if my sister was as miserable as I was. I wondered if God would do some great miracle for me, like He did for the saints we talked about in Catholic school, and get me out of here. I wondered if God would deliver me... before it was too late.

These are all things too heavy for any child to have to think about, and yet millions of kids are thinking about this kind of stuff every day, for they, too, are being abused by selfish people; and it breaks my heart.

Perhaps some of you can relate to the things I am sharing. And now you know there's a reason why you feel so broken, even decades after the fact. The good news is that you, too, can be healed; put back together and restored by the love of God. There is hope for the hurting—there is hope for all of us.

Life could be so much better all the way around if everyone understood this one simple truth.

THINGS are to be used; PEOPLE are to be *loved*.

Safety

Boy, I needed to be loved, with a pure love that wanted nothing in return. I desperately needed a place of safety as I waited for my deliverance, and I got not one, but two: Granny and my maple tree.

I wish I had understood back then that just because God seems silent, doesn't mean He doesn't care.

Chapter 3

From Demons To Drink

But whoso shall offend one of these little ones which believe in me, it were better for him that a millstone were hanged about his neck, and that he were drowned in the depth of the sea. Matthew 18:6

Matthew 18:6 has some very strong words for those who willfully harm children. I sure wouldn't want to be in their shoes come Judgment Day.

Always remember: Things are to be used; people are to be loved. We are all here on earth to love one another, not to use one another.

When people use other people for their own selfish greed or lust, major damage occurs to both parties. The perpetrator becomes more vile, hard hearted, and filled with self-loathing, and the victim is damaged in too many ways to categorize on a psychological level. Once the damage is done, it takes love, patience and understanding to mend the brokenness inside.

The world is a mess. That is why God sent His son, to make us whole; to fill us with His spirit, to restore our broken hearts, and to heal ALL who are beaten down by the devil.

How God anointed Jesus of Nazareth with the Holy Ghost and with power: who went about doing good, and healing all that were oppressed of the devil; for God was with him. Acts 10:38.

But sadly, as a broken child, when my time in the maple tree didn't relieve my torment I slowly turned away from Christ, and more and more to my own devices. Not a good idea. One day I had the bright notion to start drinking booze to tamp down my anxiety. I'd heard someone say that people drank to cause themselves to numb-out, or to forget. I thought, "Hey, maybe that's the ticket."

One night, when Mama and Daddy were out, I went to the liquor cabinet and took a couple of swigs of some horrible tasting bourbon called Ancient Age. I did this for one express purpose; to go numb, to forget, to not care. Even though the stuff gagged me and burned all the way down, my hope was that if I could get a few stiff drinks into me, then I could pass out, and be so gone that nothing could wake me up. Oh, how I craved to sleep through one whole night without the ghouls, the nightmares, and the fear of Pa.

I was nine years old.

By the time I hit my sophomore year in high school, at age fifteen, I was a full blown alcoholic. The major abuse at home had stopped, Pa had been dead for a couple of years, but the damage was done. My psyche was scorched earth; windswept tumble weed, blowing aimlessly about inside. I had only two primal instincts left: survive, and block out the pain inside.

All I could think about during the day was where my next drink was coming from. How could I get a hold of more? How could I hide it from my parents and teachers?

Here I was, the quintessential 'All American Girl,' very popular, wholesome, good looking, straight-A student, an athlete, and a cheerleader; but totally miserable, messed-up, and desperate on the inside. I felt like such a hypocrite. This Susie Sunshine act was just smoke and mirrors. I wanted to stand in front of the whole student body of East Rome High and scream at the top of my lungs, "Somebody please, please, help me! I am so screwed up!"

I'm sure there were friends of mine who thought, "What on earth is wrong with that crazy girl?" But, I couldn't have told them if I wanted to because I didn't know what was wrong with me. So I got 'black-out' drunk as much as I possibly could and still function the next day. I even carried vodka and orange juice in my lunchbox thermos to get an early jump on my drinking.

Yep, that was me at fifteen, a functioning, unhappy, straight-A, guilt-ridden, cute-as-a-button, scared-stiff, drunk.

Alcohol is such an unhealthy coping mechanism. But, since I still had no answers to the fear, the pain, and the anxiety in my life, I would quickly crawl into the bottle, whenever I needed an escape hatch, which seemed like most of the time.

I felt like the blackouts from drinking were safer than the blackness in my own heart as I continued to spiral down a path of self-loathing and confusion.

The sad result was that between my junior and senior year, my lack of self-esteem led me to have sex with a boy that I thought was my knight in shining armor. I'll call him 'Ronnie' (not his real name). Ronnie was Mr. 'It,' the Big Man on Campus; and I fell head-over-heels for him. I loved him so much I thought he loved me too, and that he would be my way out of Hell. When I was with him I was happy for the first time. I felt safe with him. I sacrificed my 'virginity' to him because I was already trained that this was what it took to make men really love you. And the summer before my senior year of high school, I found myself pregnant.

In 1968 in Georgia, pregnant single women did not just stay in high school and have the baby like they do today. To make matters worse, Ronnie refused to marry me.

The day my parents went to confront him about the pregnancy he came over to my house afterwards, and we went for a ride. I was almost giddy with excitement. I thought, "Oh, my gosh, he's going to change his mind, and beg me to marry him! Tell me that he wants to be a father."

Ronnie drove me to a beautiful sunny spot, turned to me with a smirk on his face, and said, "Marrying you is out of the question. But, since you are already pregnant, we could still have sex."

What! To quote Will Shakespeare, that was the 'unkindest cut of all.'

My brain exploded! I think I went into shock. I don't remember if I slapped him, yelled, or what, but I returned home in a rage and in a fog of disillusionment. How could anyone be that cruel? It was astonishing.

Later on I found out that once we had sex, Ronnie moved on to another gullible girl across town, and got her pregnant, too. So much for "Mr. Perfect."

Here was another trusted figure, whom I thought loved me and would protect me, and it turned out he wanted nothing more than to use me. I was shattered by the callous way he treated me.

But, like Matthew 18:6 said, "Woe unto them" who had used me, and abused me. They were going to reap what they had sown. I almost felt sorry for Ronnie... almost.

I think I went a little crazy after that, but I had to quickly gather my wits about me, because now I had an innocent life inside of me to be concerned about.

I stopped drinking completely. I tried to take good care of myself, I ate right and exercised. I ended up leaving school the last part of my senior year. Mama told the school I was ill. And in March of 1969 I gave birth to a beautiful set of twin girls, that I would never have the joy of raising. Knowing my home life, and my personal instability, I reluctantly gave them up for adoption. There was no way I was going to bring other innocent lives into the viper pit that had destroyed mine.

My biggest fear was that if I brought my children into that house, they too would somehow be abused. And so, I did the most gut-wrenching thing a mother can do, I gave my babies up for adoption. An aunt of mine, who was a nurse, had found a wonderful, Christian family who wanted to have more children, but couldn't. My only burning desire was, "Please, God, keep my girls safe. Please, in heaven's name, protect their innocence."

It is a miracle that I did not have a complete nervous breakdown during that time. (I guess it's no surprise that in my thirties I was diagnosed with PTSD by two different doctors.) I have never experienced more torment in my soul than the decision to give up my flesh and blood.

This added a whole new dimension of guilt and shame to my already non-existent self-esteem. I thought of myself as a slimy piece of filth, lower than a snake's belly. On the outside I still looked like Susie Sunshine, but my insides felt like my guts had been ripped to shreds. Howling anguish!

No surprise here; shortly after I gave up the twins I began to drink again—in earnest! My liquid 'friend' was always beckoning me with seducing words... "Peg, just take one more drink, and the pain will all go away." Not only did it not go away, every time I drank I would talk to whoever would listen to me about my babies. I would have a complete meltdown, and tell them what a horrible person I was.

The image that we carry of ourselves will attract those things into our lives, for good or for bad. And at this point, my self-image was really, really bad.

The roller coaster called "My Life" was about to rise to a whole new level of insanity. I was like a locomotive flying down a mountain railroad with no brakes. I was an accident waiting to happen.

The worst was yet to come because I had not yet hit my bottom.

Chapter 4

Tilt-A Whirl

"Your task is not to seek for love, but merely to seek and find all the barriers within yourself that you have built against it." Rumi

At this point in my life I was on a treadmill of anxiety, going nowhere fast.

Even though I had only completed half my senior year of high school, I was accepted into the University of Georgia in Athens, because of my high SAT scores and my 4.0 average. I took my first semester courses off-campus, in Rome, Georgia, and then in August headed to Athens, and a new layer of insanity.

At UGA I didn't really care about any of my classes except for art, so I sloughed off, and focused on having fun instead; wasting hard-earned money. I used to tell my friends that, "I majored in partying, and minored in art," which is not as cool as it sounds. I was still 'numbing' out because I was filled with guilt and shame.

One day an old high school buddy introduced me to a kind, handsome UGA student from Jupiter, Florida, and we began an intense relationship. In the end I messed that up too, because of my own broken soul. My new mantra was, "Hurt them before they hurt you." I was devolving, that's for sure.

The only good thing that came out of that relationship was seeing the ocean for the first time in my life, and it took my breath away. We went on spring break down to West Palm Beach, and I was floored by the beauty of the Atlantic's massive body of water. It seemed so cool, and clean, and powerful; everything I wasn't. As soon as we got home, I longed to return to the ocean.

After spinning my wheels for a year at UGA, I must have had a couple of brain cells left, because I came to the conclusion that all I was doing was wasting my student loan. That's when I decided to make money instead of spending it.

And so began a new avoidance pattern in my life: running. I ran to a new place, Smyrna, Georgia.

I would spend most of my late teens and early twenties running. Something bad would happen, and I would run to the next place. I was trying the 'geographic cure' for my problems, without much success because wherever I went, there I was. No matter where I ran, I couldn't get away from *myself*. I just carried my pain and disappointments with me to the next location.

About this time I wrote in my journal, "I sat in a cage of fear one day, and saw the fearless reap the joys of life." Oh, God, how I wanted to be fearless. How I longed to be free, to like myself, to love others, and to find some joy in life.

I secured a great-paying job at Meisel Photochrome Corporation, in Atlanta. It was the number one photofinishing house in America at the time, and I learned about all kinds of photo retouching and finishing. I leased an apartment with two roommates. I was making very good money, drinking less, and feeling pretty good about life in general. But my world was changing rapidly, the whole culture was changing.

In July of 1970, I hopped in a Volkswagen van with a bunch of friends from work, and we all went to the sleepy town of Byron,

Tilt-A Whirl

Georgia for the *Second Atlanta Pop Festival*. It was awesome; so many great bands were there. With over five hundred thousand people in attendance, it was bigger than Woodstock.

Yes, the times they were a changin'. And this music festival was a long way from *Ozzie and Harriet,* and Rome, Georgia.

Byron is where I shed my last layers of inhibitions. It was wild! Drugs were free flowing. People wore, or didn't wear clothes. There were First-Aid tents, Overdose tents, and babies being born. It was a mind blowing experience to be in the middle of a half a million people in the woods for three sweltering days. But, what struck me the most was that I wasn't aware of one single altercation. I never heard a harsh word spoken. From my perspective, everyone got along great, despite the lack of water, food, and facilities. I had never experienced this kind of camaraderie before, and I thought maybe these hippies were on to something. Peace, Love and Rock'n Roll!

We had camped underneath a beautiful tree, and had one of the cooler spots on the grounds, although we didn't spend much time there; too much was happening on the main grounds. *Richie Havens, Johnny Winter, Ten Years After, Grand Funk, It's A Beautiful Day, Rare Earth, the Allman Brothers,* and so many more great bands were on tap to entertain us for the weekend. I was in awe of the sheer size and scope of the event. A teeming mass of people who were all getting along!

On July 4th, 1970 I woke up sometime after midnight in the middle of the sea of concert goers. As I lay on my blanket, I beheld a sky full of fireworks, and flares floating down on parachutes. As my mind came into focus I was shocked to hear

Tilt-A Whirl

Jimi Hendrix and The Experience playing on the main stage. I had no idea Hendrix would be there. That night at Byron, Jimi played before the largest audience of his career. And it was an experience to behold.

I stood up and made my way down to the stage where Jimi was wailing away on his guitar like nobody else could. He was such an incredible musician. There will never be another like him. He was at the apex of his career. I was about eight feet in front of him, so close I could see his rings and finger nails, when he blasted out the *Star Spangled Banner*. It was phenomenal! It was electric. It was a new day. It was a new America!

Byron was a paradigm shift for me. I moved on from *Leave it to Beaver*, and entered the world of *Easy Rider*.

I have to admit, after that weekend, I was pretty full of myself. I had the world on a string, and I was feeling more hopeful than ever.

Love! Man that's what I wanted. My heart was yearning for something deeper, better, dare is say heavenly? I wanted to live in the realm of love, to rise above the petty squabbling on this earth. Could that be possible?

Alas, my new found feeling of joy and invincibility didn't last too long.

Only two months later, in September, this great musical genius, Jimi Hendrix, was dead. And a few weeks after that, Janis Joplin was gone too. Poof! Just like that. The flamboyant, hard-drinking, hard-living, smoky-voiced songstress from Port Arthur, Texas, who showed the world that rock 'n' roll was no longer just for the boys, was silenced by drugs, too.

Two icons in a row—gone. Both of them not much older than myself; and that hit me really hard. It seemed like every time I felt hopeful, or put my faith in something, it blew up in my face.

I thought, "Maybe that's the key to life: Live hard, die young, and leave a good-looking corpse?" Hhhhmmmm, maybe.

So I cruised along in a sea of questions, trying to sort out what this thing called Life was really all about. I would sing along with Dionne Warwick to the words of 'Alfie.'

> *What's it all about, Alfie?*
> *Is it just for the moment we live?*
> *What's it all about when you sort it out, Alfie?*
> *Are we meant to take more than we give?*
> *Or, are we meant to be kind?*

At the end she makes this stinging statement, "*Without true love we just exist, Alfie. Until you **find the love you've missed you're nothing**, Alfie...*" I thought, "Buddy-boy, how in the hell do you find that? True love? But... I don't want to be nothing. I want life to matter!"

I craved to know, I needed to know—is there real love anywhere in this world? What even matters? What is real?

A few weeks later I was having dinner with an old high school friend in mid-town Atlanta. After dinner, around 11 o'clock and completely sober, I started driving back home to my apartment in Smyrna, Georgia, about forty minutes away. I was driving my sweet little 1960 canary yellow Triumph TR3 convertible, when it began to rain and the temperature started to drop. I was glad I had not had any wine that night, because I needed to be alert on those dark, winding roads.

Along the way home I had to go over a wide overpass that crossed over the new eight-lane Perimeter Highway, which circled around Atlanta.

As soon as the wheels of my TR3 hit the bridge I could tell that I was on 'black ice' and I knew that I shouldn't brake or over-steer. I was traveling pretty fast when I hit the ice, and my car began to spin out of control. Round and round I went, across the bridge picking up speed. Thank God no other cars were on it because I was hurtling diagonally across the opposite lanes, and headed straight for the guardrail. I couldn't imagine how I could *not* go over the guard rail, and go splat on the Interstate below. Everything slowed down. In my mind's eye I could see the grainy old black and white 8mm movies they showed us in Driver's Ed class of those grotesque wrecks and broken bodies in an effort to make us want to drive more safely. I clearly imagined the scene of the EMT's pulling a teenager out of the front windshield after a fatal car accident, and that teenager was me!

As I picked up speed I felt like I was on the Tilt-A-Whirl at the Coosa Valley Fair. The centrifugal force was picking up more, and more. I knew what was going to happen: my car was going over the guard rail and... 'splat' onto the pavement below. I visualized the poor guys in white coats who would be stuck with the job of removing the mess that used to be *me* off the interior, and scooping my lifeless body into a black body bag. I wondered,

Tilt-A Whirl

"How do they ever go to sleep at night after seeing such carnage?"

When you are in a life-and-death situation, the mind goes into slow motion. I know because I have been in that situation a few times.

The blackness was whirling around me at a dizzying speed as the car spun faster and faster out of control. Then, I felt myself go airborne, and sail into the night. I didn't even have time to think, "Oh, crap!" before I felt that weightless feeling of being hurled through mid-air.

Suddenly, there was one last violent jerk! It was so strong that it wrenched the knit cap I was wearing off my head, and threw it into the back seat. And then... everything stopped... *silence*...

I closed my eyes and held my breath, and waited... waited... for the splat... waited for my death... which never came.

I gingerly peeked out of one eye and wondered if this was what it felt like to be dead. But, "Wait! What? Am I still here? It feels like I'm still alive!"

Maybe I wasn't splattered all over the Perimeter Highway! Maaaayyybe I was still alive! But—how could that be?

Stunned, I rubbed my hands over my face and head. "I feel okay; I don't even see any blood." I touched down the front of my body. Was this for real? Was I still here on earth?

After a bit I got out of the car. No one was around. The place was absolutely deserted. My knees were so wobbly I could barely stand up. The shock of what just happened was overwhelming. "Why am I still here? Why am I not dead?"

I looked around, and stepped back to assess my car. It was on a bizarre thirty-degree angle, teetering on top of the guardrail, like a stopped seesaw; the front wheels were on the frozen grass, but rear wheels were up in the air, hanging over the other side of the rail, suspended in the air over the highway below. My TR3 looked like a little Tonka toy, gently balanced on the guard rail by some giant invisible hand.

This was not a position that *real* car could get into! Was it?

I said to myself, "Okay, from a physics standpoint this makes no sense." I stood there, rubbing my face and wondering how on earth my car could turn around in midair, and come back to rest in that unnatural position.

I looked around the car; not a bent wheel rim, not a scratch. Even where the car was balancing on the guard rail, the paint was in perfect condition. I stood there shaking my head in utter disbelief. Why wasn't anything damaged? Why was I still here?

I looked up and down the road. Blackness. It was deserted in both directions. I could see the sleet coming down in the haze from of a couple of street lamps, but nothing else. I figured it was probably around midnight by now, and most folks had more sense than to be out driving on a night like this. Duh!

I was still in a daze, feeling nothing: not scared, not thankful, just numb, when I saw headlights headed my way. Soon a pickup truck pulled over next me and two men got out. They were both very tall and thin, but I don't recall either one of them ever saying a word to me. They looked at my car and went straight to the back of their truck and pulled out a 2x4, then came over, and used the 2X4 to pick up my car, *up* and *over* the guardrail, and set it back on the ground!

Now, a 1960 TR3 weighs 2,105 pounds. How do two skinny guys, who looked they had to run around in the shower to get wet, lift a 2,000 pound car two feet *higher* than the guardrail, and then lift it over and gently set it back on the road? That is crazy! Bizarre! It's impossible! It defies both logic and physics! And yet it happened that icy night in Georgia.

Again, I looked over my car to see if it was drivable, and everything was perfect, not a scratch anywhere. But when I turned around a few seconds later to thank them—they were *gone*! Poof! They just vanished! The two men were nowhere in sight. I could see more than a quarter of a mile both ways, and there were no tail lights in either direction. They had just... disappeared. Surreal.

Now I was really perplexed. I did not yet know the Bible verse that said, "Be not forgetful to entertain strangers: for thereby some have entertained *angels* unaware." All I knew was that two skinny men appeared out of nowhere, did the impossible, and vanished!

I drove back home creeping along at 25 mph. I was shaking so badly it was hard to hold the steering wheel. I was so freaked out when I got home I called my parents, and told them what had just happened. I just had to tell someone, to touch base with reality, to hear a familiar voice, because I was still not convinced that I was alive.

I didn't sleep much that night. When I went into work late the next day I told my boss, Herb what had happened the night before. He stared laughing because I was always the joker, doing something funny, or cutting up, and he thought I was just pulling his leg. He said, "Peg, you've come in with some wild tales for being late, but this one takes the cake!"

I turned away from him, walked straight to the women's bathroom, leaned my back against the wall, slid down to the floor, and collapsed, sobbing hysterically. I couldn't stop. I couldn't get control of myself. Finally, Herb sent someone in to check on me, and I told them through a catching voice, "I've g-g-g-ot to g-g-g-o home. I can't believe I'm not d-d-d-dead!" So I got up, and walked out.

Good old Herb caught me in the hallway on my way out, took one look at my hang dog face, and apologized. He said, "I'm sorry, I thought you were just being you—joking around. Take a couple of days off, kiddo, you look like you need it." I just nodded my head 'yes,' and kept walking.

When I said I had to go home, I realized that I meant home to Rome, Georgia, not back to my apartment in Smyrna. I needed to see people who could verify that I was still actually here on Earth. In hindsight, I now know that I was in a state of shock; and rightfully so. I'd just had an experience where the odds that I would end up dead were around 100%, and yet, here I was, in living color, still breathing. And that had not fully sunk in yet.

On the way home, traveling down old US Highway 41, I saw traffic begin to slow down and snarl in front of me. Something instinctively told me to do the dumbest thing you could think of doing in a low slung sports car, I pulled off the pavement at a high-speed and on to the grassy center median that ran between the opposite lanes. Just as I started pulling into the grass, a tire came bouncing down the highway and just missed my car's windshield! With adrenaline shooting out my ears at this point, I bumped and thumped along the unpaved ground beneath my wheels, and gawked as I passed a huge car pile up to my right.

When I got home, I turned on the news and found out that a big truck literally had a whole tire come off, which bounced down the highway, and caused a multiple car pile-up. Again, if I had been in the middle of that in my little convertible, I don't think I could have walked away unscathed.

I was like, "Wow! I almost got killed, *twice* in one twenty-four hour period! What the hell is going on?" Unbeknownst to me at the time, those childhood demons wanted me dead, but the hand of Eternal Love had saved me, not once but twice.

This scared the crap out of me, so I did what would become my pattern for the next few years; when things got crazy, I ran away!

That spinning car felt like a metaphor for my life, on the Tilt-A-Whirl, out of control, but somehow I was still here. *Why*?

Within a couple of weeks I packed my bags and said, "OK, Peg, let's go back to the ocean, let's try Palm Beach, Florida!"

Chapter 5

You Can Run, but You Can't Hide

The soul can rise from the earth into the sky, like a bird...
Anonymous

In the spring of 1971, I stealthily packed up my stuff while my roommates were at work, hopped in my sports car, waved good-bye to Atlanta, and drove to Palm Beach, Florida. I didn't even tell my roommates I was moving, which was a lousy thing to do.

I was nineteen years old, and I was in survival mode. Everything I needed fit into my tiny TR-3, and what didn't, I simply left behind.

Just before I left Georgia I had painted a self-portrait in the magic realism style. My face rising from the earth, growing out of a strong tree trunk, and it had purple, yellow and red, auras surrounding my face and long hair. It was very 'Mother Earth.' The background was a crystal blue sky with a soaring white dove overhead radiating light, as if calling me upward, to a higher plane. Around the sides and the portrait I inscribed:

The soul can rise from the earth into the sky, like a bird:
Not feeling the barriers of man, But the beauty of love, which is eternal.

I was searching for exactly what that inscription said: freedom, beauty, love, a higher plane. I took the painting and my meager belongings with me, and headed for the Sunshine State, excited to be near the life-giving ocean again.

My first week there I got a great job at the prestigious Mort Kaye Photography Studios in Palm Beach, just off of Royal Palm Drive. I walked into his posh reception area, as bold as brass, and told the receptionist they needed to hire me! (I may have been crazy, but I was not stupid.) I had never been short on *chutzpah*. At that *exact* moment, Mort Kaye himself walked out of his office and I accosted him and told him the same thing. I must have really surprised him, because he started laughing, and sent me to the photo finishing department, and said, "If Betty White (not THE Betty White) likes you, you're hired!" She did, and I was.

I later found out there was a years-long waiting list for people to even get a job interview with this world-renowned photographer. What are the odds that I would get hired within fifteen minutes of walking in? This job at Mort Kaye's was another great blessing of grace that Father sent my way. Don't tell me God doesn't take care of the ding-bats of this world, because He was sure trying to take care of me, in spite of myself.

I met a woman in Palm Beach whom we called the Motorcycle Queen because she always rode one. She was from a very wealthy family, and in the course of our conversations she told me that she was a witch. And I thought, so what. She also told me that she admired my sports car.

One day I foolishly loaned my beautiful car to a so-called friend, who thanked me by tearing first gear out of my transmission, and refusing to pay for it to be repaired. I ended up trading my beloved car to the Motorcycle Queen for her stupid motorcycle. It didn't occur to me until years later, that this woman, who called herself a witch, got exactly what she wanted—my beloved car.

A coincidence? I don't think so.

Without my TR3 I was totally hating life.

And since I no longer had four wheels, I lost my great job at Mort Kaye studios. No more visiting *Mar A Lago* (that was when Marjorie Merriweather Post still owned it). No more taking candid shots of the great Jackie Gleason at his race track opening in Hollywood, Florida. No more shooting candids of the Kennedys at charity events. No more pay checks. No more income. Not so good.

One night, during a severe thunderstorm, someone stole my motorcycle even though I had parked right by the front door. What now? After the storm let up, I went looking for clues and found my bike partially dissembled in the sand dunes in a field behind our house. The rain storm had apparently driven the thieves off before they could finish stripping it. I had just enough cash to walk to the parts store, buy the parts, and put my bike back together myself. Gross. Now I was really broke.

Thankfully, a fellow worker offered to drive me and my motorcycle all the way back to Georgia... back to my parent's house. How humiliating. Good grief, they must have been tired of me by now. I was tired of me!

By September of 1971, my twentieth birthday, I could accurately describe myself as one hot mess.

Broke and ashamed, I holed up at mom and dad's. Thankfully, they had moved from Dean Avenue to a brand-new house in another part of town. I quickly got a job at Burkhalter's Photography Studio in the sleepy little town of Cartersville,

Georgia. This was the town where I had given birth to my twins, and I had all kinds of crazy feelings; and faced with the prospect of potentially meeting them had me on edge.

I constantly wondered if their mother would come waltzing into the studio one day to have their portrait shot. I would agonize over what I would say and do if that happened. Would I have the guts to let them go again? Or would I fight like a mother tiger to get them back? All of this was just too weird to dwell on. Instead, I worked at making the place as clean and successful as I could, just in case. If they did show up I wanted them to see a responsible, hard-working woman of whom they could be proud.

I took a failing portrait studio, totally in the red, and turned it into a good money maker. Shooting studio portraits with my Minolta twin-lens reflex camera came very naturally to me, and I did all of my own positive and negative retouching. I was very good at what I did. After all, I had been trained by the best, Miesel Photochrome and Mort Kaye. I complimented my shooting talent with a bubbly gregarious personality. I never met a stranger. My Irish grandmother used to say I had kissed the Blarney Stone, and had the gift of the gab. Perhaps she was right.

During the week I would work diligently, by myself, at the photography studio, and on the weekends I would buzz into Atlanta where I became immersed in the hippie scene. I made a whole new group of friends there. We loved to listen to music, do drugs, and hang around Piedmont Park, where all things cool were happening. I became the quintessential flower child; peace, love, and rock'n'roll.

In the hippies I found a group who seemed to want to expand their consciousness and talk about the deeper things of life. We did not want to be under the thumb of 'the man,' the *status quo*, and so we searched for a more spiritual meaning to life, asking questions like "why am I here?" When I told my new friends about my spooky visions as a child they didn't bat an eye. The usual response was, "Far f**kin' out, man!" Or, "Way cool!" Wow! Someone actually believed me now. Some of them had even had similar experiences.

For the first time in my life I felt like I was accepted, just for being me. No masks, no facade, no one wanted anything from me, I could just be Peg. I loved having the freedom to talk about things that had happened to me without fear of being judged or ridiculed.

Isn't that the bottom line though, isn't that what we are all looking for? To be understood and accepted by others?

Fortunately, I met three wonderful women there, Chris J, Judy B, and Judy J, who were all a year older than me. And, believe it or not, all three of them had also given up children for adoption right out of high school. They had met and bonded when they were all at the *Florence Crittenton* home for unwed mothers in Atlanta, and had all moved in together after they left.

When I befriended these women, who had been through the same experience I had, it was the first time I did not feel like a leper, or pond scum in my heart-of-hearts. Here were three other strong, loving women who had been faced with the same gut-wrenching decision I had, and they were moving forward with their lives. They also understood my regret, my pain, and my guilt. They understood why I was torn up inside. The four of us had an unspoken understanding. What a Godsend they were to my life.

They took me under their wings, and encouraged me, told me that I would make it through this, too. Meeting Chris J, and the two Judy's probably saved my life because it gave me a glimpse of hope that I could survive in spite of my heartbreaking decision. They made me feel almost normal.

But of the three, Chris Johnson, quickly became my closest friend. We had both come out of the same small-town USA, (Rome, Georgia), and were both looking for something more in life than a Ken and Barbie lifestyle, complete with gossipy neighbors who had their nose in everybody's business.

After I met Chris J, I saw a poster that read, "A friend is one to whom you can pour out the contents of your heart, chaff and grain alike; knowing that the gentlest of hands will take and sift it, keep what is worth keeping and with a breath of kindness, blow the rest away."

Unbelievable. I had finally found that kind of friend.

Although only a year older than me, Chris became both a friend and a mentor. She was what I called an 'old soul.' She was wise beyond her years. She was also the person who first introduced me to the hippie movement, gave me my first hit of LSD, and many other firsts.

We would all pile into a car on Friday nights to go see all the great bands of the day, and party like it was 1999. Atlanta was a clearing house for all the great up-and-coming musicians of the day like *The Who, Mountain, Black Oak Arkansas, Grand Funk*, and more. There was a feeling of love and camaraderie that was just what I needed at the time.

But the dark side (and there always is one) were the pseudo-hippies who would rob you blind, steel your stash, and leave you broke. It was during this time that my good friend, Donna, got picked up on a minor drug bust by two cops, and was violently raped. I remember my shock and dismay when she showed us her chest, and the three deep cuts that ran diagonally across her flesh where one cop had literally torn through her skin while ripping her blouse off. That incident obviously damaged my trust for the Boys in Blue.

But through it all, my friend Chris J was a safe harbor. She and I would have deep talks about all kinds of stuff. She was the best friend I ever had. She was the only one I had ever been completely honest with about my fears and shortcomings, and she took it all in with a calm equanimity. Nothing shocked her. I try to emulate that same character trait today.

During the week I would work in Cartersville, and on Friday night I'd head to Atlanta for the weekend. Chris J and 'the Judy's' lived in an area a lot like the Haight in San Francisco. Their bungalow was just two blocks from Piedmont Park. *Joan Baez, The Allman Brothers*, and so many other great bands would play in the park for free on the weekends. Drugs were bought and consumed freely, and for the most part, everything was 'groovy.'

On Sunday night I would head back to Rome. And when I was there, I still needed my safe place, like my old maple tree back on Dean Avenue, a place where I could relax and think. I found the perfect spot one evening, out on Little Texas Valley Road, in Armuchee, Georgia.

There was an old iron bridge that crossed over Little Armuchee Creek. It's not very big, only few car lengths long, and there was hardly ever any traffic on it. I drove over it once in the daytime, and came back later that evening by myself to check it out. I pulled my car (now I had a blue VW Beetle) past the bridge, parked it on the side of the road, climbed up on top of the steel trestle, and lay back on the cool metal span. It was so peaceful and so quiet, I was totally chill. I had a Miller Lite in one hand, and a joint in the other, and poured out the cares of my heart to Whoever might be up there listening.

Lying atop the bridge, I was soothed by the creek that gurgled beneath me, and immersed myself in the starry heavens as the orbs peeked out of the inky night sky. It was magnificent. Once again, I had my 'God spot.' Although, to be completely honest, at this point in my life, I was no longer sure about the God thing, and even less sure about Jesus. Was Jesus even a real person or not? Did he even exist, or was he a myth too?

But, at least I had my 'safe place,' my bridge on which to ponder these questions.

You see, I had sort of given up on God and Jesus when I was thirteen. Sitting in the choir loft of St. Mary's Catholic Church one morning (nursing a major hangover), I looked down on the church crowd. There was Dr. So-And-So, he was having an affair with my friend's mother. There was Mrs. X, she was the most hateful gossip in town. When it came time for communion, I watched those hypocrites get up and take it, and thought, "What a load of horse s**t! They are going through the motions, but they are terrible, selfish people. What's the point of coming here? Just to look good?" So I got up, walked out the side door of the Catholic Church, and haven't attended mass since.

The Byron pop festival had moved me light years away from my rigid Catholic upbringing, and my new friends in Atlanta had moved me even further. I suppose I became an agnostic. I began to meditate, study numerology, astrology, and alternate universes. With the aid of pot, LSD, psilocybin mushrooms, peyote tea, and the *Moody Blues*, I mentally journeyed to new places, constantly searching for answers.

The bottom line though—I just wanted to know what life was really all about. I wanted some Truth, with a capital 'T.' I didn't want to be 'Alfie', and get to the end only to find out I'd done it all wrong. I was tired of the perpetual question marks; I wanted a few exclamation points!

Little did I know I was about to get some of those answers in a most terrifying way. And that old iron bridge played a major role in it. A seminal event (pun intended) was about to take place that would change my life forever.

You often hear reports on the 6 o'clock news of missing girls who disappear and are never found; I was destined to be one of those sad statistics. You can run, but you can't hide if you continue to draw catastrophe into your life through your own heartfelt beliefs about yourself, your own inner script.

In the not too distant future I would be taken over that very same bridge, my 'safe place' deep into the Georgia woods, by a rapist who wanted to blow my brains out with a gun.

It is literally by the grace of God that I am alive today to tell you my story; but far too many young women are not as fortunate as I was.

Chapter 6

I Want Answers!

Grief can be the garden of compassion. If you keep your heart open through everything, your pain can become your greatest ally in your life's search for love and wisdom. Rumi

During my hippie days I was mostly dazed and confused, but I still wanted answers.

Looking back I understand the old adage, be careful what you wish for, because you may get it; and not always in the way you expect it. I was seeking truth, and got a big dose of it through a very painful lesson.

One gorgeous spring day a very handsome man I'll call 'Harry,' came into my photography studio. He struck up a conversation, and we enjoyed each other's company. Pretty soon he started coming in a couple of afternoons a week to talk with me. He was very clean cut, not my kind of guy at all, but he surprised me by broaching topics I cared deeply about, spiritual things; just the kinds of conversation I was drawn to.

"Will you walk into my parlor?' said the Spider to the Fly." This fable tells of a cunning Spider who ensnares a naive Fly through the use of seduction and flattery. It is a cautionary tale against those who would use flattery and charm to disguise their true evil intentions. Oh, how naive I was; Harry was the Spider and I was the Fly.

Harry and I had fascinating discussions about numerology, astrology, *I Ching*, and of course, God. He seemed incredibly knowledgeable about all things spiritual. He would come in late in the day, around four thirty, and stay until closing. I never asked him any personal questions; I just enjoyed our *tête-à-têtes*.

Shortly after Harry's visits began I noticed that when I would be in the back of the studio alone, retouching in the dark room area, I could sense a shadowy figure standing over my shoulder, just out of my peripheral vision. A wraith, watching me. I could feel its presence right behind me so strongly, I would turn around very quickly, trying to catch a glimpse of it—but there was nobody there.

All the hair would go up on the back of my neck because this was the exact same feeling I'd gotten when the apparitions appeared at the foot of my bed as a child.

Hey, I was twenty years old now, all grown up. I didn't have to be afraid of the Boogeyman anymore, did I? And yet, the evil presence would be so thick I could cut it with a knife. I tried to chalk this up to my imagination, but I wasn't having much luck with that. For weeks I had the overwhelming sensation of being watched in the back room of the studio, and I couldn't shake the eerie feeling.

I mentioned it to the one and only person I felt comfortable talking to about my fears, my best friend, Chris J. She told me that it might be an evil spirit, and that I needed to watch my back. And I blurted out, "What are you talking about? Evil spirit? Do you believe in that kind of crap?"

Much to my surprise she said, "Yes. Absolutely!"

I Want Answers!

That answer really threw me for a loop. Chris told me that she had recently been looking into Christianity. What?! You could have knocked me over with a feather. I had moved away from the Church because of its hypocrisy, and here was my most trusted friend, the one person I looked up to, telling me that there may be more to Jesus than I thought.

I was like, "Yeah, right, Jesus and the Tooth Fairy."

But, when I told her about the creepy feeling in the photography studio, she didn't just blow me off. She told me that when she was in Florida for a few days, a man had tried to get into her car and attack her. She said she had rebuked him in the name of Jesus Christ, and he had fled.

I was thinking, "Girl, are you for real?" But I looked in her eyes, and she was dead serious.

I sort of rolled my eyes at this, but since I was pretty open to all philosophies at the time, I thought, "Hey, why not?"

For the most part I just remember being thankful that my friend was all right, and that her assailant had not harmed her.

This was back in the day when I, myself, carried a loaded gun in my car. A nickel plated Colt Python, a sweet little snub nose that fit right inside the elastic door pocket of my blue VW. I carried a good bit of money home every night from the studio, and I knew there were people who knew I worked alone, and might try to rip me off.

After my friend Donna had been brutally raped by the police, I certainly wasn't going to depend on them for help. I decided if

I Want Answers!

anyone tried to harm me, I would shoot them through the car door, and ask questions later. Could I have really pulled the trigger? At that time in my life I would say definitely—yes.

Contrary to urban legends, hippies weren't all peace and love. Many of them were the worst of the worst, in constant search of quick money for drugs; preying on the weak and the innocent. Remember, Charles Manson was a 'hippie.'

Anyway, for weeks the good-looking, clean cut, Harry, kept dropping by and talking to me, and the spooky feeling of being watched grew stronger and stronger; but at the time, I had not correlated the two. I just saw him as a harmless guy who might have the answers to a few of my questions. The Spider and the Fly.

The Bible says that Satan can present himself as an angel of light. (2 Corinthians 11:14). I reckon that's what Harry did. But, what price would he exact for the answers I was seeking? I was about to find out in a very painful way.

Chapter 7

A Bridge Too Far

Bridge–noun: a structure spanning and providing passage over a gap or barrier.

In the back of the photography studio, I couldn't shake the creepy feeling of someone watching me, and it brought back my old childhood fears with a vengeance. I found myself going to my bridge out in Little Texas Valley more and more often, for comfort. I'd lay up there, talking to the Universe, smoke a joint, and think, "Ahhh! All is right with the world." And it was... at that moment.

One day in late June, handsome Harry came in to talk, and stayed around longer than usual. It was past closing time, and as evening approached he asked if I wanted to go to his place to look at his book collection.

Books. What could possibly go wrong, just looking at books? Oh, boy, I was about to find out—*plenty*!

Have you ever walked into a situation with your eyes wide open, expecting it to be a good thing, only to have it turn into a complete disaster?

We drove up to a nice little place out in the middle of nowhere, surrounded by woods and farmland, but not another soul in sight. His place was what we call a double-wide down here in the South, but it was neat, and clean as a pin. When we entered the front room, what was supposed to be the living/dining area, Harry had turned into a huge library. The room was covered in bookshelves on three walls, floor to ceiling. I could tell at a glance that they were old expensive books, leather bound, gold letters on the binding, and thought, "Wow, this guy is smart."

I also noticed how dark it was inside. The summer sun was still shining brightly, but the bookshelves covered the windows and so it was really hard to see inside.

We were sitting on the sofa talking, when I looked over at Harry and suddenly his teeth looked like vampire fangs! What? I sort of blinked, and looked away, and when I looked back he had a little smirk on his face, like he was in on a joke that I was unaware of, only now he looked normal. I was so shaken that I excused myself to go to the bathroom, looked at myself in the mirror, and splashed cold water on my face. I thought, "Okay that was weird. My biggest childhood fear—vampires. Girl, get a hold of yourself! Are you having a flashback from some LSD trip, or what?"

When I was a kid, I never went to horror movies, especially Dracula, but not even the Werewolf, or Frankenstein. My nerves were already stretched as tight as piano wire, and I didn't need to pay good money to scare myself more than I already was. So I stayed away from all that goofy stuff that kids are so drawn to because I just didn't want to see it. It freaked me out.

Color me stupid, but I chalked up the vampire incident with Harry to the darkness of the room playing tricks with my eyes, or perhaps some latent drug in my system, and I put it out of my mind.

It reminds me of the old joke about slasher movies, when the voice in her head is saying, "Get out! Take your keys and go home!" Unfortunately, I didn't heed the warning.

A Bridge Too Far

After a while, Harry asked if I wanted to have supper with him. And I said, "Yeah, cool." He followed me back to Rome in his car, and even came into my house and met my parents. They were probably shocked that I bought such a clean cut, square looking guy home with me, and not one of my typical long haired, bearded friends.

We took Harry's car to go have pizza. It was an older model, with a bench seat in the front. At Pizza Roma we continued to talk about life, death, God, religion, you name it. We had a really long conversation about Jesus Christ, and whether he really existed or not.

This was a work night, and so I did not have much to drink, maybe one mug of beer, but I was really enjoying Harry's company, mainly because of the topics we were discussing. Was this guy Jesus real? I wanted to know.

After pizza it was just getting dark, and I had this sudden urge to share with Harry something that was very precious to me, my safe place; *my* bridge on Little Texas Valley Road, and I directed him there.

We were still talking about Jesus as we neared the bridge. As we got closer I was overjoyed to share this special place with such a cool new friend. But, much to my amazement, when we got to the bridge, and I exclaimed, "Stop, this is it!" But Harry kept right on going.

I said, "Hey! Wait a minute, that's my bridge, right here!" And Harry looked at me, and said in a voice that would make your skin crawl, "I have given you knowledge about Jesus, and now you have to *pay*..."

A Bridge Too Far

Puzzled, I said, "Pay? How?"

To which he coldly replied with a sneer, "Your *body*."

I started laughing and said, "Yeah, right. You're kidding. Right...?" Unfortunately—he wasn't.

Harry kept driving down the deserted road, surrounded by the ever darkening woods. I had heard at the end of that particular road there was an old abandoned church where Satanic rituals were rumored to be carried out. But he stopped before we got that far. This was all too creepy.

He pulled way off the side of the road, edging the car into the woods, and then casually leaned across in front of me, opened his glove compartment, and took out a revolver. He flicked it open to show me the bullets, fully loaded, all six chambers, and nicked the gun closed.

Pointing the gun at me, he said in a most casual tone, "You can stay in here with me in the car... or you can go out *there*... with *them*," pointing the barrel towards the dark woods.

I almost fainted from the adrenaline rush, because I intuitively knew what '*they*' were out in the woods, the wraiths, the demons that had terrified me as a child. And I knew they would somehow tear me limb from limb. I saw a vivid mental picture of myself ripped to shreds by some demonic wild animals, my body rotting in the woods, never to be found. It was grotesque.

I turned from the window to look back at Harry, who had now taken on the visage of a wolf man, glassy-eyed, and his face was covered with fur. What the hell was going on here?

A Bridge Too Far

Believe it or not, I was not afraid. I was just stunned. I thought, "Well, if I'm going to die in this damn car tonight, I'm not going to be a coward. I won't give this S.O.B. the satisfaction of making me cry, or beg. I have already been through too much sexual abuse in my life. And I am tired of it."

At that point Harry cocked the loaded gun and held it against my temple, and some kind of unnatural calm came over me. I became hyper-alert. It was like everything was happening in slow-motion, and I was there, but at the same time I wasn't there. It was like I was observing the whole event, and thinking, "This can't be happening to me."

I am not going to go into detail of exactly what Harry did, suffice to say, he violently raped me, and blood was shed.

Somewhere in midst of this defilement, an image of my friend Chris came to mind, and I could hear her telling me about the man who tried to attack her. She had shouted, "Get out of here in the name of Jesus Christ!" and he had fled.

I remember thinking, almost sarcastically, "Jesus, *if* you *are* real this would sure be a great time to show up!"

Shortly after I had that thought, everything changed. Harry flung me to the other side of the car, like I was attacking him, and a look of shock and fear came across *his* face. This was quite a turn of events.

He seemed panicked, and screamed, "I've got to get you out of here! I've got to get you out of here!"

A Bridge Too Far

I just kept my mouth shut, tried to straighten myself up the best I could, and skeptically nodded, "Oookaaaaay..."

Then, I saw a dark shadow in the shape of a man's body rise up and *out* of Harry's body and flow up through the roof of the car. It passed right through the roof, and it was gone. Poof! It looked exactly like the shadowy figures in my childhood bedroom. All I could think was, "Holy shit!"

As I was trying to compose myself and remain calm, a huge wind came up; a zephyr. I'm talking pine trees bowed over from the force of that howling wind. It was like nature itself was pissed off.

And to top it all off, it began to *snow* on us! There was an intense, swirling snow that began falling all over our car. Now, this was late June, in Georgia. It was over eighty degrees outside. I felt like I was in some awful B horror film, where nature goes berserk. I would have thought it was all a bizarre hallucination, except here I was, wide awake, and it was happening to me.

As the weather got more intense, Harry really started freaking out. I was thinking, "What the hell is going on here?" but I was also holding on to his words, and hoping beyond hope that he would really take me out of there, and maybe even take me home.

Harry turned the car around and started racing back to town. Mind you, he was the one who now looked panicked. Like Alice in Wonderland, "Things just kept getting curiouser and curiouser."

I continued to stay as calm as I could, and hopeful that maybe, just maybe, he would really let me go. I hoped that somehow I would make it through this night alive.

A Bridge Too Far

He was driving the car like a bat-out-of-hell, and yelling to be heard above the howling wind. He screamed, "All those books you saw in my house, they were all books on the occult. That whole collection. I began conjuring up demons some time ago, but I don't conjure them up any more, they now come to me, and make me do *their* bidding."

And then the freakiest part of the whole night happened, he said, "These demons have been watching you ever since you were a little child, and they want you dead! And they tasked me to do the job."

I thought, "Kill me? Why? I'm *nobody*. I'm not important."

What immediately came to mind was my mom telling me that I loved God from the time I could speak. She said she would hear me talking to someone in my room, and when she asked who I was talking to I would reply, with a beatific smile, "To my guardian angel." She said I was a very happy baby, always laughing, and I had the sweetest disposition when I was young. Of all her children, she told me, I loved Jesus the most.

Of course, that was before Pa got a hold of me, and my world came tumbling down.

What Harry told me freaked me out more than the rape. So many things began to fit together, from my childhood abuse until right here in his car. But the part that scared me the most was not knowing how to protect myself against these demons now. I didn't have a clue. How could I keep them from coming back? How could I keep them from killing me?

A Bridge Too Far

The wind continued to howl as we raced through the dark empty streets of Rome. It was like the earth was having a meltdown. Harry drove me home, and (this is really unbelievable) walked me to my door, and said in a completely normal voice, "Can I call you next week to go out again?" (What? You have GOT to be kidding me!)

To which I replied as coolly as I could, "Sure. Absolutely," knowing there wasn't a snowball's chance in hell that I would ever get near this guy again. As soon as I stepped over the threshold, I locked and bolted the door, and held my back against it, shaking like a leaf.

Everyone in the house was asleep. So, I took about a two-hour shower trying to feel clean, all to no avail. I was awake most of the night wondering, "How on God's green earth do I keep this from happening again?"

I did not call the police to report the rape, thinking about my friend Donna. I was a hippie, so they would probably just rape me, too. I didn't tell my folks, I didn't want to upset them. And what was the point? What was done was done. There was no one I could tell except Chris J, and she was out of town.

My safe place, my bridge, was now obliterated, torn from my heart, wrapped in a Nightmare on Elm Street. Stolen, along with my peace of mind.

The only thing I knew for sure was that rape is not about sex, it is about power, degradation, and humiliation. And, if Harry was to be believed, it was about killing me, a good person, after humiliating me first.

A Bridge Too Far

I felt a tiny modicum of success in that I had survived the whole ordeal, and that I had not begged or cried out once. But, this experience broke my spirit so badly that it would be years before I could cry again about anything.

Rape is all about power and control. It violates the whole person. The soul is wounded long after the body heals. Harry was a repeat of my childhood; once again, I was taken against my will, at the whim of another's lust.

That night Harry took away more than my dignity, he took away my safe place. He took away my trust for people in general. He destroyed my faith in myself to have the right instincts about people. Dirty Harry murdered a part of me, in my soul, in my psyche, and it would take years for that to be restored.

But—he did not take away that tiny sliver of hope that there might be something else out there, a Higher Power who had saved my life that night. Maybe, just maybe, calling on Jesus had actually worked.

I crossed a psychological bridge that night: If I had previously been unsure about the existence of a spirit realm, that night removed all doubt. I had just been caught up in the dark side: rape, murder, death.

I had yet to learn that there are two spiritual kingdoms: the Kingdom of God, and Light, as well as the kingdom of darkness, and they both affect our lives. One for good, and the other for ill.

The message Harry spoke to me, "The demons have wanted to kill you for a long time," rang completely true in my heart. I didn't understand it then, but years later I would put all of this all together.

I remember thinking, "Logically, if there are bad spirits out there, like Harry said, there must be good ones too. How do I find out about those?"

That night I had seen supernatural powers at work first hand. I had heard about spiritual phenomena in religion class from the nuns. But those were positive events, not rape and murder.

Did good miracles happen in real life? And *had* Jesus just saved my life? What I experienced in the howling madness, deep in those Georgia woods would change my life forever... in both good ways and bad.

That fateful night with Harry, I crossed a bridge too far. I should have left when the spooky things started happening in his house. And that one disastrous decision almost cost me my life.

And yet, mercifully, some unseen hand had delivered me. I had just experienced the supernatural, up close and personal—and I needed to find out more about it. I needed protection, now more than ever. I needed answers.

And so, I did the one thing that seemed so natural to me—I *ran*!

Chapter 8

High Anxiety and Low Expectations

The Devil went down to Georgia. He was lookin' for a soul to steal.
—Charlie Daniels

The devil went down to Georgia, looking for a soul to steal—mine—and he had failed miserably. But he was not giving up yet. And the 'Harry experience' had left me very badly shaken.

Within the week I had given my notice at Burkhalter's Studio, packed my bags, and headed as far away from Georgia as I possibly could by car: the West coast, all the way to Seattle, Washington and then down to the Bay Area.

I left Georgia with high anxiety and low expectations.

I was traumatized, freaked out, and scared of my own shadow. I didn't expect much to go my way. I was a broken woman. But I had to get out of Georgia, and as far away from Harry as humanly possible. It bothers me to this day that I didn't have the *chutzpah* to turn him in, due to my fear of the police. The one regret I have is that he might have hurt some other woman. I can only pray that our night in the woods literally scared the hell out of him, too. And hopefully he got out of the occult altogether.

After what I began to refer to as 'the incident,' my friend, Dee, and I loaded up her old VW and headed west. It comforted me to have a female traveling companion, especially a sturdy Nordic blonde, who also happened to be six feet tall. I fondly remember Dee as the Friendly Giant. In a fight, I probably would have been the more aggressive of the two of us, but her size did help me relax... just the teeniest bit.

On July 4th, 1972 we stopped on the side of an Interstate highway somewhere in the Midwest, and watched a fireworks display. As we stood on the side of the road, mesmerized by the spectacular bursts of color, I asked myself one question, "What are you expecting out of this trip, Peg?"

And my answer was three simple words, "To stay alive."

We soon made it to Colorado, and to the spectacular Rocky Mountains. We took our time, hanging out and visiting camp grounds in the evenings, located on magnificent rivers. We would crash in our sleeping bags at night, under the stars. Just what my jangled soul needed. My 'church'—nature.

We heard through the grapevine that there was something big going on in Granby, and we decided to check it out. There were rumors that the *Moody Blues* were going to play a concert on a meadow, high in the mountain meadows near Granby. And I said, "Color me there. Let's go."

When we arrived, it took us most of the day to hike up the mountainside. I was wearing Frye boots with no socks, and had a sleeping bag tied around my shoulders by a thin cord, not nice wide backpacking straps. When we got to the top, my feet were bleeding, and I had two long cuts on each shoulder where the ropes had sawed through my skin. Ouch! But we soon found a lovely group of fellow travelers who invited us to share their meal, and who tended our wounds.

After that grueling all-day hike it turned that the *Moody Blues* were not coming after all, instead it was the first gathering of the Rainbow Family, a group of hippies who still gather at places around the world to this day. Oh, well. We were on an adventure, right?

In the dwelling next to ours, was the president of the UFO Club of America. There was quite a mix of everything up there in Granby, about every philosophy and belief you could think of.

The Maharishi something-or-other came up there too, decked out in soft orange robes, surrounded by a gaggle of followers. There was singing, dancing, chanting, and tambourines. It was kind of like a really long version of the old Coca-Cola commercial, "I'd like to teach the world to sing, in perfect harmony..." For a brief moment in time, we were living that commercial. Harmony.

There was a stunning mountain lake in the midst of the camp. It was freezing cold, but we still used it to bathe and swim in. If you smoke enough hash, nothing really bothers you, not even freezing water.

Much to my surprise, there was a lot of talk about Jesus Christ up there, and something called 'the Rapture.' I think that was the Rainbow Family's thing. Apparently they were waiting for Christ to return to Earth, or something like that, and I wondered, "Where has he been all this time?" I was absolutely clueless about any of these kinds of beliefs.

Most folks today are not aware that the hippie movement was intimately tied to the Jesus movement. It was more than just 'turn on, tune in, drop out,' many of us were searching for answers. Or, as the *Moody Blues* sang, we were "In search of a lost chord." As diverse as the group was, we all had one thing in common, we all knew that something was missing in our lives, inner peace.

As hippies, we were rebelling against the horrific war in Vietnam, against racial discrimination, against 'The Man' (a name for those in authority who were abusing their power), and against a government that was lying to the American people through their teeth. We considered ourselves peaceful rebels. And when you really think about it, wasn't Jesus the greatest rebel of all time? He didn't fit the mold, the social mores of his day, either. He was misunderstood in his own time (and still is), and he turned the world upside down when he said, *"Love your enemies. Pray for them that despitefully use you."* Please, tell me a more revolutionary statement than that.

That idyllic sun-filled week restored my faith in humanity to some degree. But it was very short-lived. My bubble burst the very day we came down off the mountain.

Dee and I went to a restaurant in rural Colorado, and we both felt everyone staring at us like we were Martians. I looked around and realized that everyone in there was a Native American except for us, and here we were, two lily-white, hippie girls with long flowing hair and torn blue jeans with flower patches on our clothes. We stood out like two sore thumbs. It was just the opposite of how we had felt on top of the mountain. The patrons' disgust for us was palpable, like they couldn't wait for us to leave their establishment.

That was my first real taste of prejudice directed at me because of the color of my skin. It was unnerving. I immediately remembered the blacks during segregation, and thought, "Well,

Georgia is not the only place on the planet where racism is alive and well." Thank God, even as a teenager raised in the South, I was for racial equality. I had many black friends, and vociferously embraced the civil-rights movement led by Dr. Martin Luther King.

Although being in that diner was super-scary at the time, I was also strangely consoled to realize that the South didn't have a corner on prejudice; it just shifted when you changed locations, from one group to another. Like the prejudice I found directed against the Chinese when I lived in San Francisco. Unfortunately, hate and prejudice comes in many colors, and is not limited to any one particular people or location, but it is always wrong.

When we left the diner the sun was just going down, and I noticed one guy in particular, an ugly man with greasy dark hair and a long scar on his pock-marked face, who had been surreptitiously eye-balling us the whole time we were there. We ignored him, pulled out of the parking lot and drove until about two that morning. Then, too tired to pitch a tent, we pulled off in a deserted rest area, and fell asleep in the VW.

Suddenly I was wide awake, and there was the dark-haired guy from the restaurant, with his face against our window, wild eyed, and holding a tire iron in his hand. I kicked Dee's seat to wake her up, rolled down the front window, and yelled with all the confidence I could muster, "What in the hell do you want?"

He held up the tire iron and said, "I thought maybe you needed help." Yeah, right; a man follows us six hours across state lines to lend us a hand that we didn't need at three o'clock in the morning. I don't think so!

I said, "Get the hell out of here!" shoved the half-asleep Dee over to the passenger's seat, cranked the V-Dub, put it in reverse, and took off like a scalded cat. I drove the rest of the night, until mid-morning, and we found another rest area with more people, that felt safer. Once again I wondered how I had been able to scare him off. There were two of us, but he had a weapon, a tire iron, and could have easily overcome two sleeping women in the middle of nowhere.

Finally we made it to Seattle, where we stayed for a couple of weeks, and traded in the V-Dub for an old Metro Mite milk truck. I laughingly referred to it as my 'Hippie RV.' We threw in a mattress, a bag of fruit, a jug of water, a can of Top cigarette tobacco in the back and, as we say in the South, we were now living in high cotton. I painted a big five-foot high butterfly on the back doors. Ensconced in such luxury, we were off on the next leg of our adventure; California, here I come!

We headed south, to San Francisco by way of Route 1 that runs along the spectacular Pacific Coast. I constantly marvel that one country can hold so much diversity of natural beauty within its borders. If you have never traveled across these great United States by car, or RV, you've missed some amazing sights.

Along the way, we would come across different hippie communes, and drop in and hang out for days, or weeks, before moving on.

We spent several weeks in one particular commune in Takilma, Oregon, another fairy book place. I'll never forget that experience. There was such a feeling of harmony. Everyone was so easy-going and laid back: it was a real 'chilled out' vibe. We originally drove up to it by way of a river, late one afternoon. There were a whole bunch of folks skinny dipping and we hopped out of our milk truck, and joined right in. I remember diving into the water and seeing these beautiful round stones covering the bottom of the river bed. I was dazzled by the way the afternoon sunlight shafted through the water, and reflected off the rocks, an unreal kind of beauty. It was a kaleidoscope of light and color. One of the most beautiful sights I have ever seen, to this day, and I was stone-cold sober.

Since 'the incident,' I had stopped drinking and doing hard drugs altogether. I would smoke a doobie every now and then, but I thought it best to have my wits about me in light of my recent traumatic events. But in Takilma, I felt safe enough to take one last trip on LSD. A clean batch of Clear-light had just come in, and it looked like everyone had decided to take a communal trip. I thought, "How can I pass this up?"

We all dropped acid around supper time, and it was one of the most beautiful nights of my life. I don't encourage anyone to try LSD, and I am not proud that I did, but this book is written in full disclosure. This was part of my life, a part of my personal journey in seeking out truth.

All night long I wandered through the peaceful woods by myself, fascinated by the tall, tall trees, their bark, the stars bursting forth from the heavens. I lazily sauntered from hut, to teepee, to shack; sitting around fires and talking to fellow travelers in this journey called Life. These were gentle, kind people whom I had never met before that night, welcoming me into their abodes. For that brief shining moment I seemed to be in the midst of one of those rare universal harmonic times. I felt totally safe. I felt at One with the Universe.

Someone had a lovely illustrated book called, *Tiger Flower*. I still own a copy of that book. It is a story about a tiger that goes to a land where everything that was big is small, and everything that was small is big. The tiger is relieved because he no longer had to be King of the jungle, he could relax and hunt flowers instead of killing prey.

The book is about the tiger's search for inner peace in the midst of an upside-down world. That sounded a lot like my own quest, looking for peace in an upside-down world. That LSD experience was the one of the few times I had what was commonly referred to as a 'good trip.'

And even though that trip may have *seemed* beautiful, Satan can pose as an angel of light. I know that he gave me a 'good' ride in hopes that I would do even more drugs, but I decided to stop that night. I'm sure that it was a great disappointment to the kingdom of darkness that I did not become a drug addict.

When it comes to drugs, and alcohol, I know that I, like millions of others, was duped into going down that dark jungle path into the devil's lair. At first, I used them as a crutch, an unhealthy coping mechanism trying to numb the pain from my childhood; instead they just opened my mind up to even more demonic manipulation. Not one good thing came out of my using drugs or alcohol. And thank God, I am still free from their pull today. I have been drug and alcohol free for over thirty years, and have no desire to ever use again. My head is in a great place; drugs and alcohol would only spoil that.

High Anxiety and Low Expectations

After a few weeks, Dee and I reluctantly said goodbye to the good folks of Takilma and moved on to San Francisco. Traveling through Northern California was breathtaking. The Redwood forests have trees so big we could literally drive our car through them. There was lush greenery everywhere. Leaving behind those warm welcoming communities, we were totally unprepared for the harsh reality of San Francisco. It was like stepping from heaven into hell.

We had met up with my cousin, Ruby, in Seattle, and she had told us about her college in the Bay Area, called Lone Mountain. The first night we got into town, we parked our milk truck in their parking lot and crashed. Early the next morning we decided to check out the ocean, and drove to a dilapidated area called 'Play Land,' at the end of Balboa Avenue. This place was very run down, but I didn't pay much attention to that, I was so enthralled by the Pacific Ocean.

I had to go to the bathroom, and I left Dee in the truck while I searched for the facilities. I saw a doorway cut out in a concrete wall, marked Rest Rooms, and figured, this must be the place. Along the way there I had passed a group of girls, hanging out and sitting on a low concrete wall. Being nine o'clock in the morning, I didn't think much about it. Hey, I was from Georgia. I had never heard of gangs.

As I turned and went down the concrete stairs, that creepy feeling went up the back of my neck again. I went in the last stall, thinking that if they came in I'd have more time to react. When I came out of the stall, I slowly opened the door and breathed a huge sigh of relief when I saw that there was no one in sight.

High Anxiety and Low Expectations

I went to the sink to wash my hands, looked in the mirror, and my heart sank. The gang of girls came flooding down the stairs into the bathroom and surrounded me. The leader was almost six feet tall, and the girl next to her held out a shiny switchblade knife.

In those days I carried my money and my driver's license in a small silk pouch which I cinched around my belt loop, and tucked inside the waistband of my jeans. Ever since 'the incident' I wore a choker with a cross on it around my neck, thinking that like the old Dracula movies, maybe the cross would protect me from harm.

And where was my six foot tall friend Dee when I needed her? Out in the truck.

The girls clambered into the room, and circled around me. The tall one grabbed my necklace and stared to twist it, choking me. She had such a vicious look in her eyes and asked, "Ya got anything for your head?" meaning drugs, while the other woman was now brandishing the knife near my face.

I squeaked out, "Excuse me, I didn't understand you." And she repeated the sentence while starting to rub her hand over my body, and pat me down.

When she started frisking me, and shoving her hand down into my pants, that did it! I could feel the rage welling up in my body. I had not let a guy with a loaded gun scare me, and I sure as hell wasn't going to let this wretch scare me. I calmly wrapped my fingers around her wrist, looked up, straight into her eyes, like I could chew her up and spit her out for breakfast, and said, in a low and growling voice, "I have absolutely *nothing* that you want or need." She looked shocked!

I slowly pulled her hand away from my necklace, and threw it off of me. Much to my surprise, her eyes got wide, and she backed off. She was scared of ME! All of the girls looked stunned when she did that, but they backed away from me too. The circle of death parted like the Red Sea, and I calmly walked out and up that long flight of concrete stairs, back into the morning sunlight. As soon as my feet hit the pavement up there, I ran like a cheetah toward the milk truck, jumped in and sped out of the parking lot, that is, as fast as I could speed in a Metro Mite milk truck.

Dee, of course, was sitting there totally oblivious to what had transpired. When I told her what happened in the bathroom, I got the typical response from her. She just kind of yawned and said, "No big deal." The story of my life. No one ever really *heard* me, except Chris J. No doubt, Chris J. would have been amazed, proud of me, and would have given me a high five.

What a way to start the day, we hadn't even had breakfast yet. One thing was for sure, this place was not Takilma. But I figured, what the hey? I am still alive. I had beaten the Grim Reaper one more time, and my day could only go up from there.

I thought again about Harry-the-rapist, telling me that the demons wanted me dead. I thought back to my car going off the bridge, the pile-up I avoided on US 41, the man who had followed Dee and me from the restaurant in Colorado, and now this gang of girl thugs in the bathroom. But for some inexplicable reason, I was *still* alive.

High Anxiety and Low Expectations

Yes, I had high anxiety and low expectations, but at least I was alive. And that counted for something.

I didn't know about guardian angels back then, powerful spirit beings who protect those who are heirs of salvation; but I must have had a few running interference for me. And I want to take a moment here, right now, to thank mine, because I'm pretty sure I put a couple of them into early retirement.

The devil went down to Georgia, lookin' for a soul to steal, but so far he hadn't stolen mine. Something, or Someone was working overtime to keep me out of his clutches.

Chapter 9

The Agony of Defeat

"Seeking what is true is not always seeking what is desirable."–Camus.

Months later, I wound up in Lake Tahoe. On a whim I had decided I wanted to learn how to snow ski. I had grown up on the lakes of Georgia, water skiing since I was seven, and I thought, "Why not try snow? I'm only young once."

By now Dee had long since departed back to Georgia, and I had earned enough bucks to get myself another sports car, a shiny little red Fiat 124 convertible.

With only a backpack in tow, and my trusty white cat, Zelmo, sitting on my shoulder, I drove from Sausalito to Lake Tahoe, where I didn't know a soul. I just felt it was the right place to move. When I drove up the long mountain roads I was in for a very pleasant surprise.

Lake Tahoe is an enormous, amazing deep blue lake surrounded by snow-capped mountains, huge skies, and forest, forest, and more forest. It is breathtaking. It is, without a doubt, my kind of place.

South Lake Tahoe was like a fantasy land. If you wanted to find the most spectacular landscapes, and amazing views in America, to me, this was the place to be. It reminded me of a Maxfield Parrish painting, and yet it was quite real. After traveling much of the world today, I still consider Lake Tahoe the most beautiful place on Earth.

The Agony of Defeat

To save money, Zelmo and I drove to a State Park around sunset. I put my sleeping bag on the ground, and was getting ready to crash when I could see a Park Ranger approaching, and thought, "What now?" As he got closer I could see his long, blonde hair hanging past his Smokey the Bear hat down to his shoulders, so I figured, he's one of us, how bad could he be?

Much to my delight it turned out to be a fellow called Ranger Terry, who knew a good friend of mine from San Francisco. He offered to let Zelmo and me stay on his screened in porch for a couple of days, until I could find someplace safe to crash.

What are the odds of that happening? Another miraculous event. Once again that unseen hand of amazing grace touched my life. A Higher Power was definitely looking out for me.

I looked for jobs in the photography or printing fields, but anyone in Tahoe who had these normal jobs never gave them up, and I couldn't really blame them. It was such a beautiful place to live, who would want to move? After pounding the pavement with no takers, I was fast running out of money. I reluctantly came to the conclusion that if I wanted to stay in Tahoe, and wanted to eat any time soon, I had only one choice—the casinos.

I had come to Tahoe to learn to snow ski, not to work in the clubs. I had zero-point-zip desire to work in the ritzy-glitzy gambling casinos. They were the furthest thing away from my earthy lifestyle that I could imagine. But hunger can do strange things to your ethics. Before I knew it I was working at the world famous *Harrah's* Casino in South Lake Tahoe; first as a keno runner (wearing a totally humiliating outfit) and then as a black-jack dealer (a definite step up in both pay-scale and attire).

The Agony of Defeat

I was so gregarious and out of the box that everyone liked me. I think the Southern accent helped, too. I was soon nick-named "The Crazy Tomato from Georgia." That about summed me up. My drinking had picked up again, after all, I could get all the free drinks I wanted with drink tokens, and my inhibitions would go down the more my alcohol consumption went up. Since I worked the swing shift which started late afternoon and went until the next morning, I also took a lot of "white crosses" a mild amphetamine, to get me through until my shift ended at 3 or 4 o'clock in the morning. I met all kinds of people still up and partying at that hour: both famous and infamous, movie stars, entertainers, professional gamblers, downhill racers. *Harrah's* was 'the' place to be in the early 70's, and a petri dish to study the human condition.

In that mishmash of culture, one thing I learned in the casino was that rich or poor, black or white, everyone had their problems, and few seemed to have any tangible solutions. Obviously the casino offered the simplest Band-Aid to those problems; numb yourself out with drink, drugs, gambling and entertainment. Right?

I was making more money than I knew what to do with. I soon settled into a beautiful little home near the base of Heavenly Valley ski resort; a little red and white chalet with a white picket fence. I shared this with a couple of other women who also worked at *Harrah's*.

I was living 'high on the hog' that's for sure. But oddly enough I was still miserable.

The Agony of Defeat

That's when I really began to worry. As Camus said, "Seeking what is true is not always seeking what is desirable." Here I was, living the dream, all that one could ask for in the senses realm; money, friends, boyfriends, sports car, skiing, and all of this in the most beautiful setting on the planet—but I still felt empty. I knew I had a hole in my heart that none of this 'stuff' could fill.

Inside I felt like one of those Olympic skiers on the old ABC, *Wide World of Sports*. In what should have been my shining moment, all this success, there was no "thrill of victory," only "the agony of defeat." This was supposed to be the prize, the successful life, but I just felt empty and defeated. Chalk up another bone crushing wipeout on the slopes of Life. Have you ever felt that way?

I hadn't yet learned that pain and joy come in through the same door. Since I had spent most of my life walling off my heart from emotional pain, even though I had all these great things going for me, I couldn't enjoy them because I couldn't feel *joy*. No tangible success could eradicate the darkness in my soul. It was a well of grief and shame.

Whatever I did, wherever I went, my brokenness was still with me. My heart was damaged goods. No matter how chipper or upbeat the 'Crazy Tomato from Georgia' seemed to be, in reality my inner pain and insecurity were choking all the joy out of my life.

I recognized the same pattern in many of the celebrities I met in the club. The world was their oyster, they had fame and fortune, and yet most of them were still empty: anxious, depressed, and paranoid.

The Agony of Defeat

So many opportunities opened themselves up to me in Tahoe. I met wonderful, influential people who wanted to mentor me, I was cast in a small part in The Godfather, Part II (which I didn't show up for on my day of my shoot), I had handsome boyfriends (all of whom I cheated on), and I had terrific friends, who I treated like crap. No matter how many good things were going my way, I was self-sabotaging my life at an astonishing rate. I was one hot mess.

I was very confused because, as messed up as my childhood was, I had still been a loving and compassionate child, always wanting to give to and help the less fortunate. But by the time I got to Tahoe I was living the reverse of the Golden Rule. My inner voice said, "Screw others before they can screw you!" I became a full blown-cynic. I determined that everyone was out to use everyone anyway, so I may as well get my pound of flesh first.

I began to objectify people. After all, people had objectified me all of my life.

I had totally lost sight of God's order for life: **Things are to be used, *people* are to be loved**.

And that's the state of the world today, everywhere you look people seem to love things, but not one another. We objectify human beings for our own purposes, and then wonder why we are so miserable. Like John Travolta's famous line from *Saturday Night Fever*, "All the world is dumping, even humping is dumping." That about summed it up.

I had first noticed my hard-heartedness a couple of years earlier, when I was still hanging out in Atlanta. I was on Piedmont Avenue, one sunny afternoon, around 4 o'clock. As I was walking down the street I thought I heard a firecracker go off. No. I looked up and saw that a woman had been shot about fifteen feet in front of me, in broad daylight. Everything moved into slow motion. She was a short blonde, wearing a black jacket, and yellow blouse, sprawled on the side-walk, on her back, with a dark red hole in the middle of her chest. The contrast of the blood on her yellow shirt was embossed in my brain. And there was a man with a gun running down the street. Her pimp, maybe? Or, a drug deal gone bad? And I was the closest person to her.

When I was a child, my immediate instinct would have been to run to her, and give her aid; but instead, at nineteen, I crossed the street, and watched the drama unfold from a distance. As people gathered around her, and police sirens began to wail, I stood there, in that darkened doorway, and thought, "What the hell has happened to you, Peg? You have become an unfeeling monster, and everything you used to abhor." I didn't even know who I was anymore.

Two years later, in Tahoe, I had gone even further down the black rabbit hole. It seemed to me that the hallmarks of society, as I saw it, were lust, greed, and oppression. Most people were takers, not givers. It is not too strong to say that the world, by-and-large, has sold out to Satan and his hateful ways.

What kind of person are you? A giver or a taker?

God's cure for the human condition has always been love; not man's selfish love, but God's unconditional love, and kindness to our fellow man. But rarely do we see those attributes in practice today. That's why Mother Theresa was such a phenomenal human being, she embodied those selfless traits.

The Agony of Defeat

As crazy as this Tahoe gig was, I continued reading everything I could get my hands on, and searching for that illusive thing called 'Truth,' not knowing that God has promised to show me the way if we would seek for Him in sincerity. The Bible says so.

Ask, and it shall be given you; seek, and ye shall find; knock, and it shall be opened unto you For every one that asketh receiveth; and he that seeketh findeth; and to him that knocketh it shall be opened... If ye then, being evil, know how to give good gifts unto your children, how much more shall your Father which is in heaven give good things to them that ask him? Matthew 7:7,8,11

When I look back today, I can see that God was just waiting for me to ASK Him. But I was still looking for love, and truth, in all the wrong places.

There I was, living the high life and still searching, searching, searching for answers, all to no avail. I read all the time. I had always been an avid reader. When other little girls were playing with their Barbie dolls, I was reading the World Book Encyclopedia. I didn't understand much, but I kept reading it anyway. By the time I was in the fifth grade, I was giving the nuns fits; my personal reading list included: *The Catcher in the Rye*, *Lord of the Flies*, and *Animal Farm*. Not particularly acceptable reading for an eleven-year-old girl in Catholic school.

In Tahoe I was reading everything I could get my hands on. I loved to hike around Emerald Bay on Lake Tahoe, find a sunny spot, and ruminate, just lie in the sun and think about life. I was in search of a lost chord, in search of why was I here.

I read all of Herman Hess, starting with *Siddhartha*, Robert Heinlein's *Stranger in a Strange Land*, Frank Herbert's *Dune*. There is a remarkable passage in *Dune* about dealing with fear, "I must not fear. Fear is the mind-killer. Fear is the little-death that brings total obliteration. I will face my fear. I will permit it to pass over me and through me. And when it has gone past I will turn the inner eye to see its path. Where the fear has gone there will be nothing. Only I will remain."

I printed that passage out and read it several times a day. Here was the answer, how to deal with fear. Hallelujah! How exciting. And that's when I got the bright idea that I should DO everything I was afraid of. Which turned out to be a really, really bad idea. More on that later.

I read the moving, and insightful *Man's Search for Meaning* by Viktor Frankl, where he talks about hope. This book is a compelling autobiography about Viktor's survival in a World War II death-mill called Auschwitz, a Nazi concentration camp. Frankl goes into great detail about the psychology behind why some prisoners died in those brutal circumstances, while others survived. He linked survival to having a positive image about one's future, in other words: hope. Frankl believed that the more vividly you could imagine a positive future for yourself, the greater your chances of survival were.

Well, that book really depressed me because I had no vision for my future. I couldn't see past my next drink, or my next bike ride. That's when I started thinking I might as well die young, because what difference would it make... to anyone? The only person I felt a connection with was Chris J, and we hardly ever saw each other any more.

The Agony of Defeat

On a friend's recommendation I immersed myself into the *Urantia Book*. There was one chapter that talked about the crucifixion of Christ more vividly than I had ever heard in Catholic school. It talked about Jesus' feet being only three feet off the ground during his crucifixion, and painted a picture of how Mary and the others were up close and personal when this whole thing went down. I could really sense how his loved ones were feeling his pain. It was the opposite of some sanitized painting where the participants were there, but emotionally detached. That was the first time I really felt what it must have been like for Mary to watch her son, with all the blood and gore from what the Roman's had done to him, hanging on that cross with spikes through his arms and legs. This description threw me for a loop. It felt real. I thought maybe the crucifixion of a man named Jesus, did happen after all.

I read all of Carlos Casteñeda's books, which took me in whole other direction, spiritually speaking.

I was on the horns of a dilemma, torn between The Doobie Brothers', *Jesus is Just Alright with Me* and The Rolling Stones' *Sympathy for the Devil*:

> *Please allow me to introduce myself,*
> *I'm a man of wealth and taste*
> *I've been around for a long, long year,*
> *Stole many a man's soul to waste*

(that sounded all too familiar)

> *And I was 'round when Jesus Christ*
> *Had his moment of doubt and pain*
> *Made damn sure Pilate*
> *Washed his hands and sealed his fate.*

The Agony of Defeat

Pleased to meet you,
Hope you guess my name
But what's puzzling you
Is the nature of my game.

What puzzles most of us is the devil's game. Not understanding what life is all about and why life happens the way it does.

I would listen to that song and think, "If the devil's not real, he sure gets a lot of attention." I would ride aimlessly around the small streets of Tahoe on my ten speed bike, for hours on end, thinking, thinking, and thinking. What is truth? Does anyone have any answers? Was what Harry told me true? Where do I go from here? I'm supposed to be living the American dream right now, but I still feel miserable inside.

My favorite spot was Eagle Falls, overlooking Emerald Bay. I'd buzz up there in my little sports car, literally on top of the world. If you look up 'dazzling' in the dictionary, you will see a picture of Emerald Bay. It is one of the most stunning vistas on the planet.

Dressed in cut offs, a t-shirt, and hiking boots, I could spend all day outdoors. With my long blonde hair, braided down my back, I was ready for my close-up, Mr. DeMille. Still looking good, but feeling wretched on the inside.

There was a large flat rock where I would lie in the sun and take naps during the day. Like my maple tree, and my Little Texas Valley bridge (before 'the incident'), this was now my safe place. Only now I didn't think so much about the goodness of God, I was thinking much more about the effects of the devil on men's lives. After a year in the casinos, the idea of the goodness of man was looking pretty dim and worn out. For all its glitter and glamour, the casino was a dark and lonely place, the belly of the beast, it held the allure of fulfillment coated in fool's gold.

Even while overlooking Emerald Bay, one of the most breathtaking spots in the world, my mind was filled with images of the depravity and greed I saw every night at the blackjack tables; so many people from all walks-of-life, trapped by their own neuroses and hedonism. Where was the Love?

The next book I picked up, Gurdjieff's, *Beelzebub's Tales to His Grandson*, took me down an even darker path. Like water swirling down a drain, even in this place of spectacular beauty, I felt my life force and joy leaving my body, as cynicism set in, and my heart continued to harden. Nihilism was beginning to consume me. Did anything matter?

I recount all the different books and philosophies I studied to illustrate how sincere I was in my search for meaning; but sincerity is no guarantee for truth. There were thousands of sincere authors, but which one had the truth?

Around this time a friend asked me to go see a new movie at the huge dinner theatre in the *Sahara* casino right across the street from *Harrah's*. I said, "Cool." It turned out to be *Jesus Christ, Superstar*!

Another surreal moment, here we were in the middle of "sin city" watching a rock opera about Jesus Christ. This bordered on absurdity. What was Jesus doing in Sin City?

Having never read a Bible, I didn't catch all the nuances at the time, but some woman named Mary Magdalene, who apparently had been a hooker, became one of Jesus' followers. She sang a song that moves me to this day, *'I Don't Know How to Love Him.'* I sat there thinking, "Is there a love that pure on Earth anywhere? If I came across a person like this Jesus dude, would it change my world? And why was he hanging around a hooker, anyway?"

As you can see, I was being torn between two spiritual ideals: one was light and goodness, and the other was dark and sinister. I was miserable and confused, without concrete answers, and without hope.

Have you ever been in the place where you had a thousand questions and no answers? It's frustrating isn't it?

By this point, in 1974, my life had taken on the pallor of that wrist slashing, uber depressing song by Peggy Lee, *Is That All There Is?* Was this all there was to life? Money, 'things', back stabbing emptiness? If worldly 'success' is the big secret, WTF! None of this stuff makes you happy if you're still miserable inside. If there was no cure for my internal pain, then life truly sucked.

I was falling, farther and farther down the rabbit hole of depression. I was feeling the agony of defeat. Nothing seemed real anymore. Nothing mattered... NOTHING mattered... maybe I was just a glob of molecules taking up space on planet Earth.

Burnt out and disillusioned at 22, I did what had become such a familiar pattern, I *ran*. I quit my lucrative job at Harrahs' to do.... *what*? I had NO idea. I was adrift. But still I ran, followed once again by the reality that wherever I went, **I** was still there!

I was feeling so defeated because as hard as I tried, I couldn't run away from ME!

Chapter 10

There's Ghouls in Them Thar' Hills!

The gateways to wisdom and learning are always open, and more and more I am choosing to walk through them. Barriers, blocks, obstacles, and problems are personal teachers giving me the opportunity to move out of the past and into the Totality of Possibilities—Louise Hay

More depressed than ever, I left Tahoe and moved back to the Bay Area with my boyfriend, Barry. We had a great place on Fulton Street right across from the panhandle of Golden Gate Park. I decided to take a quick trip back to Georgia to see my old friend Chris J. I wasn't sure why I was going back there except I felt lost; like there was no needle on my compass. Maybe Chris could help me.

For the long plane ride back to Georgia, I happened to pick up a new book in the airport bookshop. It had just come out and it was all the rage. Written by William Peter Blatty, it was called, *The Exorcist*.

I buckled up my seatbelt for the long ride home, and was in for one shocker of a story. *The Exorcist* was inspired by the actual 1949 exorcism of young Roland Doe. In the book the tortured soul is a fictional 12-year-old girl, in Georgetown, DC. It portrays her mother's attempt to get the daughter's demons exorcised by two Catholic priests.

As I read the story, I didn't wonder if this kind of stuff could happen; I *knew* it could happen. I just couldn't believe someone had written it down. I may not have experienced anything quite as dramatic as she did in my own life, but I had come darn close. I had seen apparitions appear at the foot of my bed as a child. I had seen my car go off a bridge and turn around in midair. I had seen Harry-the-rapist's visage change right before my eyes, growing fangs at one point, and turning into a 'werewolf' later. I had seen snow pour down in Georgia in the month of June. For goodness sake, I had been raped at gunpoint by a man because *demons* had *told* him to kill me!

Of course things like this could happen. Weird, unexplained things had happened to me my whole life. I only had to look down at the dark scarab ring I was wearing to think of another supernatural incident that had recently happened to me.

I have never cared about jewelry of any kind, but one day, shortly before I left Tahoe, I felt prompted to go into a jewelry store. There was a man working there who took one look at me and exclaimed, "I have something for you!" Since I had never laid eyes on this guy before, I wondered what he could possibly have for me. He turned and scurried into a back room, and came back out with a small leather box. When he opened it, there was the most exquisite, dark blue, scarab ring I had ever seen. Not like the ones my girlfriends wore in high school. This one was old, *very, very* old. It looked ancient. The scarab was huge, hand carved, and the gold setting was made of intricate twisted gold filigree, shaped into exquisite patterns. My mouth sort of dropped open when I saw it because of its sheer artistry.

My uncle had worked as a jeweler, so I had been schooled on fine jewelry, but I had never seen anything of this caliber before. It looked like it belonged in a museum.

I kind of wanted it, but I figured a ring like that was way out of my price range, so I said, "No, thanks" and turned around to walk out.

He ran after me, and in a pleading voice exclaimed, "No, no, no—this is for YOU!"

I thought the guy was off his rocker, but I had to admit, I felt drawn to the ring. When I told him, "Really, I can't afford it" he blurted out, "I'll take whatever you have in your pocket!" which was about five bucks. He took the money and put the ring box in my hand, and wrapped my fingers around it, while staring deeply into my eyes. It felt spooky, more like a rite of passage than the sale of a piece of jewelry.

When I got outside, I examined the ring more closely in the sunlight. It really was a work of art. Why did this guy insist that I have it? Then I looked at the back of the scarab inside the ring, and there were three symbols inscribed on it in a language that looked like Egyptian hieroglyphics. But a voice inside of me said, "No, these are magic symbols of the occult."

Hey, I don't speak 'witchy', but I had a friend at *Harrah's* who did. Aptly named Wendy, she was a bookish woman who practiced 'white magic.' So I took the ring to her, thinking maybe she could decipher it.

After she looked at the inscription, she turned pale and shoved it back at me. With eyes full of fear, she reluctantly told me, almost in a whisper, "It means 'where the four corners of the universe meet in darkness.'"

I said, "So what?"

She asked me how I got it, and I told her the story. She told me that it was a power ring, to be worn only by a very powerful witch, or high priestess. The whole time she kept backing away from me, like I was radioactive, and she looked very nervous. Then, she asked me to leave, and not to come back.

I sort of shrugged that off, and thought, "Well, since the demons hadn't killed me, maybe they wanted me to join their ranks." I thought, "What the heck?" and I began to wear the ring.

I soon found out that I could rub the ring, and ask for something... and it would happen. After a few tries, I stopped doing it because this kind of power scared me. It was too Carlos Castañeda and *Teachings of Don Juan* for me. It felt weird having power over the unseen world.

I kept thinking of what Harry-the-rapist, had told me, "I used to conjure up the demons, but *now* they control me." Is that where I was heading? But another part of me was thinking, "If you can't beat 'em, join 'em!" I know, stupid, right?

As I sat on the plane that day, reading *The Exorcist*, I looked at the ring and felt a chill run up my spine, but I didn't take it off. 'It' wanted to stay on my finger.

When I reached Atlanta, two of my buddies, Joan Bird and Maynard, picked me up. These were friends with whom I used to grow pot and do psilocybin. They told me that my friend Chris J was now married and living up in the North Georgia mountains. They said she was on the faculty of a Christian children's camp, of all things. They offered to drive me up there the next day, and I said, "Cool."

When I got there I was elated to see Chris. She was newly married, and had a sweet little baby boy, named Jeremiah. But right out of the chute she started telling me about Jesus and some Bible class she had taken called *Power for Abundant Living*, she even showed me the class syllabus. I was about as interested in that stupid class as I was in having a root canal.

Even though the scenery was spectacular up in those mountains, there was an oppressive pall over the place. Granted, it was hotter than blue blazes; Georgia in August tends to get that way, but the feeling was not due to the heat, it just felt dark and foreboding.

When I walked into the main lodge, which was a huge log building, there was a giant timber rattler coiled up in an oversized pickle jar on the mantle of the mammoth stone fire place. Yikes! On the other side of the room was a giant stuffed bear; reared up on its hind legs, mouth open in a frozen growl, claws extended in attack mode. I wondered how these two menacing creatures were supposed to instill confidence and love of the outdoors into these little kids? I mean, they scared the hell out of me.

I was not feeling a good vibe here at all. Nevertheless, I pitched in and helped. I taught the kids art classes, and shared the communal meals.

The first couple of nights I crashed on Chris's screened-in front porch. But on the third night they said a guest house had become available for me to stay in. It was a big, old two-story rough-hewn rock and timber thing. Big, and no one was staying in it but me. I found it strange that it wasn't near any of the other buildings, it was way off by itself; I couldn't see any of the other cabin lights from the second story window. It felt isolated and creepy. Another "Take the keys and go home..." moment.

I settled in for the night but woke up about two o'clock in the morning after having the worst nightmare I've ever had in my life (and that's saying something). On top of all that, I had an overwhelming urge to kill myself. I could sense a dark power trying to control my thoughts, and felt like I was in a wrestling match with *something*.

I panicked and started looking all over the place for, of all things, a Bible. But guess what? There was not one stinkin' Bible to be found in that whole stupid house! I thought, "What kind of Christian camp is this? They don't even have Bibles in the cabins? Even cheap motels have Bibles!" I looked for a phone. There wasn't a phone in the place, so I couldn't call someone to talk to, or ask for help.

I finally found some stupid book about people trying to escape from Russia, and read it, trying to take my mind off these intensely overwhelming urges to commit suicide. As the night wore on, it only got worse and worse, and by early morning I found myself in the kitchen holding a sharp knife to my wrist with my hand shaking, and a voice whispering, *"Do it! Do it! Do it! Kill yourself, end the pain! Do it now! Do it NOW!"*

Using all the will power I could muster, I threw the knife down, and went back and sat on the bed, exhausted and covered in sweat. I stared out the window into the blackness of night and wished for first light.

When sunrise finally came I was already packed. I bolted over to the Lodge, which housed the dining hall, and took one last look at

There's Ghouls in Them Thar' Hills!

the menacing giant bear, looking hungry for kiddies; I glanced over at the giant timber rattler, coiled up, fangs exposed and ready to strike, and again, wondered why on God's green earth they would put such horrific things on constant display to frighten the children. That's when I started thinking of this place as 'Death Mountain,' and thought, "I'm gettin' the hell out of this nut house."

As soon as Chris J showed up for breakfast, I demanded that she call my friends, and get me the hell off that mountain. I told her that if this place was what Christianity was all about, I don't want any part of it. And I took off to wait outside for my ride.

I think Joan and Maynard were shocked when they came back to get me. I don't know what they expected to see, but I was completely frazzled. When I told them what had happened, they just kept their mouths shut and didn't comment on my strange experience one way or the other, which I thought was odd, too.

A few days later I did the one thing I knew to do, I *ran* — back to San Francisco.

[Hey, if you're getting tired of reading about my messed up life, think how exhausting it was to live it.]

All I could think of on the way down the mountain was that the camp was supposed to be a Christian place, but instead of being holy there were ghouls in them thar' hills, and I was *never* going back... or so I thought.

Chapter 11

On a Warm San Francisco Night

Double, double toil and trouble; Fire burn, and cauldron bubble
—Macbeth Act 4, Scene 1.

I gotta go! I gotta go! I gotta go!

Once again I was doing the only thing I was good at—running. Back to San Francisco I went, more disillusioned than when I had left.

I was feeling even more dejected now that my friend and mentor had no answers either. Chris J seemed to have gone off the deep end herself, with all this Jesus freak stuff. And it looked like Christianity was a bunch of crap too. I felt like I was reaching the end of my rope.

I moved back in with my Jewish boyfriend, and sold my beautiful red sports car so that I would have money to tide me over till my next job.

I bought a 10-speed bike. I would spend hours, sometimes all day, riding up and down the steep hills of San Francisco: riding, and thinking, riding and thinking, wondering what the heck to do with my life. I had already made lots of money, had a shot at fame, tried almost every drug, abused alcohol, had plenty of men, and nothing seemed to work. I had a deep dark empty hole in my soul that nothing seemed to fill.

The most appealing option to me at the time was to become a hit man; some kind of assassin for the United States government,

CIA wet work, or the military. Seriously, I thought that I would make a great killer. I was already so full of rage from my abuse, and I was incredibly physically fit. I figured that I could easily pass muster, and learn how to skillfully annihilate some dirt bags: shoot them, stab them, garrote them, I really didn't care. I could make money and release my pent up aggression at the same time. It seemed like a two-fer-one. And I would be doing our country a service.

Human life meant nothing to me at that point—not even my own. In hindsight, my mind set was obviously both psychotic and disturbing. But, hey, hurting people hurt people. And I was in to hurting someone big time. (And, don't try to tell me that there aren't plenty of people in positions of authority looking for ways to take out their pent-up aggression on others, too. It happens all around us every day.)

One foggy day I was riding my bike on California Street, right near 29th, and spotted a bizarre two-story Victorian house set back from the sidewalk. It was painted completely black. Spooky, spooky, spooky. It even *felt* spooky in broad daylight. It had a tall chain-link fence in front of it with triple strands of barb wire at the top. What on Earth was this place?

Later that day, I asked a couple friends what it was, and they said rather nonchalantly, "Oh, that's the Church of Satan. Some cat named Anton LaVey is the high priest."

I said, "Are you for real? Satan has a church?"

And then I thought "Hey! Maybe *THEY* have the answers!" I was coming unglued, and dangerously close to sticking my head into a spinning airplane propeller.

I did not realize that I was being manipulated by unseen forces, and now I was cogitating on, actually considering, going there. I figured I had studied all the Eastern philosophies, read countless books, been freaked out by my best friend's Jesus thing, and that's when I had the dumbest thought in my whole life, "Maybe the Satanists have the truth." As Charlie Brown might have moaned, "Good grief!"

This is where the quote from *Dune* got me into a boatload of trouble, '*Do the thing you're afraid of...* ' and you won't be afraid anymore. Really? On the 'Good-Advice-to-Take-in-Life' list that advice ranks at a minus five.

I shudder to think of the depth of insanity I had sunk to at this point, but there I was, considering this hair-brained idea. For the next few days I rode around on my bike, contemplating how to become part of the Church of Satan, and planning it out. "Okay, I know what I'll do. I'll knock on the front door and offer to be a *human sacrifice*! Satanist love that s**t! That ought to get their attention!"

There was obviously still a fight going on at that time for my soul, and my very life. Apparently those demons still wanted me dead.

When I thought about the nuts and bolts of what I was asking for it didn't really faze me that somebody might jam a dagger into my throat, rip my chest open and pull out my beating heart. Hey, I had seen this in the movies, right? Nor did I consider what other defiling acts they might do to me beforehand. Believe it or not, I was so lost I felt nothing anymore. I was just numb. I was sick and tired of being sick and tired. I was only twenty-two years old.

On a Warm San Francisco Night

I surmised I would be walking into the jaws of torture and death, and my rock star conclusion was, "So what?" That's how far down lie-based thinking can take a person. I think I felt subconsciously that I somehow *deserved* this.

My mind was so twisted at the time, that I sincerely believed "Death is just the next 'phase'—this tangible life is just an illusion anyway; so what's the big deal?"

Excuse my French, but no matter how you slice it, that kind of thinking is just bat-shit crazy!

Nevertheless, on a warm San Francisco night in September 1974, I garnered the courage to pull the trigger and present myself to the Church of Satan. At that point I decided I needed some extra courage, and fueled up on mass quantities of pot and alcohol.

I wish I could tell you everything that happened that night, but I can't. I do remember talking to my friend Susan Mc about what I was about to do, but I don't remember what I actually did for the next several hours because I had another blackout. I remember being on Susan's balcony, swilling Dos Equis XX and smoking a pipe, and the next conscious memory I have, I was back at my own apartment many hours later.

Did I "get me to the church (of Satan) on time"? I'll never know.

What I do recall was when I came out of my blackout around 2 o'clock in the morning I was standing in my living room on Fulton Avenue. I had set all of our drinking glasses on the coffee table, and had smashed most of them against the wall. There was broken glass everywhere. When I came to my senses, there were only a few glasses left on the table. I thought, "What the hell is going on? Why am I doing this?"

I looked at the glass I was holding in my hand, set it down, walked down the hall, stumbled into my bed, and passed out.

The next morning I woke up around 11 o'clock with a massive hangover and a horrible feeling, wondering "what did I do last night? Did I go to the church?" Terror gripped my heart because when I reached over for my reading glasses, they were gone! Then I really freaked out, because I knew that Satanists could put a spell on you if they had a personal item like that. Now I was terrified I'd invited more demons into my life! Man, I was really losing it.

Oh crap! What was I going to do now? I was going from bad, to worse. Now I was going to have demons all over me, and be defenseless against their attacks. Woe is me. The line from one of the three witches in Macbeth floated through my head: "Double, double toil and trouble; Fire burn and cauldron bubble." Had I jumped out of the frying pan and into the cauldron?

I thought that maybe this is what it feels like to be on the brink of insanity. Lunacy! Madness!

I was sitting there in a cold sweat, in a manic state when I felt a presence in the room. But this one seemed friendly, and life affirming. It felt like—light.

Then I heard an audible voice say, "Peg, go back to Georgia."

I must have been nuts, because I answered it, and said, "Why? I just left Georgia."

On a Warm San Francisco Night

The presence was so strong I couldn't ignore it. I figured this must be a spirit too, but it had the reverse effect of my childhood encounters. It felt like a glorious wonderful presence, pouring peace and love and light into my being. It felt comforting, like an angel with a flaming sword, there to protect me. Whatever it was, it made me feel strong, and peaceful, and settled.

Then the voice said, "If you don't get out of here *now* you're never going to make it out."

I got up to check my cash on hand. I had been keeping almost $2,000 in a cigar box from selling my car. But, when I looked that morning, I had exactly $120 left in the box. Okay, what happened to all my money? Someone must've ripped me off.

So, I phoned the airlines, and a ticket to Georgia cost $119.50.

I would end up going back to Georgia with literally fifty cents in my pocket. What a cliché.

Okay, I was running again, but this time one thing had drastically changed—by the time I got on that plane to Georgia I was a broken woman, and I knew unequivocally that I had hit my bottom! There was no place left to turn.

Part II:

The Restoration

For what is a man profited if he shall gain

the whole world, and lose his own soul?

or what shall a man give

in exchange for his soul?

Matthew 16:26

Chapter 12

Running On Empty

For what is a man profited, if he shall gain the whole world, and lose his own soul? or what shall a man give in exchange for his soul?
Matthew 16:26

I got back to Georgia feeling decimated. I had spent most of the plane ride thinking about what I would do when I got back to Rome. After my insane plan to offer myself as a human sacrifice to Satan, I knew that I'd lost my rational mind. Who wants to have their own heart cut out in satanic ritual abuse? Perhaps someone who had given up, someone who was still badly damaged from childhood abuse.

I decided on two possible roads: one, I would just stop eating and starve myself to death because I was sick and tired of being sick and tired; or two, I would voluntarily commit myself to a mental institution and let the drugs take me out of my personal hell.

Remember, I had just been to Rome a little over a month before this trip home, but it felt like years had passed. I had just turned twenty-three, but I was so tired, so worn out, I felt more like a hundred years old.

But hey, I still had Gurdjieff's trilogy, *Beelzebub's Tales to His Grandson* in my suitcase, along with the vinyl LP, *Tubular Bells*, the theme music from the *Exorcist*. The devil was happy to keep occupying my mind with his sick music and literature.

I didn't know when my flight touched down in Atlanta, that Satan's days of running me ragged were about to come to a screeching halt.

When I walked into my parent's house that day, the first thing Mama told me was that Chris J was in Rome because she had just had major surgery, and wanted me to come and see her. Thank goodness Chris was not up on 'Death Mountain' or I never would have gone.

I drove over to Chris's house around 4 or 5 o'clock in the afternoon, and there was my sweet friend, in the bed, looking very haggard. She told me she had half her lung removed due to cancer, and had just gotten out of the hospital.

I was in shock! Chris was like the hardy German milkmaid, the kind you would picture in a beer-garden carrying 24 mugs on a single tray. She had this huge personality and a mane of wavy red hair that immediately got people's attention no matter where we went. She was always the self-assured one. To *see* her in such a fragile state brought me to my knees. She was the strongest, most capable woman I had ever met, and she looked so hollowed-out and weak lying there in that bed.

Here she was newlywed with a tiny baby. What the hell was happening?

I asked her if there was *any*thing at all I could do for her, and she said, "Yes. Go meet this woman named Larkin. I want her to tell you about Christ."

I leapt out of my chair, thinking back on the debacle of the Christian camp and I spat out, "Not only no, but HELL, no! You have no idea what happened to me up there at your stupid camp! I don't want anything to do with *your* Jesus."

At that point, Chris began to struggle to get out of her sickbed, and said, "If you won't go, I will get up and take you."

At that moment her mama rushed into the room and shouted at me, "What are you doing to my daughter! Why are you upsetting her?"

I tried to assure Mrs. Johnson I wasn't doing anything to harm Chris, and in her mother's presence, Chris made me promise to go see Larkin as soon as I left her house. Grudgingly I said, "OKAY, okay, okay... Just get back into bed." And she collapsed back onto the pillows.

I had no idea how very sick Chris was at that time, and how just the act of getting up was a supreme sacrifice for her, but she did it because she loved me.

So, I drove over to the Tamassee Apartments, mumbling curses under my breath the entire way. I walked up a flight of stairs and knocked on the apartment door, hoping no one would answer. Much to my chagrin, a woman immediately answered the door, like she was expecting me.

Larkin was a skinny, Italian version of Angela Davis. She had a big smile, olive complexion, and the biggest afro I had ever seen on a white girl. She wore a simple plaid shirt, torn up jeans, and seemed very laid back. Instantly, I liked her and felt relaxed. I sensed a kindred spirit.

I went inside and we talked for a while. She told me about her recent time in the slammer for, I think, a drug bust, and how the Lord had gotten her out of jail. I said, "The Lord can get you out of... jail? Why would He care about a druggie?"

She corrected me, "Ex-druggie, and He cared about me because He cares about everyone."

I was gob-smacked! Did God really get druggies out of jail? How utterly, awesomely cool. Now *that* could come in handy someday. I had already been arrested once, for going one hundred and three miles per hour in a forty-five mile per hour zone, driving under the influence, and resisting arrest. I didn't ever want to go back to jail.

She said she had a Bible fellowship right there in her apartment, and invited me to come back over the next morning for coffee. Hey, the Church of Satan was a bust, so why not find out what the White Angela Davis had to say?

When I got there the next morning the same two friends, Maynard and Joan Bird, who had taken me to see Chris J on Death Mountain, were both there with Larkin. Okay, so she's hanging out with my friends that I used to get high with. What kind of group is this?

We all sat around her minuscule dining table, drinking coffee and telling tales. Around 11:00, they adjourned to the small living room, and I picked up the coffee cups to go wash them in the kitchen. As I was standing over the sink, washing up, Larkin yelled in from the other room, "Hey, Peg, do you want to hear from God?"

Immediately everything went into slow motion, I took a step back from the sink, and watched the coffee cup fall from my hands, and shatter on the kitchen floor. Without even stopping to pick up the pieces, I turned around, grabbed the kitchen door jam and leaned out to see what the three of them were doing, but they were just sitting there, chillin.'

I took another cautious step out of the kitchen, and examined the room for wires, speakers, or any other kind of hocus-pocus devices they might have hidden to make me *think* I was hearing God's voice, but I couldn't spot anything fishy. I was hyper-aware at this moment, after all, a lot of really weird stuff was already happening to me, and I wasn't really game for more.

I recall even now how the sunshine shafted into the living room that morning, making the little apartment look almost like a holy place. Kind of like it glowed.

I warily came over and sat on a chair; and without any fanfare Larkin began to pray a simple prayer. Not a memorized Catholic kind of prayer, but it was more like she was addressing a friend, or a close relative. She prayed with a familiarity toward God that I had not experienced before. Then Joan Bird spoke in some foreign language, and followed up with a message in English. It was something about God's unconditional love for us, and how much we blessed Him.

What? WE BLESSED GOD?

You have got to be kidding me! I didn't even like myself, how could I possibly bless God?

Then Larkin did the same thing, and although her message was different, it was still uplifting and beautiful. And then Maynard gave a message too, but his was just in English.

I sat there with my mouth hanging wide open. All three of them sheepishly smiled at me and watched for my reaction. In the simplicity of that moment, I had a seismic shift taking place inside my heart. Something in my mind was going off: Ding! Ding! Ding! Ding! Ding! Jackpot! Jackpot! Jackpot!

I felt, deep down inside, that it really WAS God speaking to me through those hippies. This wasn't an intellectual decision; it was a gut-level response. I asked, in awe, "What was that?"

And Larkin answered, "A believer's meeting. Like in the book of Acts that was speaking in tongues with interpretation and prophesy. God gave this ability to His kids on the day of Pentecost so He could talk directly to us, in real time. So we could know the score, and the same God is here with us today. God is alive, and He loves us."

Man, I had already seen so much spiritual phenomenon, but other than that morning in San Francisco, when the voice told me to go back to Georgia, this was the only other manifestation from the spirit realm that felt *uplifting*, and clean. It made me feel better. I felt alive.

From my past experiences I knew for sure that the devil was real, because I had seen his work in many different incarnations. But that day, at the Tamassee apartments in Rome, Georgia, I *knew* for the first time in my life, that **God** was real too!

I had just heard words from heaven that spoke directly to my heart and, in an instant; I knew this was the real deal. Thank you Chris J! Thank you White Angela Davis.

What a relief. I was feeling a stone move off my heart, just a fraction.

I said, "Wow! I want to do that, too." So I started going to Larkin's bible fellowship three or four times a week for an informal bible study they called Twig. Like the leaves on a tree that produce good fruit.

You're probably thinking, "And Peg lived happily ever after." Don't I wish?

Nope. Just because I found something good, didn't mean that I didn't have to work to keep it. The battle in the spirit realm was still raging all around me. God will put it out there for us, but as the Good Book says, He expects us to seek Him with our whole heart. That was my part—it had to be my free will decision.

*But if from thence thou shalt **seek the LORD thy God, thou shalt find him, if thou seek him with all thy heart and with all thy soul.** Deuteronomy 4:29*

And that's what I did; I went after God like a Texan on a pork chop. I had finally found the Truth, and like a starving man, I wanted to gorge myself on it. So, I came to fellowship faithfully, I began to read the Bible, and I studied everything I could get my hands on.

And since I had tried everything else, I figured, what have I got to lose by trying this? Plus, it sure beat signing myself into a mental institution, hands down.

But, I won't lie to you, other than Larkin, Joan and Maynard, nobody at that fellowship liked me. At twenty-three years old I was in rough shape; from drugs, booze, and an unsound mind. I was angry, surly, and hurt. I had a chip on my shoulder the size of Alaska. At that time I was still giving and receiving plenty of 'hurt.' I didn't want to be around myself, so why should anyone else want to be around me?

I would come to fellowship stoned, or tipsy, usually holding a bottle of beer, which I would casually put on the coffee table during Bible study. No one told me to stop behaving that way, or that it was disrespectful; but they also didn't tell me there was a three-week Bible class coming up, because they didn't want me in it. Honestly, I can't say that I blamed them.

But, I was so hungry for the truth, I just kept showing up. I had a voracious appetite for the things of God. I had gone to Catholic school for eight years: eight years of nuns and daily 'religion' classes, and we NEVER once opened a Bible! What kind of religious training is that? I thought that was incredibly odd. What were they hiding from us in Catholic school? Could it be they were scared for us to read—the Truth?

After a few weeks, I could feel something new, stirring deep in my bones. Could this be what hope feels like? I was on the brink of finding answers to questions I had been asking my whole life. After all, I had been willing to become a human sacrifice at the Church of Satan just to get at one thing—the Truth. Now I realized I didn't have to die to find it; but that finding Truth was actually fun and exhilarating.

One night, on the reel-to-reel tape we were listening to, the teacher said in a booming voice, "You are never so far down that God's love is not deeper still. He didn't send His son to save the self-righteous, but those who *know* they need saving."

And boy did I know I needed saving. I had been running, running, running on empty, but God had His loving arms around me the whole time; through the good times and the bad. I now believed that Jesus was the Messiah, and that God raised Him from the dead. What a great feeling. I had a savior, and I finally had a protector.

Right after 'the rape incident,' the most burning question on my mind was simply, "IS Jesus real? Is he an historical figure or just some fairy tale made up to keep us in bondage?" That little Bible fellowship was the first place that had ever answered those questions for me, and it was a resounding, Yes! He lives.

Slowly, it began to sink in that God did love me. That He was not all pissed off at me. That I was not going through life with one foot in hell, and the other on a banana peel.

I learned that God Himself talked to men who wrote a book describing His love for us, called the Bible. Men wrote it, but God authored it. Cool.

Yes, it did have some do's and don'ts, which He put in there to enrich our well-being and happiness, like a parent teaching their child, "Look both ways before you cross the street," or "Don't touch a hot stove." But, not because God is some Grand Poo Bah potentate, or a slave master trying to bind us to drudgery; it's just the opposite. He laid out the ways of life because He is our loving Father, who wants to save His children from unnecessary pain and suffering in this world. Jesus said, when we know the Truth it makes us free.

No one wants me to reach my full potential more than God does. And no one wants to bless us more than He does. He wants to make our lives better in every way. And since He is the Author of life, He knows exactly how to do that.

I was particularly moved when we read about Jesus; and how kind and understanding he was to everyone. That was a news flash to me. It turns out Jesus didn't go around condemning people; he went around healing people, and blessing them all the time. He made their lives better.

For God sent not his Son into the world to condemn the world; but that the world through him might be saved. John 3:17

That verse was quite an eye opener for me. Jesus didn't come to condemn me, he came to make me whole; to save me from myself, and the insanity of the world. He constantly spoke words of forgiveness and hope to everyone. I was amazed to find out that Jesus was never unkind to anyone—ever.

I so wished that my Granny could have been in that fellowship with me, she would have loved it. What an example Christ gave us. Could I ever be that kind to people? Could I let go of the hate and bitterness that had taken root in my soul? I sure hoped so.

The only folks Jesus ever tangled up with were the religious leaders, who were spiritual leeches; compounding people's misery, not alleviating their pain.

I understood this because I had run into those kind of creeps all my life; takers, not givers. Charlatans. Jesus confronted them because he wanted to point out their lies to the common folks. He wanted to open people's eyes, and put a big "BEWARE of Frauds" sign on those fakers. To paraphrase Jesus, "These pompous religious jerks are not good for you. Watch out for them! They are vipers."

Thanks for the heads-up, Jesus, because the same thing is happening today.

One night at fellowship, I got some major answers to those miraculous, life-saving interventions of my past, we were reading in the book of Hebrews and came across this verse, *"Are they [angels] not all ministering spirits, sent forth to minister for them who shall be heirs of salvation?"* Hebrews 1:14. Like a bolt of lightning, I understood how my bacon kept getting pulled out of the fire, those wonderful angels. Now so much made sense: my car turning around in mid-air, being delivered from Dirty-Harry, scaring off the man who followed Dee and I, finding Ranger Terry in Lake Tahoe. God, my Father, knew all along, that I was going to come home to Christ; He knew I was an 'heir of salvation' and His angels had protected me all those times.

I especially remembered that moment during the rape, when I thought, "Jesus, if you're real, this would be a great time to show up." Moments later the rapist seemed to come back into his right mind: and the demon went through the roof, and the wind blew, and the snow fell, and Harry took me home... and I LIVED!

That was not a coincidence, but Divine intervention in response to my silent cry for help. Wow!

When it comes to God, you can run but, thankfully, you can't hide.

He's got His secret agents, His angels, watching over you until you make the decision to come home to Papa, where you always belonged. And even after that, they are still with you.

Of all the hundreds of books I had read, all the people I had talked to from 'holy men' to rock stars, from millionaires to bums, from the Ritz to the pits, the Bible made more sense in a few weeks than I had found in the last twenty-three years of my life. And I was searching diligently for answers.

I remembered sitting in the maple tree as a kid, asking God to show me the way, asking Him for answers, and now my childhood prayer was being answered. Back there in the maple tree, I had believed in Jesus. Back then I believed he died and rose from the dead for me. How had I lost that connection? I came to the conclusion that it didn't really matter. All that mattered was I had it back. Like the prodigal in Luke 15, I had come home to Papa, and He was rejoicing!

God is not bound by the limits of time and space as you and I know it. He is omnipresent; which means He is everywhere present, simultaneously, He fills the universe. He is omniscient, He knows all. If you ask, how can that be? I can only tell you that I do not even understand how electricity works, but I believe it, and use it every day. Don't ask me to explain God, no man can. We must decide to believe, or not believe. That's why it's called faith. But like turning on a light switch, I see the evidence of His presence in my life every day.

In that little fellowship I realized for the first time in my life that I was not a mistake; that I was not born for someone else's sick gratification. I was born to be a child of the living God, the King Eternal. And He loved ME even if no one else did. He loved me enough to send His son to die for me.

When it came to my search for Truth, I was no longer running on empty; I was filled with God's love and forgiveness—and He keeps right on filling me, one day at a time.

Chapter 13

And Then it Happened!

The people which sat in darkness saw great light; and to them which sat in the region and shadow of death light is sprung up. Matthew 4:16

By this time I had broken my engagement to my boyfriend back in San Francisco, and informed him that I was not coming back. He begged, pleaded and cajoled, he even had his mother call me and try to convince me to come back, but I had found what I was looking for, and if he wanted to join me in Georgia, fine. If not, *Sayonara baby*!

And much to the dismay of my detractors in the Bible fellowship, I went out and got the requisite number of people signed up for the Bible class, which meant I was in it.

I did this by walking into stores in downtown Rome, along Broad Street. If the clerk was not otherwise engaged I would smile, walk up to them and say, "Did you know you have more potential power in you than Niagara Falls?" I made that bold statement based on what I was learning, that we had the power of the living Christ inside us once we were born again, and that we could do the same works, the signs, miracles and wonders that Jesus did. Which I thought was awesome!

Some people looked at me like I was crazy, others said no thanks, but some wanted to hear what I had to say, and within about ten days I had the rest of the seven students needed to run a class in our area. Hallelujah!

And Then it Happened!

It was a three week, twelve session, thirty-three hour class, so it was a big commitment.

Around the second session, very disturbing things started happening to me. I would be driving home at night and all the stars would start 'spinning,' and look like they were falling out of heaven onto my car, which made it very hard to stay on the road. Grotesque apparitions would wake me up in the middle of the night, and literally throw me out of bed. Kind of like the wraiths that plagued me as a child, except these were much more violent. I would tell them to be gone in the name of Jesus Christ, and they would go, but these episodes left me shaken.

By then I knew enough Bible to understand that I wasn't wrestling against flesh and blood, but against the demons that had tried to kill and control me since I was a child. They'd had their hooks in me for a long, long time, and they were not happy to let me go. They were going to fight for me to stay under their power 'til the bitter end.

Something that amazes me to this day is that people think if something is from God it will come to pass easily, and without any opposition. I have experienced just the opposite. If a thing is from God I find there if usually a great deal of opposition from the dark side. This is why children of God need to learn to stand fast against the wiles of the devil, which they can only do by effectively wielding the sword of the Spirit.

The Bible doesn't tell us a whole lot about angels and demons, but it does say that they are spirit beings: angels being the good ones, and demons being evil. And both angels and demons can come into manifestation in the physical realm under certain conditions. They are all sentient beings who have a mind, and will of their own. (See Appendix 1.)

The will of those particular demons, back in 1974, was to keep scared little Peggy in their clutches. They were counting on my childhood fears to keep me in bondage. But now I had some Truth under my belt, and the Truth sets us free!

Folks, like it or not, we are in a spiritual war. And this war is for the hearts and minds of mankind. If Satan can't keep you from being born again, he surely wants to keep you from enjoying the new birth and the more abundant life. And that was exactly where I was at twenty-three; born again, a child of the King of the Universe, but still being racked and ruined by demons. They had been playing me like a pin ball machine for such a long time... *ping, ping, ping,* and they did not want to give up their turf.

One afternoon, just before session five, I drove over to the Tamassee apartments to talk to Larkin. I told her that I didn't know if I could finish the class because the spiritual pressure was getting too hot. She suggested I go and pray about it, and I said, "I'll *think* about it."

I'll never forget what Larkin replied, she said, "Well, don't think and think until you hurt your thinker."

It's good that she did not pressure me to make a decision right on the spot, because most likely I would have quit. You can't pressure anyone into wanting God. Each of us has to decide that one for ourselves.

After I left Larkin's, I drove out to a life-long favorite spot of mine, the lake at Berry College.

And Then it Happened!

Berry is one of the most beautiful and unique college campuses in the world. Its campus has more than 27,000 acres of fields, forests, and Lavender Mountain, the largest contiguous college campus in the United States. There are so many spectacular settings out there, but the lake was my favorite place of all. I had been coming here from the time I was a tot to enjoy its soothing tranquility. After I got my driver's license I would take my Granny out there. She loved it too. And Chris J and I often came out to the peaceful lake to soak up some sun, play our guitars, and sing. It was a majestic place. Sadly, it is no longer there.

On that beautiful October day in 1974, I drove my dad's Chevy Malibu to the side of the lake and parked it, taking in the blaze of the fall colors: dazzling reds, golds, and yellows. Magnificent! Stupendous! In the fall months not many places on Earth can beat North Georgia for sheer beauty.

I put the windows down, and inhaled the crisp smell of autumn, mixed with the pungent tang of Georgia pine. I sat back and closed my eyes. Pure bliss mixed with painful indecision. I leaned my head back into the seat and I whispered, "Help me, Father."

Could God really set me free from this lifelong demonic harassment, or was I just asking for more trouble by taking this class?

As I sat there, soothed by nature's splendor I pondered the question, "Should I continue this class, and my pursuit of God, or should I just give it up?"

There I was, in this idyllic setting, with my brand new Bible on the seat next to me, but inside my stomach was in knots. In anguish I cried out, "Lord, *please* help me! *What* should I do?"

And much to my surprise He answered me, and said, "*Read Galatians.*"

Shocked to hear His voice, I said, "Okay."

I was brand new at this Bible reading stuff, and Galatians is a pretty hard book to understand even for the seasoned believer, but I obediently began at chapter one, verse one, and muddled through the book wondering, "What on earth is this guy Paul talking about?"

When I got towards the end of chapter three, the payoff began to happen, it said, "*For ye are all the children of God by faith in Christ Jesus.*" Galatians 3:26.

That part clicked for me. "Okay. I believe that I am now a child of God by faith in Jesus Christ; therefore Satan has no legal authority over me. So why are these demons still free to attack me?"

I kept reading, "*Now I say, **That the heir, as long as he is a child, differs nothing from a servant, though he be lord of all**; Even so we, when we were children, were in bondage under the elements of the world...*" Galatians 4:1,3.

Well, good grief Charlie Brown! I certainly understood that verse. I didn't need to be a scholar to catch its meaning. It said that an heir (a child of God), could be lord over all, but still living like a slave under the bondage of this world (demons), because he or she did not know their true identity.

It would be like having a million dollars in the bank, but you had never been taught how to write a check to access the funds. Those demons were still harassing me because I was still a little unsure that I had the God-given power and authority to tell them to bug off. I had yet to embrace my legal sonship rights.

Hhhmm. Now the Lord had my full attention. I knew that I was still living like a slave to fear, to insecurity, to alcohol, to anger, and to a host of other traits that were eating me alive. I knew that I had been a prisoner of my own pain for decades. And so, I kept on reading.

Galatians said that even though I had been set free from the enslavement of the 'elements of the world' (including demons and my past) through Christ Jesus, I was still living in bondage because I did not yet know who I now was in Christ, and that robbed me of my spiritual authority. The picture I saw in my mind was Jesus had opened my prison door, wide, but I was afraid to walk out. At that moment, at Berry College, I was still afraid to claim my God-given power.

I needed to grow up in my understanding of the things of God, of my royal inheritance, and reach out and take it. Take hold of my freedom in the name of Jesus Christ. Something in my heart said, "Peg, that's what has been happening to you these last few weeks in fellowship—the struggle for your freedom. Christ has already set you free; now you need to embrace that liberty, claim it for your own. Cast off the yoke of bondage."

I had to cast off the bondage of fear, the yoke of worry and anxiety that is too heavy for any of us to bear. I had to learn to stand my legal ground and tell those demons to buzz off, in the name of Jesus Christ.

Our flesh is totally insufficient to win in spiritual warfare. That is why we need to use the supernatural power that our Father has given us. We must learn to effectively wield the sword of the Spirit.

And right then and there I had a seismic, paradigm shift!

I kept on reading, and verse nine literally leapt off the page: *"But now, after that ye have **known God**, or rather are known of God, how turn ye again to the weak and beggarly elements, whereunto ye desire again to be in bondage?"* Galatians 4:9

I rubbed my eyes and read that verse again and again. This posed the all-important question; now that I knew Christ and had been set free, WHY would I want to go back into bondage?

My prison door had been opened. Walk out, girl! Take a hold of your freedom in Christ.

Why would I want to go back, be enslaved, to the miserable life I had been living before Christ set me free? Why would I want to go back to those actions that left me feeling sad, and used, and empty inside, when a whole new life was ripe for the picking? And that new life was right here, at my fingertips. Why would I let those demons steal even one scintilla of my joy for one more second?

Boom! I made up my mind right then to walk in my new found freedom.

With crystal clarity, I realized my decision was a resounding, NO! I will not go back to my old ways. I won't. I will go forward with my Father, into the fullness of Christ. I will finish the class and ...THEN IT HAPPENED...

And Then it Happened!

Suddenly, I do not know if I was in the body or out of the body, I was transported to a place of peace, and love, and light, and joy unspeakable. It was terrifying and wonderful all at the same time. I was in a different dimension.

I knew in my spirit that I was in the presence of God.

I felt a sweet pure love exploding from my solar plexus like sunlight shooting through every fiber of my being: through my mind, the backs of my eyes, and into my limbs. It was a feeling that is beyond words; filled with overwhelming sensations. Like information was being sensed rather than spoken. I felt weightless and timeless.

I was flooded with a knowing that God loved me, and always had. Every molecule just 'got it.' I knew that this was God's unconditional love flooding through me!

For the first time since I was three years old, I felt pure, and clean, and holy.

I 'heard' this mellifluous voice saying...."*Peg, I love you. I always have, and I always will.*" And at that moment I not only felt loved, but I felt like I was *worth* loving.

All the shame of my past was washed, clean clear away.

I had never, ever felt this kind of love and acceptance from anyone. I innately understood that God's love for me was in spite of my past, and because of the sacrifice of His dear son. I knew it was something that I could not earn: I could only accept it. So, I let go and just went with the flow.

I fell madly in love with Jesus for all he had done for me, and madly in love with my heavenly Father for thinking up this whole plan of redemption.

God's love filled every pore of my body, every neuron in my mind. I was transported to a place of complete safety, security, and above all, Love—Love like I had never dreamed was possible. It was pure, it was holy, and it was real.

I knew that there was a Power, a Person, Who loved me, warts and all. I knew that that Person was God. The Creator. The King Eternal. The First Cause. HE loved me; and had never given up on me. Astonishing!

In that moment I knew that anything was possible—even a life without fear, and self-loathing. **I knew that I could finally be free** of the **demons attacking me at will.**

I felt holy, and clean, and happy, and alive. I was transported.

In a moment of time I felt washed, baptized, changed. It was like someone took a holy Roto-Rooter to my soul and sanitized me clean clear through. I felt a love that passes understanding surging through me. And to this day there are no words to describe that experience. It was so far beyond anything a human being can imagine. It changed my whole life.

The words that kept being impressed upon my soul were, "*My daughter, you are loved! You are loved! You are loved.*"

To quote Charles Finney, I felt like, "The Holy Spirit... seemed to go through me, body and soul... Indeed it seemed to come in waves of *liquid love*, for I could not express it any other way."

That day I knew beyond a shadow of a doubt, that my life was not a mistake, but I was here on this Earth for a purpose, and by Divine destiny. I was born to experience this kind of Love—not to be abused.

Then I saw a vision of myself, standing in front of others, telling them about the love of God. To my mind that felt like blasphemy because, having been raised Catholic, this was something only a priest could do. But the vision persisted, and my heart embraced it and said, "Yes. Yes, Lord. I am humbled; if this is what You want me to do, just lead the way." And, by His grace, I have shared the message of His love with countless others since that day, more than forty years ago.

I don't know how Saul felt on the road to Damascus, but this was my Damascus road moment. I stayed in that euphoric state for quite some time. I did not want it to end. I wondered if, when it was over, I would ever be the same again. And the answer is, no.

At some point I realized that my face hurt from crying; crying tears of joy, and relief, and appreciation to God for revealing His love to me.

This was highly significant, because I had not cried since 'the incident.' I had developed such a hard heart, such a shell to protect myself, that for years I never shed a tear. But that day by the lake, all my defenses came down in the name of Love, and I opened my heart to trust Him, Who had loved me all along.

That day the Lord began creating a new heart in me, one filled with confidence in Him, that He would be with me and protect me no matter what. I could finally relax and let myself grow tender again (once a very scary thought), by trusting Him to protect it.

That very day, I gave Him my whole heart. I turned my life over to His care. What a relief. What freedom! I knew I had an Ally with me, both now and forevermore.

I just sat there for a long time thinking, letting the moment sink in; God loves me! GOD loves me! God *LOVES* ME! God loves **ME**! Unconditionally and forever. Wowee, wow, wow, wow! That is some kind of truth.

And that day the Lord showed me that my history was not my destiny. I may have been shaped by my past, but I was no longer a prisoner of my past. With His help I could now decide my own fate. The puppet strings were cut!

I thought, "My life can change for the better, starting today. Of course I'm going to finish the class." And suddenly I had that feeling inside again... I had hope!

Like Dorothy in the Wizard of Oz, for me, life went from black and white to Technicolor in a moment of time. I saw that God's love is so much bigger than we humans can ever grasp, we just have to soak in as much as we can and hold on to it. I 'saw' clearly into the spiritual realm that day; that light excels darkness like a rocket ship excels a biplane. There is no comparison between the power of the Living God and the wiles of the devil. And, I have never been intimidated by a demon since that miraculous day by the lake.

The definition of a miracle is: "an event not explicable by natural or scientific laws. An event attributed to a Supernatural Being and

And Then it Happened!

His *interaction* with mankind, often suspending natural laws for a period of time." That day by the lake fit the definition of a miracle to a tee, and it would be the first of many more to come.

By now a few hours had passed. I drove back to the apartment to tell Larkin that I would finish the class. She opened the door and took one look at my face, which was red and swollen from crying, and she must have thought I was enraged. A look of shock mixed with fear crossed her face, and she ran and locked herself in the bathroom. I didn't blame her. This was how most people perceived me, a violent loose cannon, ready to explode.

It took some persuading to get her to come out of the bathroom, but I kept tapping on the door, saying, "Hey, I came back to thank you, not to hurt you. I'm gonna' finish the class."

When she finally did emerge, she just looked at me skeptically and said, "Uh, really...?"

I reached out and hugged her, and thanked her for all she had done for me. I guess she was still in shock because for the first time since I'd known Larkin she was speechless.

You may have noticed, but we do not live in a spiritually-minded society. Believers often make the mistake of thinking that because God shows us something great, other people will understand it too, which rarely happens. Most of the time they think we're nuts, and that's exactly what happened to me with my 'conversion' story.

No one believed me. When I shared about my heavenly encounter by the lake, they said, "That crazy girl, why would God talk to *her?*" (I've heard that a lot through the years.) But He did talk to me, and He still does.

And all of their doubt and skepticism could not dim what the Holy Sprit Himself had done inside me that afternoon. He took an emotionally bankrupt girl from Georgia, and put her back together again. Unlike Humpty Dumpty, the Lord was able to restore the shattered pieces of my soul.

That day I knew deep inside that He believed in me, and that was all that mattered. I was starting to understand the truth that, "You and God always make a majority."

But I had also asked the Lord, "Why would you show such grace to a sinner like me?" And His answer was simply, "Why not?"

Then He added this little caveat, "And, because I knew you would DO something with that revelation." God is not wasteful. People do not hear from Him very often because He knows beforehand (omniscience) that they are going to ignore his message. I did not.

"This is a faithful saying, and worthy of all acceptation, that Christ Jesus came into the world to save sinners; of whom I am chief." 1 Timothy 1:15.

I might have been the chief of sinners, but my Father saw me as His beautiful clean daughter. He knew that I would take His message of love and redemption to a hurting world, long before I could imagine myself actually doing that.

Don't get me wrong, I still had lots of work to do. Now, my inner man was all cleaned up, but I had to establish a **beachhead of**

new thought patterns in my mind to 'put on' my new identity in my daily living. I needed to put on my new self image, the one given to me by grace. I was no longer a slave, but an heir of God and a joint-heir with Christ.

But now, after that ye have known God, or rather are known of God, how turn ye again to the weak and beggarly elements, whereunto ye desire again to be in bondage? Galatians 4:9.

There is no way I was turning back to the weak and beggarly elements of this world that had held me in bondage for so long. So I just gave myself over to the Lord. And I immersed myself fully into the things of God.

That day in October 1974, really was the first day of the rest of my life, as well as the first day of the best of my life. I have never been the same since that close encounter of the God kind.

I held all these things in my heart, realizing that not too many people have this kind of experience. And if others chose to doubt mine, and make fun of me, that was on them. I am here to tell you—things like that can happen, and do happen to people all the time. God is still all powerful, and He can communicate with us any way He wants to.

GOD IS LOVE—and Love is a real thing. I got a supercharged dose of it that day by the lake, not because I was so good, but because He is so good.

Never, ever, ever let anyone talk you out of God's love for you; it is His most precious gift to mankind. It is the Pearl of Great Price. Once you have found it, never let it go.

And Then it Happened!

Through the years I have had many other close encounters of the God kind, but I will always cherish the first one the most. That was when I knew that my heavenly Father loved me, warts and all. And I knew deep down in my bones that God's love is real, that His presence is real, and that He is real. My search for the truth had ended, and my new life had just begun.

The words of Matthew 4:16 came flooding into my heart, "The people which sat in darkness saw great light; and to them which sat in the region and shadow of death light is sprung up." That's what happened to me at Berry College in 1974, the light sprung up.

A young Blaise Pascal, the French mathematician and philosopher in the 1600's penned these words, "There is a God shaped vacuum in the heart of every person which cannot be filled by any created *thing*, but only by God, the Creator Himself."

Young Blaise was absolutely right.

That day by the lake the God-shaped void in my own heart was filled by His presence, and then it happened... the Living God stepped into my life and filled me to the brim with Him.

Chapter 14

From Victim to Victor

But thanks be to God, which giveth us the victory through our Lord Jesus Christ. 1 Corinthians 15:57

In October 1974, I also received my first miraculous physical healing. I loved to drink coffee and they served it at every fellowship, but after I would take a couple of sips, my stomach would clench in pain. I had been diagnosed with a bleeding ulcer. I don't know if that is common for a person as young as I was, but there you have it.

One night Larkin offered me a cup, and I told her my situation. She said, "Why would you want to stay sick when Jesus Christ has healed you?" Great question. And she asked me if I would like to receive healing, like Jesus did in the gospels.

I cried out, "Yes!"

She laid hands on me, prayed a simple prayer, and handed me the cup of coffee. Tentative at first, I sipped it down, and to my amazement, I was pain free, and stayed pain free. Praise God! That was the first of many miracles that would touch and heal my body.

Physical healing is beyond cool, and is so needed in our lives, but for me, the greatest miracle has been the healing of my soul; as Christ filled that deep longing in my heart for him, I understood that the Lord *is* my deliverer, my rescuer, and my comforter.

"He reached down from on high and took hold of me; He drew me out of deep waters." 2 Samuel 22:17.

I will try to describe how my new relationship with God and His Son felt: it was like I had been drowning in a vast ocean of confusion, and ugliness. I was gulping down dirty water, and going down for the third time... when Jesus pulled up in his shiny wooden Christ Craft, drew me up and out of the murky waters, and into his loving arms.

Then Jesus took me to his own home, washed me clean, and gave me new garments. He then escorted me to a lavish supper, and introduced me to our Papa. There I found out who I really was; an heir to a vast fortune of love, health, wisdom, and power, an heir to the Kingdom of God.

The Lord imbued me with confidence, and self assurance, and sent me back into the world, with these simple words, "Go forth, and Love others the way I have loved you."

And with a wink he added, "And you might want to love our Father with all your heart and soul, after all, this Kingdom of God thing was His idea."

How true.

Colossians 1:13,14 says, "God rescued us from dead-end alleys and dark dungeons. He set us up in the kingdom of the Son he loves so much, the Son who got us out of the pit we were in, got rid of the sins we were doomed to keep repeating." All we have to do is reach out and accept His invitation.

God is the King Eternal. The Kingdom of God is over all. He originally bestowed kingship over the earth to Adam and Eve, who later transferred that precious gift to the serpent, through disobedience. But God's plan all along, was to send His Messiah into the world, to be the gateway for mankind back into God's Kingdom. So that God's will can be done in earth as it is in heaven through His children, His royal heirs. That's why Jesus is the King of kings.

There is no joy on earth that compares to the new birth, and discovering the real you, the person God meant for you to be all along. That is the most exciting discovery you will ever make.

And no one is ever so far gone that they are outside the everlasting arms of God. No one is ever so far down that God's love is not deeper still. I know because the Lord of all Creation revealed Himself to a broken down, hardhearted woman from Georgia; and He continues to love me unconditionally, on my good days and my bad. He never gives up on me, even when I give up on myself.

And He will do the same for you.

By this time, I had burned my bridges to California, broken up with my fiancé, and decided to stick around Rome. I was ready for a fresh start, and surprisingly enough, the city of my birth seemed sort of a fitting place to do that, to come full circle.

I got a good job, and moved into a beautifully restored old two-story Victorian house on Avenue A, with Larkin and Joan Bird as my roomies. The house had a big lovely porch, and was right in the heart of town.

Unbeknownst to me, this home had once belonged to my own great-grandmother. My dad came over to visit one day and told me this had been his grandmother's old home, and he showed me a brick in the basement where he had carved his initials as a child. Again, full circle.

My dad also told me a lot of his family history. I found out that as messed up as my maternal grandfather, Pa, and his ancestors were, my dad's side had been just the opposite. I came from a long line of devout Episcopalian pastors and preachers, dating back to the early days of the founding of Georgia. Many of them were circuit rider preachers; who braved the elements, and the Indians, as they traveled on horseback to share the gospel of Christ. All they carried with them was what would fit in their saddle bags, and a burning faith in the living God. They were genuine men of peace, and faith.

So along with generational curses on Pa's side, I had also inherited a boat load of generational blessings from my dad's side. All I could say was, praise God!

Over the next few weeks I did some spiritual house cleaning in my own life. Lord knows, I was doing my best, but I still had many bad habits to get rid of.

To start with, I still wore the occult 'power ring' that was given to me up in Lake Tahoe inscribed with the symbols, "*Where the four corners of the universe meet in darkness.*" By now I knew that it was a demon magnet, calling them to my location. But it was so old and exquisite, the artist in me hated to get rid of it; that dark blue hand carved scarab, set in expertly designed gold filigree. It had to be hundreds of years old. It must have been worth a great deal of money, and I could have used it at the time. But every time I thought about selling it, I heard a firm "No" in my spirit. Why pass such an evil talisman on to another person's life as a magnet for the same demons?

I couldn't very well 'put the dogs out' of my life if I kept inviting them back into my own house, so I knew I needed to get rid of that ring.

Very early, one misty morning, just as the sun was coming up, I walked over to a bridge about two blocks from our home. The mist was so thick you could cut it with a knife. I felt like I was in a B horror movie, which was an appropriate setting for the action I was about to take. I took off that exquisite ring, said a prayer asking for God's forgiveness and protection, and threw it into the swirling currents of the Oostanaula River. It was a hard thing to do, to obliterate something of such craftsmanship. But I knew it was the right thing to do.

Throwing that ring in the river wasn't just a sign of my involvement, it was a commitment. I had skin in the game. I walked back to Avenue A, missing the cash, but feeling a huge sense of relief.

Real change often takes sacrificing things we have grown comfortable with, but which are bad for us. And Lord knows, I was willing to change. I *needed* to change. And the first step to lasting change was to become obedient to the promptings of the Spirit. Hence the ring thing.

Next, I got rid of my Gurdjief books. After reading how Jesus dealt with Satan and demons in the Bible, Gurdjief sounded like some kind of confused nut job spouting out gobbledygook. He offered no solutions to life whatsoever, only ridiculous opinions that led to nowhere. So, Gurdjief went into 'file 13' otherwise known as the trash.

Next, I threw away my favorite music album, *Tubular Bells*. I was lying on the floor listening to it one day, and could physically feel the darkness encroaching upon me. In a moment of clarity, and knew that it too, had to go. I broke it in half and threw it away.

I'm not saying that everyone who gets saved has to get rid of a bunch of stuff; it's a very personal thing. But for me, these three items opened doors in my mind to demonic spiritual attacks, and invited the hounds of hell back onto my turf. It was my own freewill decision to shut those doors. And I am thankful that I did.

For we wrestle not against flesh and blood, but against principalities, against powers, against the rulers of the darkness of this world, against spiritual wickedness in high places. "Wherefore take unto you the whole armour of God, that ye may be able to withstand in the evil day, and having done all, to stand." Ephesians 6:12,13.

The average Joe thinks life is comprised of what we can see, smell, taste or touch; when the greater realities of life are all taking place in the spirit realm. To succeed in life, we must know how to take a stand there. It seemed stupid for me put on the whole armor of God while throwing a rattle snake inside with me. That's why I got rid of the things that spiritually invited the demons back onto my turf.

You see, once a person is born again of God's Spirit, Satan has no more legal rights over them—none whatsoever. But, being the thief that he is, he assigns demons to try to come back in the 'side door.' When we entertain ungodly thoughts or actions, we open that door again, and put out the 'Welcome' mat. The child of God, in essence, invites the demons back in. This is usually done through ignorance. Hosea 4:6 says, *"My people are destroyed for lack of knowledge."* God is talking to His own children who lack the knowledge about how the spiritual kingdom operates, and through ignorance, they don't know how to walk as a son. That was the lesson in Galatians.

Now I say, That the heir, as long as he is a child [immature, unschooled], differeth nothing from a servant, **though** *he be lord of all… Galatians 4:1*

That verse in Galatians 4:1 was becoming more and more clear to me. I was a son of God, but *if* I didn't know how to use my spiritual power over the devil, he could still mop the floor with me.

Well, I was done with that scene. God had put me in the Catbird seat, and it was time to step up my game.

The new birth comes with a ton of privileges and responsibilities. Salvation is by grace, but putting on the 'new man' our new nature, created in Christ Jesus, takes discipline, surrender, and a change of habits. This is called renewing the mind. It takes time and effort to change your thinking, to believe that you are a *bona fide* child of God; righteous and redeemed, literally part of a new family, God's royal family.

I approached renewing my mind like I approached athletics. Methodically. Training for a 5K is hard, but we do it to achieve a level of success. Retraining our mind to new ways of thinking is hard, but we do it to attain success in Kingdom living. And Jesus is there to cheer us on, and to coach us every step of the way.

Hey, when we know better, we do better. Right?

And it worked. By the spring of 1975 I was doing miracles like Jesus did in the gospels. One night, when we were running a Bible class in our home, a woman named Cindy fell out of her chair, started foaming at the mouth and writhing on the floor. As you can imagine, the whole class was in shock.

Larkin was leading the class, and she motioned for me to take care of the situation. I thought, "What? You're the leader. *YOU* take care of her!" But I jumped in anyway, trusting God to show me the way to relieve this poor woman's suffering.

Cindy's husband and another man picked up her convulsing body, and carried her to the rear bedroom. When they put her on the bed I had no idea what to do, so I got quiet and asked God, "What do I do?" (Brilliant move, eh?)

I felt inspired to place my hands on her shoulders, and I began to pray for her *silently* as the two men watched, their faces full of apprehension. I closed my eyes and prayed, "Father, relieve this woman from this pain, bring her back to us, and make her whole."

And to all our amazement, the seizure stopped! And she instantly sat up, perfectly fine, and in her right mind.

All of a sudden her husband William, a big strong hulking man, burst into tears. I thought he would have been relieved that his wife was okay. So, I asked him, "What's wrong?"

Choking with tears he said, "Normally when Cindy has one of these seizures it lasts at least half an hour or more. I've never seen her come out of one so quickly." In other words, he was crying tears of joy because he knew that God had performed a major miracle for his wife.

A few minutes later, to the astonishment of the rest of the class, the four of us walked back in with Cindy, who was completely well, and she took her front row seat. The true God most definitely did *not* give Cindy that seizure, the Adversary did. It was the true God who **healed** Cindy. What a way to finish a Bible study, with the whole class witnessing a miraculous gift of healing right in their own midst. It was an electric evening.

Verily, verily, I say unto you, He that believeth on me, the works that I do shall he do also; and greater works than these shall he do; because I go unto my Father. John 14:12.

What a simple promise Jesus made to his followers. God doesn't call the qualified, he qualifies the called. God can work through any of us who have the heart of a child, who trust Him implicitly. That's where my heart was that night, trusting Him, not myself.

The next day Cindy went to the doctor and he could find nothing wrong with her. What I had not known the night before was that she was also battling cancer, and she was healed of the cancer as well as the seizures. Glory to God for doing even MORE than we had asked of Him, and for honoring the simple faith of His child.

Right out of the chute I was involved in many signs, miracles and wonders, because I had a heart to serve. I didn't think about the mechanics, I just believed I could do what God said I could do, and I did it. I knew that I knew, that when Jesus said we could do the same works that he did, he meant it.

A few weeks later Larkin decided to move back to Atlanta, and asked me to take over the fellowship. I reluctantly said yes, but again wondered, "Why me?" There were others who had been around a lot longer than me. But then it hit me that I was the only one out of our group who had consistently exhibited the faith to DO the works that Jesus did. I was the only one to really step up and walk the talk.

And so I said, 'Yes' to Larkin's offer. Between God's illuminating talk with me at Berry College, and the last several months of applying the Bible, I believed what He had shown me in the vision by the lake of me teaching others the Bible.

God doesn't call the qualified, He qualifies the called. He's not asking for perfection, He just asking for our participation and cooperation with His plan.

Something inside changes when you begin to understand that you were born to be born again. (John 3:3.) Your self-esteem goes up. You begin to believe that you are here on earth for a purpose; to get to know God and tell others about Him. And that every good thing that has ever happened to you in your whole life, ultimately came from God. *"Every good gift and every perfect gift is from above, and cometh down from the Father of lights [God], with whom is no variableness, neither shadow of turning."* James 1:17.

That verse really set me free. It was such a joy to understand that the true God only puts good in our lives. All the bad came from Satan. And you can take this to the bank:

God is ALWAYS good, and the devil is always bad.

The Bible clearly says that it's the devil who is the author of the bad things that happen to us in life: *The thief [devil] cometh not, but for to steal, and to kill, and to destroy: I [Jesus] am come that they might have life, and that they might have it more abundantly.* John 10:10.

Jesus came to deliver us from the devil, and all the misery he puts on mankind. And in exchange, Christ gives us a more abundant life. That's a great deal by anybody's standards. Who would not want that?

And even though my self-esteem was still a bit shaky, I was getting better and stronger every day. My mind was becoming more clear; I was able to hold sound thoughts, and make better decisions. I was still drinking too much on occasion; it would take me another few years to kick that habit for good. But compared to the first 23 years of my life, the improvement I experienced in a matter of months was nothing short of miraculous.

The more I studied the Bible, the more I understood why things happen the way they do. There are spiritual laws that govern life and, like the law of gravity, we can either work with them or against them.

Obviously, it helps if you know what the spiritual laws are, hence the Bible. Otherwise you go through life blind in one eye, and can't' see out of the other. Or as God said, "Destroyed for lack of knowledge."

The more I embraced God's ways, the more joy I felt. Much to my surprise, the bitterness and resentments of my past were evaporating. Instead of being bitter about all that had happened to me, I began to glimpse how truly broken the people were who hurt me. I thought of the words that Jesus spoke from the cross,

"Father, forgive them for they know not what they do," and thus began my journey of forgiveness.

I'm not saying these people were unaware of their actions, I'm just saying they were highly damaged, and never got help themselves. I found the burning hatred in my heart being replaced with compassion, and understanding.

Don't get me wrong, I'm not a 'doormat for Jesus.' I never have to interact with those people again. But I needed to let go of the resentment and the bitterness inside of me, for *my own* sake. I started turning them over to the Lord. I made a conscious decision to start forgiving: not because **they** deserved forgiveness, but because **I deserved** peace.

And I had an epiphany: I would not be defined by my past. I had been prepared by the events of my past for great things. Instead of wallowing in self-pity, I began to see my past as one giant lesson which prepared me for my life's purpose, to be a compassionate pastor and healer. I possessed a genuine empathy for those who are beaten down by life because I could relate. I had been there, done that. More and more I wanted to do anything within my power to alleviate the suffering of others. What a change from where my head was at only one year earlier.

I had a deep well of certainty in my soul that if God could deliver me, as messed up as I was, He could deliver anybody. And that gave me tremendous confidence to step out into the deliverance ministry.

This did not all happen overnight, it took years. But the seeds were planted at Avenue A, my starting point.

As my understanding grew, it became more clear than ever, that in my darkest hours, God never left my side. He was there, loving me, holding me, protecting me, and keeping me alive until this very day. He was just waiting for me to reach out and love Him back... just a little; to open my heart to Him so my healing could begin.

The Lord impressed upon my spirit that Jesus was with me through all the horrible things I had experienced, and he himself wept to see Little Peggy so full of fear and pain. It tore his heart out to see what a grown man was doing to an innocent child. Jesus couldn't overcome Pa's free will, that would have broken the spiritual laws, but he protected me in ways I am still finding out about today. He saved me from death on multiple occasions, and brought me out of the darkness and into his marvelous light.

Isaiah 9:6 says, Jesus (*Yeshua*) is called the Prince of Peace (*Sar shalom*), which perfectly describes his ministry and personality. He IS the Prince of Peace. And through him, I was finally getting some peace of my own.

Jesus threw open the prison doors of my heart, and I walked out of decades of bondage—free to be my true self, my best self.

I was now more than a conqueror through Christ. He filled me with his peace and joy, and I knew somehow, that the rest of my life would be the best of my life. And that's the gift of hope!

I may have been a product of my past, but I was no longer a prisoner of it. Jesus had set me free, and because of him, I was making the move from victim to victor.

Chapter 15

Love Will Find A Way

"Where Love is God is." Tolstoy

The nucleus of all miracles is Love. And God is Love. The greatest miracle in my life was when God revealed to me that truth, that He *is* love.

For years I had cried out in desperation to Him, searching for answers, and Love found a way to give me the desire of my heart. He led me to that little Bible fellowship and opened my eyes to the wonders of His plan for man, to be heirs of His Kingdom of love and light.

In that quaint old house on Avenue A, I was soaking in this Bible like a sponge. Every day I was learning more of how deep, how wide, and how rich God's love for man is. I learned more truth in a few short months than I had in eight years of Catholic school, and all my searching in between. In God's word I found a bonanza of wisdom and truth. I found the pearl of great price, something worth spending my life for. Finally, I was getting answers to the BIG picture, to "Alfie's" question: "What's it all about?"

It's all about Love.

Those were exciting, life-changing days, where I was transitioning into a new way of thinking and living. Every day more light bulbs were turning on in my head. A big part of my growth came with the knowledge that **all good things come from God.** HE is at the center of *every* good thing that has ever happened to you or me... ever. (James 1:16,17.) Just chew on that for a minute. This was the total opposite of what I had been taught all my life.

It turns out the whole Bible is a love story. If you read the final chapter, LOVE wins, big time. And that's **the whole point of being here on Earth, to love and be loved**. To be in a relationship with God our Father.

Radical! The "Love" belief system was sure working for me: love is way more powerful than hate. I could think of lots worse ways to spend my life than loving.

The old Southern preacher, Rufus Mosley summed up the meaning of life this way: "The goal of History is the utter triumph of love over hate, of good over evil, light over darkness, of joy over sorrow, health and healing over disease and discord, and life over death – of Jesus Christ over everything unlike himself." And since Jesus is Love, that is a very good thing. Love wins.

At the same time I was learning more about the sinister kingdom of darkness: that Satan, the Serpent, the devil, or whatever you prefer to call him, was the *source* of <u>ALL</u> the pain and misery in this world. The Devil's goal is the antithesis of God's. Satan is pure evil, God is pure love. Satan's goal is to make man's time on Earth as miserable as possible, in every way imaginable. That's just who he is. He's a snake who's going to bite with venom because that's his nature.

God's goal is to redeem mankind, to give us richly all good things to enjoy, and to give us eternal life in His Kingdom. What a difference.

Your day-to-day living, as well as the salvation of your soul, depends on which side you choose: God's or the devil's, light or darkness, good or evil.

For this purpose the Son of God was manifested, that he might destroy the works of the devil. 1 John 3:8.

Satan is an equal opportunity destroyer, man, woman, child, or baby, he doesn't care.

Well, Praise God, and pass the peanut-butter! Jesus came to destroy the works of the devil, and set the captives free. That's us. And he did it because he loves us, and we need his help.

God's plan always was to have children whom He could bless, and heal. To restore the soul/life of whosoever calls on Him in faith, and make us whole. This was abundantly evident in Jesus' ministry.

How God anointed Jesus of Nazareth with the Holy Ghost and with power: who went about doing good, and healing all that were oppressed of [beaten down by] *the devil; for God was with him. Acts 10:38*

Jesus went about healing ALL who were beaten down by the devil. God wants everyone to come to Him through His son so that they, too, can be restored; and then use their supernatural power to help one another along the way. That's pretty hard to square with most mainstream religions, who teach that God kills or gives you a terrible disease to bring you closer to Him. Really? That defies logic. That would be child abuse. And God is never abusive. He is Love, and healing, and restoration.

Love is the greatest power in the universe. And it was love that caused Jesus to live, die, and be raised from the dead in order to redeem mankind and set us free from the curse of Adam.

When we were utterly helpless, **Christ came at just the right time** *and died for us sinners.* Romans 5:6. That's all of us.

This may come as a shock, but life isn't all about your little rice bowl, it's about God's whole family. He created us; He designed us, to be the recipients of His love and blessings, and to invite others to the party, so that they can be loved too.

Avenue A was a time for me to test the waters to see if this Love stuff actually worked. I am a gal who wants empirical evidence. And I got it. There wasn't a day that went by where I didn't see a miracle. The Lord was so gracious to me to prove Himself faithful, whatsoever I asked in believing, and did not doubt in my heart, I received. Just like Jesus said I would.

That was when I learned one of the all time great spiritual laws, the law of believing: WHAT YOU BELIEVE, IS WHAT YOU WILL RECEIVE IN LIFE.

The natural man says, "Seeing is believing." But the spiritual law says, "Believing is seeing/receiving." First you believe and *then* you receive His promises. This is counterintuitive to human nature. That's why it's called walking by faith.

The law of believing works both positively and negatively.

Wherever I continuously harbored fear and anxiety in my heart, I would attract negative results into my life. But when I went into a situation focused on the goodness of God, trusting His desire to provide for me, then I would have a positive, godly outcome. Empirical evidence.

To put it another way, "As a man thinks in his heart, so is he." Proverbs 23:7. This is an ancient spiritual law, and it cannot be broken.

Rather than living in fear of 'when's the other shoe going to drop' or 'this can't last', I began to work my mind and cultivate a confident expectation of something good.

Psalm 23 says that goodness and mercy shall follow me all the days of my life, and I embraced that promise. The more I *expected* good things, the more they manifested in my life. It's a spiritual law. Even though I still had some areas where I harbored fear and insecurity, I understood that life is a growing process.

God's not looking for perfection, He's looking for participation. So get off the bench, suit up, and learn as you go. You will have some setbacks along the way, I call those 'growing pains.' But here's the deal, if you don't try you have already failed.

The true God is not so much about rules and regulations as about love and forgiveness. The Law of Love supersedes all other laws of man and nature. When you walk in love, you will 'naturally' do the right thing because you will be in tune with Love itself, God.

Once I learned these basic laws, I needed to put them into consistent practice. When I would set my mind on God, and claim a promise from my heart, it came to pass. When I would fear and doubt, it did NOT come to pass. Empirical evidence: I got the same results every time I applied God's spiritual laws, for good or for ill.

And all things, whatsoever ye shall ask in prayer, **believing** [trusting God], *ye shall receive. Matthew 21:22*

Trusting God is such a simple concept, but not so easy to apply. Most of us were not taught to trust Him as children. So, I had some changing to do. Mentally, I went to work, making the spiritual walk a new habit. I began taking charge over my own thoughts. Like training a puppy I would bring my mind back to "What does God say about this?" And then tell my mind, "Sit! Stay on that idea." This is a lot harder than developing a muscle skill-set. Changing our core beliefs is the most challenging thing any of us will ever undertake.

I had so many unhealthy thought patterns including: rebellion against authority (even God's), low self-esteem, and fear of the future. I had to make the effort to let go of the negatives, and groove new healthy thought patterns. No one could do that for me, not even God. That was my job.

Once I needed $80 dollars to take a class, I asked God to help me, and believed that He would. Within 24 hours a photographer called me to paint a backdrop for $50, which I quickly accepted. That same afternoon a piece of art I had in a local craft store sold for $30. There was the $80. I did my part, and God did His: I was learning to work in partnership with the Creator. How cool.

One weekend I needed to go to Atlanta, and a friend called me out of the blue and said they were going to Atlanta; did I want to ride along? When I needed a new job, I made my supplication known to God, laying out how much I needed to make, and how many hours I desired to work. He led me to a fantastic part-time job in a print shop for a major building company that paid more than I had asked for, and with fewer hours. That was when I learned that God could give me more than I asked for, but not less than. And that He is all about working smarter and not harder.

That's when Ephesians 3:20 became my mantra: *"Now unto him that is able to do exceeding abundantly above all that we ask or think, according to the power that worketh in us."* The Good Lord was willing to do exceeding abundantly above all I could ask or think IF I trusted Him. Man, what a deal! Miracles and blessings follow when you have an intimate relationship with the Creator of the Universe.

I was taking baby steps, learning how to be led by the Spirit, and how to cast my care upon Him. My mind was set at ease, knowing that I would never have to face life alone again. What a comfort. I was forging a bond with my heavenly Father; my Protector and Provider.

And that took me back to those childhood needs: to be chosen, to be loved and to be accepted. I felt all of those things in spades. God summed it up in Ephesians 1:3,4—"God... has blessed us with all spiritual blessings... in Christ... and he hath chosen us in him before the foundation of the world, that we should be holy and without blame, before Him in love..." God chose us. God wants us. He loves us. We matter to Him. Before He made the cosmos He wanted you and me, children whom He could love and take care of.

In other words, you and I are the *WHY* of creation!

We all know what it feels like to be chosen or left out. Maybe you excelled at math, but were the last one chosen for team sports. Maybe you got asked to spend a day fishing with your dad, or you got left at home with the girls while your older brother got to go. The inner longing in every human heart is to matter, to belong, and to be chosen. And right there in the Bible it says: you were wanted and you are chosen.

Ephesians 1:4 further elucidates this mind-blowing truth: "Even before he made the world, God loved you and chose you." If you reverse engineer that statement, it really knocks your socks off—God created the universe so that He could make a home for you. That's quite a reality sandwich. God, who, needless to say, is pretty smart, chose you and wants you as part of His family. You matter to Him.

He's just been waiting for you to choose Him back. You know, to operate that pesky little thing called free will. Just the act of coming to God, and asking for His help gives Him great pleasure!

WE make God happy. We fill a need in His heart. I'd say that make us pretty special.

I know it takes a paradigm shift to grasp that you are chosen and loved by the Creator of the heavens and Earth, but that's the truth. And He loves you, warts and all. Come to Him just as you are, and watch the healing begin.

The more I embraced my new self-image, the more I was able to relax, and enjoy life. And the amazing part was, this salvation thing would work for anybody, any place, any time. Through His son, God reached out to a hurting world, and said to everyone, "Are you lost? Are you hurting? Here's the way home to Papa."

God is no respecter of persons, only of one condition, do you believe Him? Do you realize that you need Him in your life, and that He wants to help you?

Just like John 10:10 said—the first twenty-three years of my life Satan tried to steal from me, kill me, and to destroy my sanity. That's why I was so beaten down and crazy back in San Francisco. Only an insane person would want to join the Church of Satan. But those days were gone. I was regaining a sound mind. There was a new sheriff in town, and his name is Jesus. And with him by my side, I was in the Catbird seat. The world was my oyster, and I meant to start winning for a change.

I'm not saying I had arrived that first year, but my train had definitely left the station. I was on the path to a new and better life.

Life is 10% what happens to you and 90% what you do with it. I knew I had grabbed the brass ring, and I wasn't about to let it go.

On Avenue A, I quickly grasped the concept of "use it or lose it", and after all those years of pain and searching, I didn't want the crumbs, I wanted the whole loaf. For years I didn't own a television, or go to movies; not because of some religious ideal, but because I wanted to spend every waking moment saturating my thoughts with the things of God. I had free will, and that was my personal choice. Now that I had a taste of spiritual freedom, I wanted more. I craved to have full restoration, and was committed to investing the time and energy to attain that goal. Like anything worth having in life, it was going to take time and effort.

So began my road to recovery, the inner change from victim to victor, and the complete makeover of my psyche. As a new believer, I understood that I had to guard my new found liberation like a mama bear guards her cubs, with a certain ferocity. I did not want to go back to my old way of living, or thinking. So, I rolled up my sleeves and went to work on ME.

I may have been born at night, but I wasn't born last night. I applied my common sense to understand that my mind didn't get messed up over night, and it wasn't going to get straightened out overnight. Granted, my spirit was perfected in an instant, at the time of the new birth, but it would take time to change deeply ingrained mental habits.

When I was a kid, I used to hike through the woods of North Georgia, often using a machete to cut a path to a new fort, or tree house. That's how the mind works. We have these neural pathways we have grooved over the years, some of which lead us to a toxic dump. We have to let those paths grow over, and cut new ones that take us to God's peace and joy.

Thoughts are things. They are real. They are the seeds of the life you currently lead. If you plant tomatoes, you don't grow cucumbers. If you constantly plant fear and lack you cannot produce peace and prosperity.

If you want a better life you have to do two things: start planting new thought seeds, and start carving out godly thought trails/habits in your mind. Start dwelling on and confessing truths that line up with God's word. And make that your new habit. There is no abundant life without God's truth at the center of it. Truth makes us free.

Finally, brethren, whatsoever things are true, whatsoever things are honest, whatsoever things are just, whatsoever things are pure, whatsoever things are lovely, whatsoever things are of good report; if there be any virtue, and if there be any praise, **think on these things**. Philippians 4:8.

Most folks are thinking on just the opposite of the list in Philippians, they are dwelling on past hurts, ugly slights, lies, and worrying about everything that can possibly go wrong. They flood their minds with anxiety and worry.

To live abundantly we must choose to think like Philippians, and that is the basis for renewing the mind, thinking on the good, honest, uplifting things in life. It's like a Rorschach test, two people can be in the exact same situation, one will see only the bad and be full of fear, the other will see the best, and ways to make it work in their favor. This attitude of glass half-full thinking doesn't just happen, you have to work at it. Looking for the best in life, cultivating thankfulness, and above all, trusting God to be your wing-man.

I was so excited about what I was learning, I wanted to share the wealth with anyone who would listen. Pretty soon I had 30-40 people coming to my Bible fellowship six or seven nights a week; souls like me, who were hungering and thirsting for truth. I had no idea how so many people were hearing about our fellowship, but I was thankful they were coming. It was an electrifying time in my life.

But, as human nature goes, at one point there began to be dissension among the 'old timers' regarding my leadership. They couldn't even get a class of seven people together, and here I was, touching dozens of lives daily in a positive way, and they thought they knew better than me? The proof was in the pudding, I was growing and helping others, they were stagnant and jealous. They weren't seeing results in their lives, so they wanted to tear me down to their level. No thanks.

This is why bad things happen in our world, because people *think* about doing bad things. By the way, these were the same hypocrites who had wanted to throw me out of fellowship when I first started attending, citing I was 'too messed up to ever change.' Thank God, they were wrong.

Larkin, who had turned the fellowship over to my care, came back from Atlanta to set things straight in the fellowship. She suggested that I go hang out at the nearby Waffle House while she met with the dissenters in my living room. I wasn't too excited about that proposition, I wanted to be there to defend myself, but I obediently went anyway.

Upset by all the backbiting, I just wanted to go into the diner, and sulk in a back booth by myself, and lick my wounds. I certainly didn't feel like talking to anyone. But, when I walked through the door the place was jam packed, and there wasn't a single booth available. Reluctantly, I had to find a seat at the end of a very crowded counter. I was not a happy camper.

I found one lone seat at the far end, between two men, and squeezed in. I plopped down, and opened up my Bible on the counter, and ordered a grilled cheese and coffee. Still sulking, and mumbling under my breath, I tried to read, but found it difficult to concentrate on the words.

This red haired skinny guy, sitting on my right, kept leaning over and glaring at my Bible. I was getting more and more annoyed, when he looked me straight in the eye and said, "Hey, you and I work for the same boss." I gave him my best withering "Don't bother me' scowl. Nonplussed, he repeated, "you and me work for the same boss."

Irritated, I said, "What do you mean, the same boss? Do you work for Mr. Manis?"

Then he tapped his finger on the pages of my Bible, he said, "No, the one who wrote that book. We work for the same Boss."

I was gobsmacked! Speechless, even.

He said, "You run that Bible fellowship up there on Avenue A, don't you?" Puzzled, I replied, "Uh, yeah, I do."

"I send a lot people up there." he offered. (Well, that answered one question, where all those people were coming from.)

I queried, "Then why haven't you come yourself?"

He looked ever so sincere and said, "That's not *my* job. My job is to send them to you." And the way he looked at me, it was like he was seeing right into my heart, and it caused all the hair on the back of my neck to stand up. It was as if he was seeing down into the very depths of my soul. Wow! Freaky.

And then I had a 'woman at the well' experience, like in John 4:29 — this perfect stranger told me all the things that were in my heart. He addressed my fears, my insecurities, my past, and my loneliness. He also praised me for my desire to help others.

My mouth dropped open a couple of times because I wondered how on God's green earth this *stranger* could know all these things about me; things that I had never told a living soul? How did he know my life story? How did he know where I worked, and where I lived? It could have been very creepy, except I did not feel one bit scared.

In fact, I felt like I had known him all my life. Even though he looked a bit rough, and scruffy around the edges, there was something calming, almost radiant about his demeanor, especially his loving blue eyes. He looked straight into mine, and I felt... peace.

He told me how proud our mutual 'Boss' was of my efforts to lead the fellowship, and that He was backing me up all the way. Can you say surreal? There was a group of turkeys up in my living room at that very moment, complaining about me. How could this guy know that? And yet here was this perfect stranger, out of the blue, delivering a message from God to me, saying in effect, "You are my beloved daughter, in whom I am well pleased." It was mind blowing.

He told me he was a local photographer, but I knew all the professionals in these parts, and I had never heard of him before. Then he pulled out a black and white photo from a notebook, and handed it to me. It was a photo of a little three-year old child, in sagging dirty underpants, squatting down by the edge of a lake, and gently petting a baby duck on the neck. That duck looked exactly like the ones I had raised when I was a kid. I almost started crying, I was so moved by the tenderness in that shot.

What that image said to my heart was: we are *all* little kids with dirty faces and poopy diapers. No matter how old we are, or how 'together' we look on the outside, inside we're all pretty much a mess, and need a lot of love and compassion to heal our wounded souls. We should all be trying to help one another, not hurt one another.

And that was exactly what I was trying to do for the folks in my fellowship, help them, because someone had once cared enough to help me.

Right there, in the cacophony of the Waffle House, I felt a deep well of compassion for all humanity rising up within my soul; even to the point of forgiving those people who were up there in my house, trying to take me down. I just felt an overwhelming sense of peace and tenderness.

I don't know what that photograph would have communicated to anyone else, but it touched me deeply—profoundly. And it helped me get my bearings, and re-establish my purpose.

That man told me things that day that changed my life forever. It buoyed my courage. Even after the bitter rejection of a handful of back-biters, after talking to him I wanted to get back in the game. I was even eager to get back and move forward, no matter what others were saying about me.

This was definitely supernatural, like the time I was by the lake at Berry College, but instead here was a man, ministering to my soul, and encouraging me in a crowded diner.

I was so deep in thought that I was oblivious to the din of the noisy crowd, but I snapped out of my reverie when I heard a noisy engine pull up in the parking lot right behind us. I turned around to look through the window, and saw an old beat up reddish Volkswagen pull in. A heavy set woman got out, and slowly walked around to the door, opened it, and called across the room, "Michael, it's time to go." And he started to get up.

Oh, man, I did not want this guy to leave. But he smiled at me, patted my arm, and said, "It's all going to be alright" and walked out the door, leaving the photograph in my hand.

"Michael?" I thought, "Why does that name ring a bell?"

I went back home and told Larkin the whole story, and she immediately reminded me of the verse in Hebrews 13, "Be not forgetful to entertain strangers: for thereby some have entertained angels unawares." She said in a matter of fact voice, "Peg, that was an angel you just talked to. Don't you remember, Michael is the archangel? He fights for God's people."

Wow! You could have knocked me over with a feather. Once again, God loved me enough to send one of His chief messengers to help me out. Man, this God stuff was awesome! Hebrews 1:14, "Are they (angels) not all ministering spirits, sent forth to minister for them who shall be heirs of salvation?" I was an heir of salvation. And one of the angel's functions was to minster to my life, to help me out of jams. That was way cool.

I remembered my mama telling me how I often talked to my guardian angel as a child. And I reckon I was. Children can connect with the heavenly realm a lot more easily than adults; but as we grow up we talk ourselves out of it. There I was, bigger than life, talking to a heavenly messenger in the Waffle House. How cool is God? Very.

That day, it was even more deeply impressed upon my soul that when my life had seemed like 'Crazy Town' when I had so many near death experiences, God was there, sending angels to minister to me. That's the reason I was still alive. And God's angelic protectors were still working on my behalf.

Through all those early years of insanity, *Abba*, Father had His hand upon my life. He was just waiting patiently for me to ask for His help so that He could reach out and bring me all the way home. To move me past surviving all the way to thriving. That's it. He was just waiting on me to get to the place where I would willingly open myself up to His love, so that He could restore my soul, like in Psalm 23.

The Lord is my Shepherd... **He restores my soul:** *he leads me in the paths of righteousness for his name's sake. Yea, though I walk through the valley of the shadow of death, I will fear no evil:* **for thou art with me;** *thy rod and thy staff they* **comfort** *me. Psalm 23:1,3,4*

Here I was, experiencing Psalm 23 in living color. He had been with me through the valley of death, and He *was* restoring my soul that very day. I mean, God had just sent an angel to the Waffle House to help me out. What else had He done for me through the years that I was completely unaware of? How often had I "entertained angels unaware"? Like the two men who had lifted my car off the guardrail in Atlanta, Georgia. What amazing grace.

I remember sitting on the back steps of my house thinking, "Man! This Bible stuff is for real." God will bend over backwards and do what He can for us, but He is a gentleman, He will never force His love upon anyone. Like Jesus said, "Look! I stand at the door and knock. If you hear my voice and open the door, I will come in, and we will share a meal together as friends." Revelation 3:20

In life there is his part, and there is our part. The door to our heart only opens from the inside. And if we decide to open up to Christ, he will move right in, and take care of us in ways we can't even imagine.

Needless to say, I kept on leading the fellowship, and kept growing in the spirit. And I ended up touching hundreds of lives from that beautiful old house at 705 Avenue A; the very house that my godly great-grandmother used to own. Through her side of the family, I inherited generational blessings, and here I was, passing on those blessings to others.

God had kept me alive through all the madness that had occurred in my youth so I could receive my godly legacy, and carry out my calling in the body of Christ, showing others the way home.

I saw the Light, but He saw me first. He had His hand on me all along, and He was still there for me that day on Avenue A, loving me, and building me up. Where God is Love is. No matter how far down you are, God will find a way to lift you up, and fill you up with His hope and promise.

Chapter 16

The Triumph and the Tragedy

Jesus came to deliver them who through fear of death were all their lifetime subject to bondage. Hebrews 2:15

While living on Avenue A, I was especially thrilled whenever Chris J would come down from the mountain to visit me. I would minister healing to her, and the cancer would go into remission. You see, I had read Luke 9:1,2, and **believed** it.

Then he called his twelve disciples together, and gave them power and authority over all devils, and to cure diseases. And he sent them to preach the kingdom of God, and to heal the sick. Luke 9:1,2

I know that healing took place for Chris, because she would go to the doctor and get a clean report. But every time she would go back up to that lousy mountain, not only would she get sick all over again, but it would come back worse than before.

I couldn't understand why Chris would not just stay away from that deadly place, and away from those negative people. Apparently her husband insisted that they stay there, and she complied. This was not the Chris I knew, she never would have kowtowed to anyone's destructive wishes. To this day, I don't know what kind of hold he had over her, but it was definitely to her detriment.

Sadly, while my life was blossoming, and getting better in every way, my mentor, my best friend, the woman who led me to Christ, was getting worse and worse. I felt so frustrated and helpless.

The Triumph and the Tragedy

After all, I couldn't force her to stay in Rome. I couldn't make her stay away from that 'Christian' camp.

One day I got the news that Chris was in really bad shape, perhaps close to the end. I knew I had to go up and see her. I did NOT want to go back to that awful place, where the demons had tried to make me take my own life, so I asked a friend, Lynn to drive up there with me for moral support.

All along the trip the Lord was preparing my heart. He warned me, in no uncertain terms, that this was going to be a horrifying experience and one of the hardest things I would ever go through in my whole life—and He was right.

I was anxious but determined; I was not going to let Chris J down, even though I knew beforehand this was going to be excruciatingly painful.

When we finally reached her cabin, Lynn surprised me by telling me that she was not going inside with me to see Chris. That sort of shook me. So I took a deep breath, got out of the car, and prepared myself to face this on my own.

It was a spectacular, bright noon day, with a beautiful blue sky. But when I got out of the car, the spiritual darkness surrounding her cabin was so thick you could cut it with a knife. It was cloying. There were three or four old ladies dressed in black, sitting on the front porch, rocking back and forth, back and forth... just waiting for death to come. They reminded me of a pack of vultures, sitting on a tree limb; it made my skin crawl.

I went in, said hello to Chris' husband, and held her sweet baby boy. Then I took a deep steadying breath, and turned to the real reason I was there, to take Chris back to Rome with me. I walked down the hallway to her room and when I turned into the doorway nothing could have prepared me for what I saw. I went weak in the knees, and thought I was going to faint. In my heart I cried out to God, "Please, please hold me up!" Even though He had tried to prepare me for this sight in the car, I was still floored by the *reality* of what lay before me.

Chris was on the far side of the room, propped up in her sick bed, and she looked like something out of *The Exorcist*. Even with the sun shining in to brighten the room, the atmosphere was dark and smothering, like a heavy fog. I found it almost impossible to breathe.

O, Lord! There was my wonderful vibrant friend decimated by the disease. My robust German milkmaid with the flaming red hair was now an emaciated shadow of her former self. She looked like a skeleton with tight skin stretched over it. She had a lime-green pallor to her skin, and most of her beautiful red hair had fallen out, except a few long wisps, that had turned completely white. This made her look ever more surreal. Her teeth had all gone dark and she had deep purple circles under her sunken eyes.

Oh, my God! She couldn't have weighed a hundred pounds. I couldn't understand how this happened so fast? It had only been a few weeks since I had last seen Chris and she looked fine then.

At twenty-four, I had never in my life seen a human being who looked this bad. And it was the person I loved and trusted more than anyone else on earth. It was like an out of body experience. I guess I was in a state of shock.

The Triumph and the Tragedy

I wanted to run! I didn't want to be there. I wanted to curl up on the hallway floor in a fetal position, and scream and cry my eyes out.

I wanted someone tell me this was all a bad dream; and that I would soon wake up; but that was not to be.

I tried to focus on Jesus, and asked for his strength. I *had* to be there for Chris J, I had to be strong for my best friend, the woman who had done so much for me. I had to be there, she had led me to Christ. She had given me back my life. My heart cried, "Oh, Lord, give me the courage to do this."

As pathetic as this sounds, after the initial shock of seeing Chris, I prayed that I would not have to touch her. But the first thing she did when she saw me was try to smile, and reached out her skinny arms, asking in a weak voice for me to come and pick her up.

There must have been angels there that day too, because it was only by some supernatural strength that I was able to keep standing, let alone go over there and pick her up. But by God's grace, I did. And she put her boney arms around my neck, and was light as a feather.

I carried her to the other side of the room where I very gently set her in a worn over-stuffed chair. How I kept from sobbing uncontrollably is beyond me. I wanted to cry so badly. I wanted to shout and scream! I wanted to beat the hell out of her husband for keeping her up here on Death Mountain. I wanted to wrap her up in that blanket and take her back home with me right that second. And I asked Chris if I could please take her back to Rome with me. But she wanted to stay where she was, with the old-lady vultures on the front porch, keeping her death watch.

Oh, how my heart broke into a million little pieces seeing my best friend in this ghastly shape.

This made me hate the devil even more. Hebrews 2:14 says that the devil has power over sickness and death; and God has the power over life and healing. At least I knew who to blame for Chris' abominable condition, but that was small comfort compared to the volcanic emotions that were exploding inside me.

How could I go on without Chris? She was my rock. She was always so much stronger than me. How could this have happened to her of all people?

Every time I tried to talk to Chris about God or the Bible, her eyes would roll back in her head, and turn white. It was like some dark 'force' was keeping her from hearing the words that could set her free. I must've been in there about three-quarters of an hour; my clothes were soaked through with sweat, not because it was hot, but because my anxiety level was so high.

Finally, when Chris looked like she couldn't hold her eyes open any longer, I knew it was time to go. I took Chris' two hands in mine, and looked her straight in the eyes, and said with all the love in my heart, "Chris, it's Christ in you"… and for the first time that day she looked back at me with total clarity, and she finished my sentence, "… the hope of glory!"

"It's Christ in you, the hope of glory" were the last words that ever passed between us, my best friend, and me. Every time I called back up there, they wouldn't let me talk to her.

The Triumph and the Tragedy

I am weeping now, even as I write this all these years later. I can't help it. It still tears me up inside. I still miss her.

How thankful I am for Chris' life. She was the only person ornery enough not to give up on a lost cause, and lead me to Christ, kicking and screaming.

Chris opened the door for me to have a whole new life, but she was not going to be there to enjoy it with me; she was coming to the end of her journey. Unbelievable. There she was, dying right before my eyes, at only twenty-five years old. It was all so senseless and surreal. Why she wouldn't come back with me to Rome, I'll never know.

Once again, I felt alone, abandoned, and afraid when I walked out of that cabin. But as we drove back down the mountain, this time something had changed. I also felt the comfort of my Savior, who had promised to never leave me nor forsake me. And I knew I had found a new friend for life, one who would never die, and his name was Jesus.

Within a few short weeks, my dear friend Chris died on that lousy stinking mountain. Oh, what a cruel, cruel blow that was.

But I determined on my way down 'Death Mountain' to live a life that would make Chris J proud of me. Many times, in the darkest times yet to come, it was that vow that kept me going.

That last day I saw Chris on 'Death Mountain' was a time of triumph and tragedy: the tragedy that my friend would soon be gone from this earth, but triumphant in the knowledge that I would see her again one day, in Paradise, where there will be no more sickness, nor sorrow, nor crying, just my happy healthy German milkmaid.

Chapter 17

Life, the Final Frontier!

*"Life is a story. You can choose your story.
A story **with God** is the better story."* Life of Pi.

I returned to Rome that day broken-hearted.

I found out Larkin was in Savannah, Georgia for the summer, running another bible class. I called her up, and asked if I could come down and assist her. I needed to get out of Rome, but I also wanted to stay busy helping folks. And the thought of being near the ocean seemed like it could be very healing. So, to Savannah I went, no longer running away from, but running to something important.

Shortly after I arrived, one afternoon my mom called and gave me the news that Chris had passed away, and my world came crashing down around me. Stunned, I hung up the kitchen phone, slid down the wall onto the floor, and everything sort of went blank. Even though I knew this was coming, I was still in a state of shock and disbelief.

Despite all the evidence to the contrary, in the back of my mind I kept hope alive that somehow, someway, Chris would pull through this. Man, when you are twenty-four years old, you feel sort of invincible, but Chris' death changed all that.

Contrary to what Captain James T. Kirk said, space is not the final frontier—*Life* is.

Life, the Final Frontier!

When we are dead, we can't love, we can't learn, we can't think, we can't change. By then it's too late. The die is cast. Life is the final frontier because it is during this life that we choose our *eternal* destiny. There's a great verse in the Bible that says, *"There is hope only for the living. As they say, 'It's better to be a live dog than a dead lion!'"* Ecclesiastes 9:4.

We need to choose our belief system wisely because this is our one shot to get it right—Life, that is.

"It is appointed unto men once to die, but after this the judgment." Hebrews 9:27

You only live once. Contrary to pop culture, we don't get multiple incarnations until we finally 'ascend.' This life is not a dress rehearsal; this is the main event, so make it count.

When I received the phone call that day of Chris' death, I sort of lost it. I went to pieces. Here I was, running a Bible class, I believed (and still do) in miraculous healing, and yet the woman who brought me to Christ was deader than a doornail. How could that possibly have happened?

My mind fragmented into a million little pieces.

Just because I was born-again didn't mean I suddenly knew how to handle a tragedy of this magnitude. That part takes growth and maturity. And that hot summer day my mind went to a very unsound place. I was overcome with survivor's guilt, the old "it should have been *me*" syndrome. I felt a sense of profound loss, and anger, and even resentment that my friend was leaving me alone here on earth to face life without her.

Of course, in that frame of mind, my old 'pain reliever', alcohol, reared its ugly head.

The next thing I knew, I fled out of the apartment in a blind rage, hopped in my old green Ford station wagon, and headed straight for the liquor store. First stop, a quart of Jack Daniels. I pulled over, unscrewed the top, and I proceeded to go on a rip-roaring bender.

It was around 2 p.m. when I left our place at Heritage Square Apartments, on the South side of Savannah, just off of White Bluff Road. I was headed for the beaches at Tybee Island, about forty minutes away. I got more and more inebriated as I drove like a bat out of hell. And to top it off, a major storm was brewing. I thought, "Here I go again with the demons and the wind."

I am sure the devil was licking his chops to see me in such a self-destructive state. And that day he almost got two-fer; because I was ready to die, too. Or, so I thought.

I had almost reached the beach, and I was screaming at the top of my lungs, shaking my fist, and bellowing at Satan, "You want to kill someone? Well, take ME, you S.O.B.!" At that very moment I was speeding around a curve, going way too fast, and immediately the brakes on my car went out. My brake pedal went all the way to the floor and *nada*! Nothing—they were gone! I had confessed it and now I possessed it, death staring me in the face.

Going way too fast, I was about to crash into a row of town houses that were set back just a little ways off the road, when I made a split-second decision, and I cried out, "Lord save me, I don't want to die!"

Instantly, without even thinking about it, my left foot smashed down on the emergency brake.

My car skidded through the sand, and spun around three or four times, and finally landed almost on its side, uphill, on a sand dune. My car was on such an incline that when I opened the door, I literally fell out of the car and rolled down the dune. But at least I was off the main road.

Drunk, crying, and scared, I looked up and saw that the storm was about to blow. The wind was howling something fierce, like a blizzard, blowing sand in my eyes and mouth. I crawled into a cement drain pipe about three feet in diameter, curled into a fetal position, and passed out in there for I don't know how long.

When I came to it was around five in the evening. The worst part of the storm had passed, but it was still heavily overcast, and everything was drenched. My head was throbbing, and my stomach felt like I had drunk a jug of sulphuric acid. I sat in that tunnel and thought, "Crap! What now?"

Staring out at the grey ocean, waves thundering against the shore, my trust was surely being tested. I queried, "I don't understand? I've already seen so many miracles of healing, why couldn't Chris J have just *one*?" I was despondent, wrenched with guilt, and pain, and loss.

In a deep funk, I staggered back to my car, wondering how in the heck I was going to drive the forty minutes back across town with no brakes. Then a little voice said, "Use your emergency brake." And so I did. I used my emergency brake to stop the car through heavy, wet, rush hour traffic, all the way back across Savannah.

Life, the Final Frontier!

The next morning Larkin and I drove to a nearby K-Mart to get my car fixed. The mechanic put it up on the lift and got under there with his shop light, going up and down the undercarriage. Finally, he stuck his head out and gave me this quizzical look. He said, "Hey Lady, how did you drive this car over here?"

"I used my emergency brake." I replied.

He looked me straight in the eye and almost yelled, "Lady, you DON'T HAVE an EMERGENCY BRAKE. Your lines are busted!"

Larkin was standing there with me when this happened, and we both looked at each other, our faces going pale. We both knew that God had saved my life in the midst of my self-inflicted, drunken pity party. He had miraculously taken me back across town, safely to my apartment, with 'brakes' that did not exist.

Shocked, I thought, "Our Father is so loving." If you ask in faith—even if you're the Bozo that caused the mess—if you ask in faith, you shall receive God's deliverance anyway. That's called mercy.

Like they said in the *Life of Pi*, "Life is a story. You can choose your story. But a story *with* God is the better story." I can certainly testify to that.

Chapter 18

Clear Shining After Rain

Negative emotions don't die, we just bury them alive.
–Dr. Jen Clark.

A couple of days after my near death experience, Larkin and I went back to Tybee Island, to the same beach where I had almost killed myself. This time I was fully sober, but oh, so brokenhearted. I was there to lick my wounds. And boy, did I my soul need some mending.

I was back on the thread, with all the crazy stuff I had done, why had I been spared?

I love King David. He could be so awesome, and yet so very flawed. I reckon that's why I relate so well to him; the flawed part, I mean. And, I love these words that God spoke to David shortly before his demise.

The God of Israel said, the Rock of Israel spake to me [David], He that ruleth over men must be just, ruling in the fear [love, respect] of God. And he shall be as the light of the morning, when the sun riseth, even a morning without clouds; as the tender grass springing out of the earth by clear shining after rain. 2 Samuel 23:3,4

I love the imagery because it represents everything right, and clean, and good. That verse promised that if we love God, our life could be cleansed, refreshed, restored, and that we could lead others to that same deliverance.

Many times, as a child, I would climb up into my tree following a rain storm after the sun had come out, and lay up there looking out over the yard. Everything glistened. I marveled at the drops of water on the leaves, and the beauty of the earth. Even the air smelled cleaner after a thunder storm. I needed that, a cleansing after the storm. I needed for my heart to sparkle, and be set right again.

We arrived at the beach around 11 o'clock in the morning. It was a spectacularly beautiful day. I left Larkin to go for a walk by myself and think. The feel of the soft white sand between my toes, inhaling the exhilarating smell of the salty sea air, was a strong juxtaposition to the gloom I felt inside. The gulls were squawking and wheeling over head, not caring one whit about my problems. Folks were out *en masse* enjoying the sun and surf.

It's funny how you can feel so torn up on the inside, like your life is falling apart, and yet the world just goes on spinning, and people just go on their merry way, oblivious to the pain of others.

My heart felt like a stone, heavy and aching for Chris J. I was feeling pretty sorry for myself. I walked on and I began to have a deep conversation with God; asking the same old question, "Why Chris and not me?"

I stood on the beach, staring out to sea, feeling like little girl lost, and yet I couldn't help being captivated by the magnificence of the soft waves across the endless horizon. Who can escape the power of their majesty?

I began to walk up the beach again. While I was pondering the immense power of the ocean and the God who made it, I came upon three or four kids digging a hole on the sand. They seemed to be having fun, but they were absolutely filthy; mucking around in the deep hole they had dug, which was now filled with filthy muddy water.

I looked to my right and focused on the clean, blue ocean, not five feet behind them, and for some reason I became incensed. I thought, "Why on earth would those kids play in a mud hole when they could play in a beautiful, clean ocean just steps away?"

I got so angry it frightened me. And I thought, "What's up with this? Why am I getting so bent out of shape over some kids in a mud puddle?" It was the Spirit of God getting my attention.

I turned again to take in the full vista of the ocean, and God spoke to me as clear as a bell. He said, "You're seeing your friend Chris, right there. Instead of stepping out and trusting me, and allowing me to heal her, she played it 'safe' and went back to 'Death Mountain.' She knew she would be surrounded by darkness, and unbelief, but it felt familiar and 'safe' to her. That's why she succumbed to her illness. Instead of launching out in faith, onto the ocean of my Love, she played in a mud hole of her own making; one of misplaced trust in her husband, and it cost her her life."

I just had to sit down. God never wanted Chris to die, but she just couldn't get it together in her own heart to accept His healing. And that broke his heart as much as it broke mine. For a fleeting moment I felt *His* sadness.

The Lord continued, "**Peg, My will is *always* to heal.** But I must have the cooperation and trust of the injured party for that to come to pass. I can't *force* my healing on anyone; they have to reach out and take it. I wanted with all My heart for Chris to receive her healing, but she just couldn't let go of the negatives people were feeding her. She trusted their words of death over My words of Life. Sadly, she made her choice. And that breaks My heart."

I sat there in the warm sun, and God's gentle words soothed my aching spirit. I was overwhelmed with the presence of God, whose love for us is bigger than the ocean, and deeper than the Milky Way. His love sustained me that day.

It sunk in even deeper that the true GOD DOESN'T KILL ANYONE.

He doesn't even make people sick. He is the author of life.

Just look at that ocean. No one even knows how many species of life are out there, no one knows how the moon affects the tides, and yet He created all that life by His mighty word. And, He can heal any disease; after all He made the human body. And Jesus paid for our healing two thousand years ago.

Hebrews says, it is the devil that has the power of sickness and death, not God. God is the Author of Life.

Here is a really important truth:

Forasmuch then as the children are partakers of flesh and blood, he [Jesus] also himself likewise took part of the same; that through [his own] death he might destroy **him that had the power of death, that is, the devil**. *Hebrews 2:14*

I sat there before the crashing waves, stunned. I had read that verse many times, but that day at Tybee it gelled in my heart, I got it. I had a *metanoeo*; a paradigm shift, regarding the true nature of God. Even after we start learning the truth about God, it takes time to put off the lies that have been drilled into our head for most of our lives.

Nobody in church had ever taught me that it was the *devil* that had the power of death.

I can remember once, at a child's funeral, the priest said that God wanted another rose petal in heaven. That made me crazy. I knew that the good God I talked to in the maple tree would never take the life of a beautiful child, and devastate their whole family, for a freakin' rose petal in heaven. Lordy Pete, religious traditions can be utterly devastating. God does not want *anyone* to die prematurely. But the devil sure does.

And just to put a fine point on this truth, here is what Jesus said to his disciples regarding little children, "*Even so it is not the will of your Father which is in heaven, that one of these little ones should perish.*" Matthew 18:14. God's will is clear, it is not His will that one of these little ones should perish. Period.

When are we going to just read what's written? It is **NOT** the will of God for a child to perish. God does not want "another rose petal in heaven." He wants all of us to live a full life, vibrant and happy. Oh, how far we need to come in understanding who God really is.

It breaks my heart that God gets blamed for things He literally cannot, and will not do. I have spent a lot of time on this one point, God's goodness, because it is vital to understanding the true nature of God, if you are going to enjoy an intimate, easy-going Father/child relationship with Him; you need to trust Him.

In Acts 10:38, Luke said that Jesus, who always did the Father's will, was sent to heal, not to harm, ALL who were oppressed of (who?)—the devil. "How God anointed Jesus of Nazareth with the Holy Spirit and with power: who went about doing good, and healing all that were **oppressed of the devil;** for God was with him." Jesus was sent to heal, and do good on God's behalf. And he was a mirror of his Father's true nature.

So, let's get this straight, who oppresses, and kills people? The devil.

Who liberates and heals people? God! Now we're crystal-clear.

It always struck me as odd that the Catholics reveled in the idea of 'suffering for Jesus' like that was a mark of true holiness. It must make the devil jump for joy to get God's children to think that God wants them to suffer. And sadly, much of Satan's work is done for him.... through God's so-called 'messengers.' What a con job.

The Bible tells us in hundreds of places that God wants to bless, bless, bless His children, and heal His children, and prosper His children. So who are you gonna' believe? Some preacher, or God? I'll go with God.

I sat on that glorious beach at Tybee, overwhelmed by God's love, and thought, "Wow! That answers so many questions. Jesus always did the Father's will. If religion is right, and God IS the author of death and sickness, then why didn't Jesus make even one person sick? Why didn't Jesus lay just *one* fatal disease on *one* person and say, 'Oh, boy, now that you are sick and dying you are really glorifying my Father.'" Jesus did not and would not.

To make the leap that God kills, or maims, or sickens anyone, makes no sense whatsoever. You know what? You have to be *taught* to be that stupid, because it defies common sense.

God doesn't make us miserable. Most of our misery is caused by our own poor choices, or choices of those around us. It's also caused by toxic, lie based thinking buried in our subconscious (more into that topic in future chapters). Because negative emotions don't die, we just bury them alive. Eventually we have to face them, or they continue to sabotage our health and happiness.

God is always there with His hand out, ready to raise you out of the pit, and put your feet on solid ground. Just ask for His help.

However, there is plenty of empirical evidence that Jesus heals, not just in the gospels, but today, even as we speak. I have personally witnessed hundreds of miraculous healings through the years, all done in the name of Jesus Christ.

Right there on Tybee Island, God ministered to my heart. I had that momentous epiphany; God doesn't harm or kill anyone. Ever. He wants to heal the whole world, if they would just reach out and let Him.

If God did half the things most people accuse Him of doing, He would be, in no uncertain terms—a child abuser. We lock people up for less. You wouldn't treat your own kids the way some people accuse God of treating us—would you? So why would you think so little of Him?

Satan is the father of lies, and he's a master of deception. He has cleverly blamed his own mayhem and depravity on our heavenly Father, and gotten away with that lie for centuries.

Why don't people use the good sense that God gave them, and just think this thing through? God is LOVE. Okay? He's ALL Love. He is not loving, He is Love. Love is kind, love is gentle, love is giving. And, God's love never harmed anyone, any time, any place. God's Love is always life-giving, life-affirming, and healing.

And, here's another shocker, God doesn't even tempt people:

Let no man say when he is tempted, I am tempted of God: for **God** *cannot be tempted with evil,* **neither tempteth he any man:** *James 1:13.*

Looks like we all have some unlearning to do. Matthew 4:1,3 says that the devil is the tempter. So, I had that one wrong, too. All this came into focus for me while I was sitting at the edge of the ocean, and allowing the Holy Spirit to speak to my heart.

The Bible says we have not because we ask not. If you want answers to life, asking God is the first step to getting truthful answers to life. Don't ask people unless you trust and respect their spiritual wisdom and motives, and even then, take it back to the Bible and see it for yourself. God is the ultimate giver of all truth.

So many preachers today are, knowingly or unknowingly, teaching error. That's why it is vitally important to study the Bible for yourself, and ask the Holy Spirit to guide you into all truth.

Jesus answered and said unto them, Ye do err, not knowing the scriptures, nor the power of God. Matthew 22:29

This is what happens when people don't study the Bible for themselves, and base their beliefs instead on whatever the Right-Reverend-So-and-So says, instead of the Author of the book. They get error; and lots of it.

Don't get me wrong, there are some very godly preachers out there, but the vast majority are only out for themselves; bigger churches, more money, a new jet, and the adulation of the people. Modern day Pharisees. That's why you must study the Bible for yourself to see if what they are teaching is correct.

Standing there that day, with the waves lapping at my feet, I thought about Jesus walking on the water, and what a cool miracle that was. Not only did Jesus walk on water, but good old Peter, at Christ's invitation, got out of the boat, and walked on water, too. Matthew 14:29ff.

The analogy God showed me at Tybee, was that the kids playing in the filthy mud hole were there because that was where they felt safe. Limited and dirty, but safe. And then He showed me a vision of myself, walking on the waves of the ocean, unafraid, knowing that His hands were beneath me. It was exhilarating to say the least. Then He showed me that, metaphorically speaking, it took real courage to step out into the vast ocean of His supernatural provision, which often defies human logic, and to trust in Him alone to keep us afloat.

That's exactly what Peter and Jesus had done, trusted God, and they both walked on water—by faith.

Peter did fine as long as his focus remained on Jesus. But, when he *saw* the waves and *felt* the wind, his five senses took over, doubt set in, and he began to sink, just like I had done in my drunken rage a few days earlier. When I took my eyes off Jesus, self-pity took over, and I sunk like a rock because of Chris J's death.

But when Peter began to sink, he cried out," Lord, save me!" Jesus did not turn his back on Peter, he reached out and pulled him out of the water; just like he had done for me a couple of days ago with my non-existent emergency brake.

I could relate to old Peter. I had been overcome by emotion, and done something very, very stupid. But even when I thought I was ready to die, Jesus was there, holding me up and keeping me alive—almost in spite of myself.

Centuries apart, Jesus reached out and saved *two* drowning people, one named Peter and the other named Peg.

Jesus is the one who gave me the 'emergency brakes' that saved my life, and got me back home, when the mechanic said I had none. That, my friends, is not just grace. That is mercy; the withholding of merited judgment. My good God had snatched me from the jaws of death again, even if it was brought on by my own stupidity. That is mercy.

The Father showed me at Tybee, that it was my lack of trust in Him, or anyone for that matter, that was my greatest enemy. I still doubted that God would do what He promised. I doubted that He would love me unconditionally, that He would be there for me when the chips were down. How wrong I was. He *was* there for me, every step of the way. I had already overcome so much, but now my own doubt was my greatest enemy.

It is fear and doubt that block the promises of God from coming to pass in our lives, and we need to ask God to help us let go of those crippling thoughts, and replace them with godly thoughts; trusting in Him at all times. Until we let go of our fear and doubt, we are still in the mud hole of life, like those little kids on Tybee Island.

When you boil it all down, we doubt God because we doubt ourselves; and then we project our own weakness onto Him.

And also, because we don't understand *how* He can do the miraculous, we doubt that He WILL do the miraculous. That's on us, not on Him.

Of course we don't understand miracles because they are *supernatural*. They defy human logic. That's why they are called miracles: events that cannot be explained by natural or scientific laws. Miracles are attributed to a supernatural being. That's why we receive miracles by faith, and not by logic.

What is impossible for man to do, is possible with God: *And Jesus looking upon them saith, With men it is impossible, but not with God: for with God all things are possible. Mark 10:27*

When Father taught me about His love through those kids on the beach, it made a huge impression on me. I have gone back to the lessons of that day, and used it as an anchor for my faith over and over again.

That day, on the beach, I made a commitment to do everything in my power to draw closer to God; to launch out on the ocean of His love, and help as many people as I could "walk on water" with us. I asked Him to help me become fearless, and to show me how to trust in Him, like Jesus did.

So if you sinful people know how to give good gifts to your children, how much more will your heavenly Father give good gifts to those who ask him. Matthew 7:11

Knowing and trusting that God will never disappoint you is the best gift any of us will ever receive in this life.

We begin to know Him the moment we accept Jesus Christ. Then we build up our trust in Him as we apply what we are learning in real time, and see the results. That is how to grow up, spiritually speaking.

I understand that we all have our insecurities and lack of trust because of past experiences of being burned, but, praise God, since those fears were learned, they can also be unlearned. And as we let go of our old ways of thinking, we open the floodgates for rivers of God's blessings to flow into our lives.

There is a river whose streams make glad the city of God, the holy place where the Most High dwells. Psalm 46:4 NIV

Our Father is in the restoration business. He is in the healing business. And He wants to make our lives better in every way.

Jesus came to bring us into a Kingdom, into a Royal Family. He did not come to build big buildings with stained glass windows.

He came to offer us sonship, a new spiritual family, and to usher us into our Daddy's arms.

That day on the beach I was overcome with gratitude, and decided this is what I wanted to do for others for the rest of my life: to help others find their way home, home to God's heart. Chris J opened the way for me, she showed me the path to God's love, and I wanted to do that for others.

Even though I was still mourning her loss, that day at Tybee, I felt washed and clean again; I felt like I had a "clear shining after rain" moment. And I no longer blamed my heavenly Father, or Chris J, for her death. I let go of the anger and bitterness. I realized that the devil worked his nefarious evil to snuff out a truly promising life. And I 'got it' 'There but for the grace of God go I.'

I forgave Chris J for leaving me. I felt refreshed and at peace again. I wish everyone could experience that feeling that comes when heaven's comfort washes through your soul in a time of grief.

That day on Tybee Island I had a profound change, I had a paradigm shift regarding God's unconditional love for us.

So all of us who have had that veil removed can see and reflect the glory of the Lord. And the Lord—who is the Spirit—makes us more and more like him as we are changed into his glorious image. 2 Corinthians 3:18

I have thought back to that day on the beach countless times, and the contrast between the mud hole, and the ocean of God's love. I crave to live in the vast ocean of His unlimited Love. The life-lesson that God poured into my spirit that day has sustained me in times of immense difficulty, and has encouraged me in times of discouragement.

And I know, even if I mess up, I can come back to Him as often as I need to and receive my "clear shining after rain."

God doesn't work with the perfect, He works with the willing. And that's me, willing but flawed. Aren't we all?

Chapter 19

God Things Happen to Those Who Wait

To need God is man's highest perfection. –Soren Kierkegaard

After the shock of my friend's death I was in an emotionally vulnerable state. Satan sprung one monster trap on me and I walked right into it. I made a *really, really* bad decision that pulled the rug out from under me for a while.

About a week or so after Chris died, my old pot-growing friend Maynard (not his real name), one of the three who had been there at my first fellowship, called out of the blue, and asked me to elope. We had both come to Christ. We had dated on and off back in Rome, but certainly nothing this significant. Actually, I didn't know him very well; I knew nothing of his past, or what his future aspirations were. Despite my gut screaming 'NO!' for some reason I foolishly said, 'Yes.' To this day I do not know why.

It took him a few days to get to Savannah, in which time the Lord clearly spoke to me three times and said, "Don't do this! Don't do this! DON'T do this!" But, like a bull in china shop, I bowled forward anyway, ignoring the promptings of the Spirit.

After Maynard arrived we went straight to the Justice of the Peace. Along the way we got lost multiple times, and I kept thinking, "*Why* am I doing this?" When we finally arrived at the J.O.P., his wife answered the door, and when I walked into the room I realized the judge was blind! To me this was *another* huge red flag from God, "Peg, don't go into this *blindly!*" But I went ahead and acquiesced to a spur of the moment Braille ceremony. (And it wasn't even a shotgun wedding.) Why the rush? Was it because I felt lonely or scared after I lost Chris? I don't know. But that *one* bad decision took a terrible toll on the next four years of my life.

Note to self: NEVER, EVER MAKE A LIFE-CHANGING DECISION WHEN YOU HAVE JUST EXPERIENCED A MAJOR TRAUMA!

It turned out that my charming, handsome 'Christian,' man, was an ex-con, a serial adulterer, and a wife-beater. Oops, that one's going to leave a BIG mark.

Lordy, Lordy, I wish I had listened to my heavenly Father's warnings. Here was one more example of God trying to keep me out of the soup, but I chose *not* to listen. And I had only myself to blame. Since my inner childhood script was still one of self-sabotage and abuse, it is not at all surprising that I would subconsciously be drawn to an abuser.

Free will is one of God's greatest gifts, but so few of us use it for its primary purpose: to talk to God, and to **heed** His wisdom. Instead, we use it to make stupid, selfish, and often self-destructive choices.

We are free to choose, but we are not free to choose the *consequences* of our choices.

A lot of Christians don't want to talk about the trouble they get into *after* they are born again. Perhaps they are afraid of being judged. Sadly the new birth is no substitute for common sense and poor judgment, those things must be remedied over time. My spirit was perfect, but I still had a long way to go to have a sound mind.

Through the next few years of ups and downs, my new-found salvation was the only thing that brought any joy into my life. God's presence was the one thing that did give me a sense of purpose; and eventually the courage to walk away from that sadistic marriage.

Six months into this catastrophe of a marriage, I went to my church elders to talk about Maynard's adultery and abuse, and basically their counsel was 'suck it up butter cup.' Do not divorce him. To this day I don't know why any counselor would tell a woman to stay in an abusive, life-threatening marriage.

Their unsound advice almost got me killed.

One night Maynard really lost it. He beat me so badly that I had two black eyes, a broken nose, loose teeth, and bruises as big as saucers all over my upper body. I couldn't lay my head on a pillow for weeks because it was so bruised and swollen. You see, he had been a Mixed Martial Arts champion in Okinawa, and that night he took his full fury out on me. I thought he was going to kill me, to beat me to death. He threw me to the floor, and he was on top of my chest with my arms pinned under his knees, and he was beating me for all he was worth. When I was just on the edge of passing out, somehow I had the presence of mind to say through bleeding lips, "In the name of Jesus Christ, I command you to stop." At which point he (the demon in him) crumbled to the ground like a deflating balloon.

I wish I had commanded the demon sooner, but Maynard attacked me so quickly, and with such blinding fury, that he took me completely by surprise. It took me a moment to gather my wits. If I had not miraculously stopped him, I don't think I would be here today to write this book, and he might be back in prison.

The next morning I looked at my battered face in the mirror and thought, "He's not the crazy person; I AM for still being here!"

I remembered how Harry the rapist had said, "Satan wants you dead," and I realized Satan was still trying to kill me. Maynard may have called himself a Christian, but his heart showed otherwise. You can label a can 'pickles' on the outside and it may have 'beets' on the inside. Labels mean nothing. Actions speak louder than words. And, 'sincerity' is no guarantee for truth. There are lots of smooth-talking operators in this world who trap good women into abusive situations. And Maynard was one of them.

Of course, he begged me to stay with him after the brutal beating, just like most abusers do. All I did was point to my face and say, "Really?" as I continued packing my things.

God was doing His part, but I had to have the courage to do my part: to leave.

I packed my car, and began the long drive to move in with some friends, friends who lived 1,418 miles away from Maynard. I started divorce proceedings right away. Of course, when I left him, he began spreading lies about me, and blaming ME for our break-up. No surprise there.

One thing I learned during that time was don't bother explaining: your friends don't need it, and your enemies won't believe you anyway. I held my head high as many of my so-called 'friends' turned against me for leaving. But it was my life on the line, not theirs.

But here's the good news: That was the last time, after years of abuse at that hands of men, that any man ever laid a finger on me to harm me.

For those of you who have been in an abusive relationship, something gets fundamentally messed up in your inner wiring when people whom you love and trust betray or abuse you. I'm including the church elders here, because they counseled me to stay with that monster.

When I did get the courage to leave, God had some major blessings in store for me to speed up my healing.

My life was at another crossroads after my divorce, but this time, I had the good sense to ask the Lord for guidance, and take it. And He showed me the right place for me at that time was Bible College. Through a set of miraculous circumstances, God provided the funds for me to attend *The Way Bible College* of Emporia, Kansas.

In the rest of this chapter I will share some of the major insights I had that first year at Emporia, where God did many mighty miracles of provision and healing in *my* life. Up until that time I had been so focused on helping others, I had not even realized what bad shape I was in.

When I was in a safe environment, able to focus on my own stuff, remarkable healing took place. I finally felt worthy, like a child of God, and a royal heir to the King. Kind of like Sally Fields at the Oscars when she cried, "You like me, you like me... you really,

really like me!" Away from the negative influence of that toxic marriage, I was free to realize how deeply God loved me, and enjoy the blessings He wanted to lavish on me.

At Emporia it clicked that God was responsible for me, that I belonged to Him, like a parent and a child, and He would never let me down. My God-confidence grew in leaps and bounds.

Without the albatross of Maynard around my neck I began to heal and blossom again spiritually. In a college environment I could totally focus on my relationship with our Father. I began to make decisions with deeper spiritual insight, followed by many successes. Life was gelling. I was growing up, maturing into a stronger believer, and that felt awesome.

Here's a fact of life: the presence of God is man's natural environment. Like the apostle Paul said, "It is in Him we live and move and have our being." Acts 17:28. Our purpose here in Earth is to get in touch with God, and have a relationship with Him.

God's presence is the 'environment' we were born to inhabit; to live surrounded by His love and power. Until we learn to live *in Him*, there will always be something missing. We all need God. It is the only way we can reach our highest selves as human beings; by teaming up with our Creator. That truth really came home to my heart in 1979.

When it sunk into my *heart* that I AM God's child, and that He *is* my Father, I was filled with a new kind of confidence.

We are here to succeed in life by being in league with God, and that is the number one truth that Satan wants to steal from us; our identity IN Christ, our intimacy with God. When Satan tempted

Jesus in the wilderness, he asked him three times, "**IF** thou be the son of God..." Satan knew if he could just get Jesus to doubt his sonship, then it would be game over.

Of course, Jesus never doubted—because he knew, not only *who* he was, but *whose* he was. And even though it takes time to develop that kind of God confidence in our own lives, Jesus showed us the way. And that was the task I devoted myself to at Emporia.

Friends, life is a journey, not a destination. It's all about moving from one goal to the next, or as St. Paul said, "from glory to glory" if we are living life correctly. The key is to keep moving forward. If you have a set back, pick yourself up, and keep going. You cannot live a healthy life looking in the rearview mirror, you must focus on the road ahead, and on the next chapter. And that's what I did.

All life is spiritual. I know it doesn't always *feel* that way, but it is. At bible college I was also developing my ability to use my spiritual powers to a greater and more consistent degree. The first part of my life I had been plagued with demonic phenomenon, but that year I began experiencing heavenly miracles on a regular basis.

My shackles came off in 1979. Granted, it took me a few months to realize how oppressed I had been under Maynard, and how I had lost my self identity. While I was married to him my spiritual growth was hampered dramatically, being hamstrung by our toxic relationship. When I walked out of that mess, I felt like a woman who had been swimming with weights tied to my arms and legs, and now they were gone. I was filled with a feeling of buoyancy. Of lightness. Of freedom. And I didn't feel alone—I felt complete.

That's when I had another 'aha!' moment; who could take better care of me than God? No one. I started to walk like the heroes of faith in the Bible, trusting God, and doing the works that Jesus did on a more consistent basis. I was becoming very adept at heeding God's call, and walking by the Spirit, as listed in 1 Corinthians 12:7-10: speaking in tongues, interpretation, prophecy, word of knowledge, word of wisdom, discerning of spirits, faith, miracles and gifts of healing.

That was also the year I began to receive emotional healing. Jesus said he came to preach the gospel to the needy (humble), and I knew I was needy. I needed a restoration of my heart. I was emerging from a mess, and I asked the Lord to take me—and make me better. I was humble, and ready for instruction. I was more than ready to quit being a punching bag. I was ready to become a full-blown victor, instead of a victim.

The Lord knew that after almost five years of abuse I was very weary, I was faint, in fact, I was utterly worn out. I needed above all to have my inner strength renewed. I needed and wanted to feel empowered. What a wonderful change that would be.

The following verses from Isaiah gave me solid keys to achieve that goal:

He giveth power to the faint; and to them that have no might he increaseth strength. Even the youths shall faint and be weary, and the young men shall utterly fall: But they that wait upon the LORD **shall renew their strength**; *they shall mount up with wings as eagles; they* shall run, and not be weary; and they shall walk, and not faint. Isaiah 40:29-31

What a load of TRUTH! Those verses healed my heart like sunshine on an open wound. The emphasis was on 'He.' God was going to do these things for me, if I pressed in to Him.

So, let's break this down. *"But they that wait upon the LORD,"* the word 'wait' means to 'bind together with, or to join with.' It's not a word that represents time so much as a condition. Isaiah said that if I chose to bind my heart to God's, to join with Him and let Him lead the way, He would and could heal me. No more going off half-cocked without seeking His will; I had done that once too often, and suffered the consequences. I had to learn to push pause, and wait and listen for Papa's counsel by including Him in ALL of my decisions. In other words, to do two things: to make the Lord, my closest confidant, and to make my prayers a dialogue instead a monologue. That's why God gave us *one* mouth and *two* ears; we are supposed to listen to Him more than we talk to Him. And that takes practice.

That was a scary thing to do, since my trust level was so low. Turning my life and will over to God took courage. But, I wasn't playing games, I was serious. I just said, "Here Lord, you are the Potter and I am the clay." Give me a makeover from the inside out.

The next line, *"Shall renew their strength."* 'Shall' puts this promise in the absolute tense, but 'shall' also implies time. Becoming mentally whole and stable was going to take some time. I didn't get broken overnight, and I wasn't going to get fixed overnight. But I knew that if I stuck with God's program, everything that people, the devil, and 'life' had stolen from me could be fully restored. Hallelujah!

The result of pressing into God is, "*They shall mount up with wings as eagles.*" This is a very interesting metaphor. It was not lost on me that the eagle is the serpent's natural enemy. In a fight between an eagle and a serpent, guess who wins? You got it, the eagle. In the old logging camps they would train eagles to hunt and kill rattlesnakes, to keep the loggers from getting snake bit. Old Satan himself was called a Serpent in the Garden of Eden. Without God teaching us how to mount up with wings of eagles, people just keep right on getting 'snake bit.'

God was showing me how to never get 'snake bit' again, by joining together with Him. By listening to Him, trusting Him and walking in His wisdom; then the Serpent could no longer bite me at will, and sink his poison fangs into my life. This was the answer I had been seeking since I was a child. My thirst for how to keep the demons from racking and ruining my life was finally slaked.

And like an eagle, God was taking me to a place higher than I had ever been before, a place I could never have gotten to on my own.

Eagles see life from a higher vantage point. They have extraordinary eyesight even from far away. Thinking like an eagle, problems that used to look like mountains to me now looked like molehills. With the Lord leading the way, I could vanquish those adversaries who had once seemed so daunting.

And, here's the kicker: "*They shall run, and not be weary; and they shall walk, and not faint.*" I loved to run back then, and nothing felt better than getting that second wind, to get in 'the zone.' That's what I wanted spiritually, to tap into that second wind of strength, and stamina that comes from the spirit of God within. To get into 'the zone' with Him.

I did learn how to tap into my 'eagle' inside, and I became Satan's greatest threat. What a turn of events. What a banner year 1979 was for me.

In Isaiah I found simple keys for winning in life: trust God, bind together with Him, let His presence renew your strength, put on your eagle's heart, and believe that His Spirit will empower you when you are faint. Let Him do the heavy lifting. That's a winning combination for success.

Keep driving into your heart, 'I am what the word of God says I am. I can do what the word of God says I can do. Therefore, I DO!' Build your **reliance on God**, that's what will fortify and strengthen you, because you are relying on the strength of the Creator of heaven and Earth, not your own fleshly weakness. This allows the Lord to reinvigorate you from the inside out, and that's better than Gatorade. Working as a team, joined with God, you can run and not be weary, and you can walk and not faint, because the Lord Himself will be your strength and your second wind. How encouraging.

That is how you go beyond simply believing His **promise**, to trusting the **PROMISER**.

It's not the words in the book that have power, it is the One who backs up those words that brings them to pass. When you grasp that, you and the Father are grooving as one.

I ate, drank and slept those verses from Isaiah 40. They were 'tattooed' on the inside of my eyelids. They burned like a fire in my belly and were the anchor that kept me moored to my new found God-confidence. There was Someone greater than myself to whom I could turn in every situation. Partnering with God proved to be electrifying. Almost every day I was surprised by some new miracle: from friendships to finances, from better health to being asked to participate in a special project. It was awesome. My life was humming with joy and purpose.

I was allowing the Holy Spirit to illuminate His truth in my mind, and make it living and real in my heart. Like Jesus said to Peter, 'Flesh and blood has not revealed this to you, but my Father who is in heaven.' Bam! That's how life is supposed to work, being led and fed by the Spirit.

In little old Emporia, Kansas, my life was taking on a new zest, and a whole new dimension. I can't begin to tell you how thankful I was to be there.

This great change was happening because it finally gelled in my heart that **thoughts ARE things**. Thoughts turn into tangible things and events. They either bring good into manifestation, or the lies of Satan, depending what thoughts we chose to embrace.

Much of my sanity was restored that year just by studying the Bible, and being in a safe environment; out from under the constant abuse from Maynard. As my thinking patterns cleared up, I saw what a silly puppet I had been for the first part of my life, and that Satan was the puppeteer. I was pushing thirty, and it was high time for me to get my act together. As the eyes of my understanding opened, I cut those strings, and became my own woman; actually, I became God's woman, which is even better.

That concept is beautifully expressed in 'The Little Prince' when the fox tells the boy, "People have forgotten this truth," the fox said. "But you mustn't forget it. You become responsible forever for what you've tamed." Well, God had 'tamed' me, so-to speak, and I was more than happy to have Him take responsibility for my life. I gladly placed myself under His protection and guidance.

Here's a reality check: we were not created to be windup toys that get cranked up and left on earth to bump into walls for the rest of our lives. Humans are beautiful, sentient beings, intricately designed to hear God's voice, and to have an ongoing relationship with Him. After all, He created us in His own image.

We were born to be born-again, to be a 'chip-off-the-old-block'

I could hear Jesus whisper to my heart, "Hey, Peg, I gave my life, suffered and died, so that you don't have to suffer all the time. I came to redeem you, to restore you so that you can learn to love yourself. I came to give you a good and blessed life, not to struggle all the time. *Capiche?*"

Okay, Jesus, I got the memo.

I was bowled over by Jesus' love; a man I never met, who got the stuffing beat out of him, and died to save my hide. That is absolutely amazing. Totally heroic. Jesus came to do for me and in me, that which I could not do for myself. Like he said, "Greater love than this has no man, that he would lay down his life for his friends."

Did that mean I was Jesus' friend? I was starting to think so.

I thought back to the time Peter got out of the boat and walked on the water. (Matthew 14:22-33) What faith that took on Peter's part. But, when Peter took his eyes off the Lord, and he began to sink and cried out, "LORD, save me!" Jesus didn't let him sink, he reached out and took his hand, and pulled Peter back up, on the water. But he did ask Peter one thing, "*Why* did you ever *doubt* me?"

Jesus could have walked away, and let Peter sink, but, that's not how he rolls. The Lord of Love is all about helping us, he's about recovery, and restoration. Jesus did not come to condemn us, but to make us whole. But he asks us the same question he asked Peter, "Why do you doubt me?"

For God sent not his Son into the world to condemn the world; but that the world through him might be saved (made whole). John 3:17.

For eight long years the nuns had drilled into my head that when I messed up God couldn't stand to even look at me. But Jesus said that when I messed up **God was <u>out</u> looking <u>for</u> me**. Not to condemn me, but to restore me. (Luke 15:20) What a difference the truth makes. He is always yearning for us to call out, "Papa, help me."

The Lord doesn't shun you in times of trouble; He seeks to help you in times of trouble. And helping you is what makes God happy. Such a deal.

Embracing that one truth regarding God's true nature got rid of a boatload of lie-based thinking, and healed many places in my broken heart. Unconditional love can do that.

They say, "You can't fix stupid," but 'they' are wrong. The Bible says, "The entrance of thy words giveth light; it giveth understanding unto the simple." [the STUPID!] Psalm 119:30. So technically YOU can't fix stupid—but <u>God</u> can.

You might ask, "Why didn't your life become all sunshine and lollipops at the moment of the new birth?"

In some areas, it did, there was an immediate change, especially in the area of hope. But the deep, subconscious, lie-based thinking that was programmed into me from my childhood, the stuff that was lodged in my subconscious, took time and effort to be rewired. And that begins with the renewed mind.

God originally set man up to have rulership, dominion over the whole earth, over everything except their fellow man. (Genesis 1:26, 27) Both male and female had this dominion. Unfortunately, they turned from God's goodness, and relinquished their authority to Satan. Bad move. Ever since that day, Satan has been the god of this age, and has taught mankind to think of themselves as nobodies, helpless, and slaves to elements they were originally created to dominate: health, weather, food, and well being. After a lifetime of feeding on negativity and impossibility thinking, we all have a certain amount of damage that only the Holy Spirit can heal.

When something good happens to most us, we simply don't feel deserving, or we wonder what is going to happen to ruin it. But when we come to Christ, we realize there is an abundant life waiting for us, and we do deserve the best in life, because Christ made us worthy by the grace of God, who wants to give us honor, and health and prosperity.

To live in an abundance mentality takes retraining of the mind. We cannot live effectively until we learn to think according to who we are in Christ Jesus. We must break out of the negative 'slave' mold of this fallen world, and be transformed by believing we are who God says we are, the King's kids. We then begin to think the way Christ thought, and do what he did. This is the renewed mind, and it is our key to power. Dr. Myles Munroe said," Renewing our minds means returning to the original mind that we had before the fall of man, a mind that loves and honors God," and understands his rightful place on earth is as an heir of God, and joint-heir with Christ. "And if children, then heirs; heirs of God, and joint-heirs with Christ." Romans 8:17.

That's the place of dominion and power. Man as God designed him to be; the head and not the tail. Joyce Meyer said, "If you want your life to change, the mind must change. Where the mind goes the man follows."

Humans are three-part beings: body, soul, and spirit.

The body is man's physical being. The soul is man's intellect, will and emotions. And the spirit is man's life force.

When one accepts Christ as their savior, in a nanosecond they receive a brand new spirit or life force; it is holy, sanctified, and immortal. They are imbued with the very nature of God. (II Peter 1:4) Wow! That is the miracle of all miracles. That is called the new birth. That is by God's doing. But appropriating the new birth in our day-to-day living is our decision. We decide how little or how much of our heavenly inheritance we want to avail ourselves to.

The lifestyle of a child of God is both miracle and practical. Once we are born again; our new spirit is perfect, but our mind, which is in our soulish part, is still damaged from our past. Therefore the mind must be renewed, or brought into harmony with our new standing in Christ. And that is the practical part of our new life. That part is up to us.

*And **be not conformed to this world: but be ye transformed by the renewing of your mind**, that ye may prove what is that good, and acceptable, and perfect, will of God. Romans 12:2.*

God is in the transforming business. 'Renewed' is the Greek word *anakainosis*, which means 'to renovate' or to *exchange* something old for something new. Transformed. So, I said, "Sign me up!"

This transformation is kind of like HGTV, where they renovate those old homes; they tear out the old rotten junk, and put brand new stuff in there that works properly. I began to ask Jesus, 'The Renovator' to guide me, and show me what patterns to tear down, and what new thoughts to put in their place. I was willing to change. I was ready for change and a full restoration. I longed for this transformation. How exciting! Have you seen the faces of those people when they walk back into their newly renovated homes? They are elated! Some of them cry for joy. Others say they can't believe it's really their home.

The renewed mind makes living life just that exciting and fresh.

I knew it was going to take time and energy to change deeply entrenched old thought patterns and habits, but the payoff would be well worth the effort. Another term for the 'renewed mind' is 'putting on the mind of Christ.' That makes me happy, just to know that it is *possible* for me to think like Christ did.

And since we all come through life damaged to various degrees, that means we all have negative thought patterns to put off, and replace with godly ones. All of us have some toxic, or lie-based thinking. The Bible calls that our 'old man' nature, and we need to change our mental diet over to 'new man' thinking to transform. We have to put down the Twinkies, and feed our mind the 'health food' of God's word.

Old thoughts like, "You are a loser, you are no good, or, you will never amount to anything" need to be replaced with new man thinking, "I am more than a conqueror through Christ Jesus, or God is with me and in me all the time, I expect the best to come my way today."

We need to mentally change channels, and tune our mind to station W-GOD, because God says, "You are My beloved child. You are a joint-heir with Christ. You are more than a conqueror through him who loves you. You were created for victory." Those are uplifting, life-affirming truths. And His truth never changes.

Do you think Jesus walked around all day full of negativity, grumbling, and anxious? No, way. He knew better. He went around praising God, and being thankful. He walked in God-confidence. He always looked to His heavenly Father for wisdom and strength, therefore he believed that he had the *powers of heaven* at his disposal, just like Adam and Eve once had. And now, so do you. That is putting on the mind of Christ.

When you put on the mind of Christ you will find yourself: praising God, thankful, loving, bold, confident, optimistic, and victorious. Can you see the difference? That is 'new man' thinking, versus 'old man' lies from our past. One is completely toxic, while the other is health food for the soul. Which would you prefer to feed on? The choice is yours.

There are many remarkable benefits to putting on the mind of Christ. Research has proven that 95% of all **physical disease** comes from **toxic** thinking, and stress: anxiety, worry, anger, resentment, and guilt, to name a few. Drip, drip, drip. Our inner thought life is either bringing life or sickness to our body on a continual basis.

Here is an every day example of why we need to renew our mind: let's say that someone steals your idea at work. You came up with it, you worked out the bugs, but they stole it. They presented it to the boss as *their* idea, and they got a big raise. Now, you are furious with 'righteous' anger.'

But Jesus said to love your enemies, and to pray for them that despitefully use you. What? You've got to be kidding me! Your flesh is saying, "No way! I want to get even with that so-and-so. I want pay back, and I want it now." Your whole body is shaking, you lose your appetite, and you can't sleep at night. Does any of that sound like its good for you? No. And if you keep this up long enough, you develop an ulcer, or even heart disease.

There is a way out—change our mind! The mind of Christ tells you to forgive that person, and turn them over to God. Let the anger go. Not for *their* sake, but for *your* sake.

I still blows my mind that Jesus, while bleeding and dying, said from the cross, "Father, forgive them, for they know not what they do."

Just stop, and think about that for a minute. That kind of forgiveness defies human logic and emotion. Yet Jesus asked his Father to forgive the very men who had brutalized and beaten him, who jammed a crown of thorns into his head, and nailed him to a cross. You know what? No one has ever offended me *that* badly. How about you?

Why is it so important to forgive? Number one, because God asks us to. But on a more practical level, unforgiveness hurts *you*. Unforgiveness is like drinking poison and expecting the other person to die. It doesn't work that way.

How do we get to the place where we deal with our enemies like Christ did? We must put on the mind of Christ, and tap into the fruit of the Spirit: God's love, joy, peace, patience, kindness, goodness, faith, meekness, and self-control. Only then can we let go, and let God. Only then can we forgive the wrong doer, and let God sort out the pieces. "Vengeance is mine, says the Lord, I will repay."

One way or another, God will take care of *you* and exalt you in due time, *if* you put your trust in Him. That is the goal in life, to trust in Him, and be more like Him.

That doesn't mean you have to say what the perpetrator did was okay, it was not; in fact, you would be smart to stay away from them, and be on guard in their presence. But it is crucial for you to let go of all the resentment and bitterness inside your own soul for your own good.

There is a spiritual law that you will reap what you sow. Most of the world calls this karma, but God said it first. He calls it the law of sowing and reaping. That's why He said, "Do unto others as you would have them do unto you." That's solid gold wisdom.

The point is, you can let go of the offender and let the laws of the courtroom of heaven take over. Then trust God to give you what you deserve in His own timing.

Humble yourselves therefore under the mighty hand of God, that he may exalt you in due time: 1 Peter 5:6.

Here's the deal: you and I will never reach Christ's kind of forgiveness through our flesh. Our flesh is weak. Only the spirit of God in us can unleash that kind of forgiveness as we put on the 'new man.' Only then can we represent God's nature and character on this Earth.

When we put on the mind of Christ, we find that we can do what we once thought was impossible; we find ourselves growing more compassionate and understanding, even forgiving those who have wronged us. In a word, we find ourselves *transformed*.

Like HGTV, most of the 'rooms' of our mind need renovating and rewiring, from the ground up. And that's what happens as we choose to replace fear with faith, anxiety with God-confidence, resentment with compassion, and anger with love. The next thing you know, you will be so blessed, you'll hardly recognize yourself; you have been 'renovated.'

I wish at the time of the new birth we could just hit an 'erase' button and start fresh with a clean slate mentally, but that's not how life works. We have to put off the hurtful thinking of our past, and put on new, godly thoughts. How do we know what godly thoughts are? Simple, study the Bible, a lot, so you have a foundation, and learn to *listen* to the voice of God.

I used to write scripture verses down on small cards and carry them around with me, and memorize them. Sounds corny, but it really helped me establish some beachheads in my mind with which to deal with the Adversary.

I took charge of how I was going to act, as well as *react* to situations. I learned to think thoughtfully and on purpose. This can only be accomplished by working in concert with the Spirit of the living God, guiding us, and revealing to our heart His way of thinking about stuff. As I embraced this makeover, I changed for the better in the most remarkable ways.

Being confident of this very thing, that he which hath begun a good work in you will perform it until the day of Jesus Christ: Philippians 1:6.

What God starts, He finishes. He wants to make you whole: spirit, soul, and body, but you have to be willing to do your part. And that begins in your mind.

This transformation is even more dramatic than the home remodels on HGTV. It's more like when that ugly furry caterpillar changes into a magnificent butterfly. One is ugly earthbound, and vulnerable, while the other one is beautiful and soars through the heavens with grace and ease.

As I committed to the task of deep inner change, I would often look in the mirror, and focus on the 'new me' the Christ in me; that part of me that was perfect, beautiful, confident, happy, and excited to be alive. The more I focused on the new me, the more I soared like a butterfly.

The renewed mind can be as simple as saying, "Lord, I've got a lot on my plate today, but with You by my side, I know we can handle it together." Or, it can be as difficult as forgiving a relative who molested you when you were a child. Both entail putting on the mind of Christ.

A great example of a transformed life is the apostle Paul. He had been at the top of the heap socially, religiously, financially, and every other way, which made him very arrogant. (And all that pride and arrogance turned him into a murderer. He went around killing Christians, and thinking that was a *good* thing.) Paul had once wielded tremendous social and political power, but he was a wreck inside. When he was exposed to the truth, he counted all of those worldly accolades as dung, compared to the joy of knowing Christ. He said, "Buh-bye" to all of that fleshly ego boasting.

Yea doubtless, and I count all things but loss for the excellency of the knowledge of Christ Jesus my Lord: for whom I have suffered the loss of all things, and do count them but dung, that I may win Christ. Philippians 3:8.

For Paul, there was no prize, or title, or accolade that could compare with the excellency of simply knowing Christ, and having a relationship with him. That's one powerful recommendation for getting to know Jesus.

That first year at Bible College I was having one paradigm shift after another. The things that I used to count so dear: what others thought about me, the big bucks, or more toys, paled in comparison to the joy I experienced in getting to know Christ, as both my savior and my friend.

Like Paul, I wanted to do everything in my power to know Christ, and the power of his resurrection. That became my driving force. I wanted to walk around, and love and heal people just like Jesus did. I John 4:17 says, "As he [Jesus] is, so are we in this world."

For a Christian living 'as he is' should NOT be a lofty goal, it should be the norm.

The key to being 'as he is in this world' is love. Love God, love yourself, and love others. That pretty much sums up the walk of Christ. Focus on love, and the rest will fall into place.

God *is* Love. And His Love can be both seen and felt.

His love changes lives for the better. Through His love we come to see ourselves as God sees us. Only His love makes it possible to put off anger, and bitterness, and resentment; towards yourself and others.

Believing in God's Love for you is the portal through which you receive all the blessings from heaven's treasure room.

And that year, love blazed a trail to God's heart for me. I started to really blossom into the person God created me to be; kind, generous, and unafraid. I was changing, in the inner depths of my soul. I was learning to trust God on a deeper level. Not just in my head, but in my heart.

Like Jesus said, we confess with our mouth (head), but we *believe* in our heart. Romans 10:9.

The heart and the mind are not the same thing. The soul is what makes you—you. And your soul houses **both** your heart *and* your mind (head). The mind is where we make our conscious decisions, but our heart is where we hold our true beliefs. Some folks use the word "heart felt" for a genuine apology, one that is not just off the top of the head, but felt deeply and sincerely, from the heart.

When we turn our problems over to God, His peace will guard both our hearts and our minds.

Be careful (anxious) for nothing; but in every thing by prayer and supplication with thanksgiving let your requests be made known unto God. And the peace of God, which passeth all understanding, shall keep (guard) your **hearts and minds** *through Christ Jesus. Philippians 4:6.7.*

In life, what we believe is what we will draw into our lives, for good or for ill. Since believing comes from the heart, not just the head, that makes our heart life singularly significant. The renewed mind will transform us to a marked degree, but deep lasting change occurs in our hearts. (We'll talk more about how to change our heart in a future chapter.)

It's what we believe in our heart, not just our head, that carries us into the presence of God. And **the presence of God is man's natural environment. Man as he was designed to live.**

We were not put on Earth to live without God. We are wired to live in His presence, trusting in Him as our coworker, the One who does the heavy lifting. That's why when we don't have God at the center of our thoughts, we feel overwhelmed.

We then, as workers together with him, beseech you also that ye receive not the grace of God in vain. 2 Corinthians 6:1

Let that vision sink deep into your heart. That is the key to transformation: knowing God, and working together with Him.

The more we purposely intertwine our life with Him, the more beautiful it becomes as we manifest the grace of God.

*Jesus told him... 'Man does not live by bread alone, but by **every word** that comes from the mouth of God.' Matthew 4:4.*

In Matthew 4:4, 'word' in the Greek is *'rhema.'* There is another Greek word translated 'word' in the Bible, which is *'logos.' 'Logos'* implies the recorded or written word, the Bible. But *'rhema'* is God's voice, His word, speaking directly to your spirit in real time. It is personal revelation given at a particular time addressing a particular situation. *'Rhema'* is dynamic, living, real time information that comes to you just when you need it. *'Rhema'* is pointedly specific. *'Rhema'* is revelation: as in word of knowledge, word of wisdom, and discerning of spirits. *'Rhema'* is how we got the Bible: God spoke to men of old, who took dictation and wrote it down. That became the Bible, the *'logos'*.

Every born-again believer has this direct connection to God, and the ability to hear His voice. You never get a busy signal when calling your hotline to heaven. But the soul is the filter. Our Father can impart much needed information to us, but if our filter is clogged, we cannot take hold of His words, and believe them.

Our mind was designed to hold GOD'S thoughts, but that means training our mind to do what it was created for.

That's why when we don't hold on to God's thoughts we become sick, miserable, and afraid. We need to put off toxic thinking (thoughts that literally fight against God's thoughts), and lead every thought captive to the obedience of Christ. If your mind is mucked up with anger, bitterness, and anxiety, it's like putting sugar in the gas tank. The engine locks up. It's like trying to have a deep conversation with someone at a loud rock concert—futile. God's voice comes in over still waters. That's why we need to cultivate quiet seas in our own heart and mind, in order to hear Him.

The more I studied the written word, the *'logos'*, the more I recognized the *'rhema'* when I heard it. Revelation, *rhema*, will never contradict the Bible, but will always line up with it. The number one litmus test for knowing if you are hearing God's voice is: does it line up with the Bible?

Under the new covenant, God speaks to us through the spirit of Christ within us.

"My sheep hear my voice, and I know them, and they follow me." John 10:27.

Genuine transformation comes when you habitually follow the Shepherd and feed on his words: heed the promptings of the Spirit, and walk in obedience.

- YOU have the power to **choose** what you think, say and do

- Choose to think on God's words concerning your situation

- Believe and act on what He tells you

- Make His will your will, and reap a good harvest in your day

For the LORD giveth wisdom: out of his mouth cometh knowledge and understanding. Proverbs 2:6.

I started out in life with my psyche under constant attack; fear, molestation, low self-esteem, guilt and shame. The demons made a shamble of my inner heart life at a very young age. But I am here to tell you that God has healed my heart, and turned my life around, and made it better in every way. I thank God for that, because out of the heart issues life.

A good man out of the good treasure of his heart bringeth forth that which is good; and an evil man out of the evil treasure of his heart bringeth forth that which is evil: for of the abundance of the heart his mouth speaketh. Luke 6:45

Do you want good things to happen in your life? Do you want good fruit? Then plant the truth deep in your heart, and reap a harvest of blessings.

As my heart was healing, it became much easier to follow the promptings of the Spirit, instead of leaning on my own understanding. Great things happened. Miracles became the norm. My faith was deepened. I became happier, more confident, healthier, and more at peace. Thanks to Jesus, my broken soul was being restored in the most remarkable way.

God didn't give us this spiritual inheritance only for 'someday' in the 'sweet by-and-by,' but He filled us with His spirit to make our lives better in the sweet now and now. Right here, today.

Life will most assuredly be great, someday, in the future, when we inherit our home in Paradise, but make no mistake, **Jesus came to give us the more abundant life here and now—today**. Because you and I face problems on a daily basis, of all shapes and sizes. What kind of Father would say, "Okay, be miserable for a few decades, and then we'll get to the good stuff." That's insane. No loving parent would withhold any good thing from their child that would relieve their suffering now.

For the LORD God is a sun and shield: the LORD will give grace and glory: no good thing will he withhold from them that walk uprightly [that's NOW]. Psalm 84:11.

Who shall not receive manifold more in this present time, and in the world to come life everlasting. Luke 18:30.

Jesus came to make your life better today. And even better tomorrow, and the next day and the next, as your trust in Him grows. He sees your life progressing from 'glory to glory.' What a great vision.

But we all, with open face beholding as in a glass the glory of the Lord, are changed into the same image from glory to glory, even as by the Spirit of the Lord. 2 Corinthians 3:18

I'm not saying bad things don't happen to God's kids, of course they do, we live in a fallen world, but I am saying that if you trust God, He will always give you the victory in and over those situations. Jesus promised that in all these things you are more than a conqueror through him who loves you. (Romans 8:37).

None of us will 'arrive' at total perfection until the resurrection, but in the meantime we are promised the more abundant life if we walk with God in the here and now. So dig into the Bible, and find out what treasures are waiting for you in this life.

That year at Bible college, I fundamentally changed the way I thought about ... well ... everything: God, life, death, goals, and the future. But the most important change was that my confidence in God grew exponentially. It gelled in my heart that He is my guardian, my keeper, and the One who is with me, fighting for me every moment of every day, even when I'm asleep.

I developed the *habit* of practicing the presence of God. And that, my friend, is some great transformation.

Renewing the mind is a lifelong endeavor; it's like breathing, you need to do it constantly. There will always be more junk to put off, and deeper truth to put on, but the key is to keep bringing your mind back to God's presence. That sounds so simple, and yet it is so liberating.

Soren Kierkegaard, the Danish theologian, said, "To need God is man's highest perfection." Masterfully said.

We can *grow* in our relationship with God as far and as fast as we want. Our growth is determined by our own hunger to know Him. That year at Emporia I lived at the feeding trough. Like the apostle Paul, I counted all things but dung, for the excellency of the knowledge of Christ Jesus my Lord. And that involved change. If we are going to let go of the negative mindsets of our past, we must retrain our minds in the behavior of an heir to Kingdom, and a child of God. Which includes studying the Bible and obeying the promptings of the Spirit. This takes work, but it is exhilarating work. And the rewards are heavenly.

Until Christ returns, there will always be more growing to do, God is infinite. But, you will come to a place where something 'clicks'. You hit pay dirt in your heart. That's when you know that you know that Jesus is the Way, the Truth and the Life, and no one can ever talk you out of it.

That year at Emporia, my train left the 'Loserville' station, and I was well on my way to Glory Land, living for and with the Master.

The Lord spent a long time waiting on me to come home to Him, and now my greatest joy was, and still is, spending quality time with my Abba Father, nurturing our relationship. My intimacy with Him grows deeper, and richer every day. I live a blessed life because I live in His presence, and I am complete in Him. This is what I was born to do.

But they that wait upon the LORD shall renew their strength; they shall mount up with wings as eagles; they shall run, and not be weary; and they shall walk, and not faint. Isaiah 40:31

That's why I say, **God things happen to those who wait.** And He never disappoints.

Chapter 20

Jesus IS Just Alright With Me

Jesus is just alright with me, Jesus is just alright, oh yeah
Jesus is just alright with me, Jesus is just alright
–The Doobie Brothers

It still amazes me that I went from a total burnout, who wondered if Jesus even existed, to a firm believer in *The Doobie Brothers* sweet refrain, "Jesus IS just alright with me." What a radical change.

People who have only known me for twenty or thirty years have no idea how radical that change was. But I know, and I will always carry a deep and profound gratitude in my heart for it.

That's why I love being a counselor, I have such hope for everyone. I don't think there is anyone who is too damaged for the Lord to restore. He has seen it all, and restored it all. Jesus died for all mankind. His love and restoration is available to whosoever will reach out and take it. And that includes you.

After Emporia, I moved to Beltsville, Maryland, where I became and in-country missionary, which gave me a whole year to put the truths I had been learning at college into practical application. Again, I had another year of signs, miracles, and wonders.

The following year I moved to a beautiful two story home in College Park, near the University of Maryland, with three roommates. That summer I was reading a church magazine, and came upon an advertisement for a trip to Israel in December. I had never thought much about going to Israel, but a voice spoke to me and said, "Peg, I'm going to *send* you on that trip to Israel." I looked around to see if someone else was in the room, but I was alone. I figured the voice must be God, so I filled out the registration form and sent it in. I then began telling everyone who would listen, that God was going to send me to Israel.

That September, when it came time for the deposit to be turned in, I had none of the required money; zip, zero. So, I called the trip organizer and said to him, "I don't have any deposit money yet, but God said He was going to send me to Israel."

To my absolute shock, he said, "Sorry, no money, no trip."

I came right back at him, "Hey! The theme of this trip is following the steps of the heroes of faith. Where's your faith?" And I hung up on him. I went in to work the next day, and asked for the first two weeks in December off so that I could go to Israel. And I continued telling everyone God was sending me to Israel.

Boy, this was a real learning curve for me. I put myself out there. I either believed God, or I didn't. There was no in-between. And everyone I knew would see the outcome of my situation.

I stood firm in my own mind. I remember looking out my bedroom window, at the evening star, and telling myself, "In a few weeks I'll be seeing you from Israel." I looked at that star as often as I could, and encouraged myself in the Lord.

I had one particularly close friend at Creative Signs, where I worked as a graphic designer. He was the shop foreman, an older gentleman named Chuck. I had told him that God was going to send me to Israel, and he tried to be kind, but I could see in his eyes he thought I was delusional.

In December, the Friday before the trip (my plane was departing the following Monday morning) I was getting ready to leave work for my two-week vacation. Chuck came into my office and sat down with a hangdog look on his face, and he said, "Pego, do you have the money to go on that trip yet?"

With a smile on my face, and full of all the confidence I could muster, I said, "Nope. Not yet. But the plane doesn't leave 'til Monday. My God doesn't promise to be early, but He's never late!"

Looking miserable, he said, "Honey, I just don't want you to be disappointed. Lots of people think they hear from God, but they don't. I don't want you to get your heart broken."

I coolly replied, "Chuck, God told me back in June that He was sending me to Israel, and I believe Him. It's just that simple. I'm going home to pack."

With teary eyes, he hugged me, and patted me on the back. And I went home... and packed.

My roommates were having a hard time looking at me, here was this crazy woman saying God was going to send her to Israel, when the trip coordinator had already said she couldn't go; she had not paid her deposit or the final installment. She had no ticket. And the plane was leaving in two days.

I didn't even have spending money saved up, because God said He was sending me to Israel, so I figured He had all of my expenses covered, too.

Needless to say, the next day, Saturday, as I continued to pack, the tension around my house was palpable. I think my roomies were getting ready to call the men in white coats to take me away. Now, I had less than forty-eight hours before the plane was scheduled to leave. What would you have done?

I just kept packing and trusting God.

That night, around six o'clock, there was a loud knock at our front door. Someone yelled my name, "Peg, come on downstairs some guy wants to talk to you."

A man I had never met was standing at my front door, and he said, "I heard that you want to go to Israel."

"Yes."

"Well," and he reached inside his overcoat pocket, "I have a ticket right here." And he pulled out the airline ticket, and trip packet. Now, just stop for a moment and ask yourself, what are the odds of that happening?

With a big smile on his face, he proceeded to tell me that he had bought the package for another person, but they could not go. Furthermore, he said that I could buy their ticket at a greatly reduced price.

To which I replied, "No, thank you" and I began to shut the door.

I could hear an audible gasp from my three roommates, who had all gathered behind me, and the man looked utterly stunned. He put his foot in the door to stop it from closing, and I looked at him and said, "God told me that *He was going to send* me to Israel. If he can bring a complete stranger with a ticket right to my front door, then that's not *my* ticket, because **God is paying for *my* ticket.**"

Was I nervous when I made that proclamation? You bet! But I was in for a penny, in for a pound. The Lord said He was sending me to Israel, and I was going to take Him at His word.

The man was flummoxed, and turned a bit red in the face, and said, "Uh, well, uh, well... may I come in?" And I opened the door. After we talked for a few minutes and I told him the full story, he smiled and said, "Hey, this ticket is yours if you want it." And he handed me the ticket, and travel package worth a couple of thousand dollars; which back in 1981 was a heck of a lot of money. Come to think of it, that's still a lot of money today.

My roommates started cheering and crying, but I just felt whole... peaceful... vindicated. This felt *right*. God had spoken and I had obeyed. Win-win.

For six long months, with no tangible evidence to back me up, I had believed that God spoke to me, and that He was going to send me to Israel. This was a mighty miracle that happened that Saturday night, and a witness to everyone I had told for the past six months, that God was going to send me to Israel. It was a *bona fide* result, empirical evidence, that God still speaks to us today, just like He did to the men and women of old in the Bible. He is the same God today, the God of the miraculous. And He is oh, so good.

> *If ye then, being evil, know how to give good gifts unto your children, <u>how much more</u> shall your Father which is in heaven give good things to them that ask him?* Matthew 7:11

The cool thing about going to Israel is, I didn't even ask God, He *invited me to go*. He said, "Peg, I'm going to send you to Israel." What I did do was **believe** Him, in my heart; and hang on to that word from the Lord. Despite all the naysayers, I trusted the Lord of Heaven and Earth more than those 'doubting Thomases.' In my heart and mind it was a done deal. Even though I did not know 'how' He would send me, I just knew that He would send me. First, I believed then I received. That's called faith.

And what I believed *could* happen, did happen.

The next day was Sunday, and our little home fellowship was bouncing off the walls. All of my roommates had witnessed my steadfast confession, "God is sending me to Israel." What a joyful day that was for everyone. And that Monday, when I got to the airport, someone walked up to me, and handed me an envelope full of spending money.

Just like He promised, God sent me to Israel. I kept thinking of that simple verse, "The just shall live by faith." Now I had a major taste of what that felt like. And He sent me there in style.

On one of our last days in Israel, I was sitting in front of Gordon's Garden Tomb, in Jerusalem, the place where Jesus was raised from the dead, when I looked up, and there was *my star*! The one that I had seen out of my bedroom window. All those months I had confessed, "One day I will see you from Israel." And there it was. I got chills. I rested my camera on top of a stone a bench for a time exposure shot, and got the most beautiful photo of my star to bring home with me. Empirical evidence.

And what a spot for that wondrous moment to take place, right next to the open tomb.

Not only is Christ risen, but I was standing there in Jerusalem, having experienced his power and love first hand right now, in the twentieth century.

When I went back to work, all seventy employees of Creative Signs were dumbfounded. They had ALL heard about my trip, for months I had been confessing that God would send me to Israel; and when my words came to pass, many hearts were tenderized and people asked to know more about my Jesus. They had witnessed someone that they knew, and worked with every day, receive a *bona fide* miracle from God.

My friend Chuck was especially blessed, and said, "Pego, if I hadn't seen it with my own eyes I wouldn't have believed that such things could happen in real life."

If that kind of miracle doesn't make you think there is a God who knows and loves us, I don't know what will.

Saint Francis said, "Witness at all times; use words if necessary." It was one thing to hear me *talk* about what God was going to do, but it was a whole other kettle of fish when they saw God come through on His promise.

People's lives were changed, not because of what I did, but because of what He did for me. Well, technically I guess it was what *we* did; Father made a promise, and I believed His promise. That's how to work in synch with Papa, He speaks—we act.

Having been exposed to the spirit realm since I was a child, it was exhilarating to learn how it could work supernaturally in my favor.

As a child, I had been unwittingly caught up in the kingdom of darkness, in the middle of so much dark supernatural phenomenon, from the demons appearing in my room as a child, to Dirty Harry morphing, and shape-shifting, to the occult.

But now I was experiencing the supernatural in a totally positive way: God had given me a life-changing revelation of His love at Berry College, 'Michael' an angel had appeared to me at the Waffle House to strengthen me, God gave me brakes when I had none that stormy afternoon in Savannah, and God audibly invited me to go to Israel, and came through with flying colors. He sent a man I had never laid eyes on to my front door with the tickets. These events were just some of the life affirming miracles that were taking place, because I was learning to trust God; to believe Him. Because of that, I was living in the realm of the miraculous, living like a royal heir in God's family.

Jesus said unto him, If thou canst believe, **all things are possible to him that believeth.** Mark 9:23.

The more I believed I was who God said I was, the more all things became possible. I believed I was a child of the King, and I was starting to seize my birthright.

The manner in which God sent me to Israel was a giant growth spurt in my faith. I was encouraged by my own steadfastness, to stay put on what God told me, in spite of the skepticism of all the naysayers. And I was truly blown away by the manner in which God brought it all to pass.

That one miracle, Israel, really helped me get out of my people-pleasing rut. During those six months, *nobody* believed me—but God believed *in* me; and that was all that mattered. Of course everyone was patting me on the back *after* it came to pass, but before I got the tickets they were just shaking their heads and treating me like I was crazy.

Well, if that is crazy then don't try to fix me, because I'm walking in signs, miracles and wonders, and it feels great!

In Israel, I was literally walking in the footsteps of faith, where Jesus, and David, and Mary, and Paul, had trod, and how many folks thought *they* were nuts? But they were the ones who were walking with God. Yes, being there made the Bible come alive in my heart, confirming that those folks were real people, just like me, who faced real problems, but who also had *real faith*. What a trip!

One sunny day when we were in a section of the 'Old City' standing on a cobblestone street our guide said, "This street led to the high priest, Caiphus' house, in the time of Jesus. You are standing on the very cobblestones where Jesus walked."

I can't explain the electricity that shot through my spirit. My feet were touching the same stones where my Messiah had walked. Where he was hauled before a kangaroo court, falsely accused, and then crucified so that I might be redeemed. It shook me to the core. I was overcome with such emotions of love and gratitude that words cannot express the way I felt.

Standing there that day, under the blue Mediterranean sky, it struck me as ironic that so many of the wealthy say they are searching for immortality, when it has already been granted in the person of Jesus Christ. He alone can give man eternal life.

My sheep hear my voice, and I know them, and they follow me: And I give unto them eternal life; and they shall never perish, neither shall any man pluck them out of my hand. John 10:27,28.

As surely as God sent me to Israel, His son gives us eternal life. You can take that to the bank.

Yes, Israel changed me, in a deep and profound way. There is something about that whole mysterious and beautiful land, but especially Old Jerusalem, and the Sea of Galilee, that felt almost otherworldly. It is charged with a certain kind of spiritual energy. Amid all the chaos and the tension that is Israel, there was an underlying sense of peace that touched my spirit, "Peg, this is your home. You will return here one day, in your resurrected body, to enjoy the splendor of Ezekiel's temple. You will see Me face to face, and know Me even as you are known by Me. And you will walk and talk with Jesus."

I will be forever grateful to my heavenly Father for sending me somewhere I didn't even know I needed to visit, and bring such a miraculous experience into my life.

In Israel I felt a synthesis (the Greek word *suneisis*) of rivers of understanding flowing together in my heart. It was a comprehension of God's plan since before the foundation of the world; to send His son, the Messiah, to save the world. To make a way for us to live the life we were created for, that is: in the Kingdom of God. To love and be loved by our Father, the One Great King Eternal, is the whole point of life.

And so much of His plan had taken place right there, in a country not much bigger than the state of New Jersey. And here I was, standing where His love plan came into fruition. I turned around, and focused on the Mount of Olives, the place where the soldiers arrested Jesus. The place where he made the greatest decision of all time; to die for his fellow-man.

Love *is* the great healer.

Love is so much more powerful than selfishness. Like abuse and betrayal mess up your wiring and damage your thinking patterns for the worse; on the other end of the spectrum, experiencing times like my trip to Israel, where God's love literally exploded in my heart, heals you in ways you can't describe, on a profound and deep level.

Proverbs says that when we receive a desire of our heart; it's like a 'tree of life' springing up on the inside.

Hope deferred maketh the heart sick: but when the desire cometh, it is a tree of life. Proverbs 13:12

I didn't even know I wanted, or needed to go to Israel, but God put the *desire* in my heart in June, when He told me He would send me. *He knew* I needed to go, even if I didn't. He was training me for the things I would do for Him in the future. As I lay claim to His invitation, my desire to go increased. And I hung in there for months. Then two days before the trip, my miracle knocked on my front door with the tickets. But it took me standing in those streets where Jesus himself once stood for the full impact of what had happened to hit me. *Yowzaah!* I was overwhelmed with a profound sense of gratitude and praise for my God, who never disappoints. Another paradigm shift had occurred.

Thankfully, I had carried all of my camera equipment with me to document my trip, and took hundreds of pictures. When I got back to the states, I put together a thirty minute slide show, synchronized to music, where I spoke live about all the places I had visited, and connected them to their Bible stories. That little production led hundreds of souls to the Lord. I presented it to Kiwanis Clubs, on college campuses, to churches, and any other group that would invite me to speak.

God knew what He was doing when He sent me to Israel—even if I didn't. He made a very wise investment into His Kingdom through all those slide show presentations, and many people gave their lives to Christ as a result of them. So, I made good use of His gift. I had been preyed upon by darkness so much in my own life; I was elated to help others get set free through my Israel presentation.

I rolled many principles of how Christ set us free into that slide show. And gave hundreds of folks the opportunity to come to Christ for the first time. I offered many inspiring examples, through the lives of the Bible characters, of how those who trusted God saw miraculous results, including my own miracle of how the Lord invited and provide the trip for me.

It ended with the resurrection, backed up by the theme from *Rocky*, with an on-screen fireworks display. The final slides were of the open tomb, and I said, "It doesn't really matter if he was buried here, or somewhere else, what matters is—he's not there—he is risen!" Cue the Rocky music, cue the fireworks. People who had seemed disinterested to attend the event were now on their feet, clapping and cheering. Grown men moved to tears. It was something.

I can't remember ever giving that show where it did not receive a standing ovation. And all glory goes to God, who sent me there in the first place, and inspired me to do the show. It felt so good to give back to others, some of the excitement, and deepening of my own faith, that I had experienced while there. Share the wealth, right?

And they went forth, and preached every where, the Lord working with them, and confirming the word with signs following. Amen. Mark 16:2

The Lord gave me the opportunity to inspire others like He had inspired me. How cool.

The whole Israel experience was an answer to a need so primal I didn't even know I had back then, an unrelenting need to feel *safe* and cared for. That included the need to feel like I mattered to *somebody*; I needed to feel loved in a completely unselfish, non-sexual way. The Israel trip ticked all of those boxes. Father offered me that trip… just because He could, and asked nothing in return. That is unconditional love.

Those needs went back to my stormy childhood of abuse; of feeling unheard and unloved. One by one, God was restoring those dark places by showing me that HE loved me, and was interested in my *personal* happiness and well-being. He patiently built my confidence in Him by showing me that I could take Him at His word, and whatever He told me He would do, He would follow through on 100%.

I remember one night, when I was about five years old, my folks took us to the Rome City Auditorium (yep, right in the shadow of the ugly she-wolf, nursing old Romulus and Remus), to see the *Passion Play* about the life of Christ. One scene in particular, burned itself into my mind, the part where Jesus was sitting under a tree, and little children, about my age, all came running up to him, and one jumped up on his lap. His disciples were very upset by this, and tried to shoo the kids away, but Jesus said, "No! Do not forbid these little children to come unto me, for of such is the Kingdom of God!"

That night, in the Rome City Auditorium, I felt like my little five-year-old heart would burst. I wanted to sit on Jesus' lap so badly. I longed to have his arms around me. I wanted to feel *safe* with a grown-up. Oh, man, how I wanted to be one of those little kids, to feel Jesus' love, and protection. I did not want to go back to my own house, where I did not trust the adults, and where I lived in constant fear.

I remember thinking, "Safe, safe, safe. Jesus, please keep me safe."

I know that there were other powerful scenes in the play, but those kids on Jesus' lap was my takeaway. I would replay that image over and over in my mind in my darkest hours, begging God to make that a reality in my own life.

And in Israel, He had. Papa brought me to the very place His son Jesus was born to impress upon my heart that I mattered to Him as much as Jesus did. I made the connection.

I got it: The Kingdom of God is made up of happy, trusting 'kids' (no matter how old we are). Now I was part of *that* Kingdom, and part of God's royal family.

When *Abba* invited me to Israel, He proved faithful. I felt like He invited me to sit on Jesus' lap. He had given me His word, "I will send you to Israel" and against all odds, He came through for me with flying colors. After Israel, I allowed myself to trust more and more in his Love, and protection. I knew I would never be that scared Little Peggy again. I now had an ally, a new big brother, and his name was Jesus.

Christ died for our sins just as the Scriptures said he would and he was buried and three days afterwards he arose from the grave just as the prophets foretold. 1 Corinthians 15:3-4

Jesus loved me so much, he died for me, so that I could experience his love on this earth, just like those kids in the *Passion Play*. I allowed myself to be folded into his loving arms, and comforted.

God and Jesus work as a tag team: God is the Creator, and the Father of Jesus, who is His beloved son. Jesus is His agent, the Messiah, and the head of the body of Christ. All power in heaven flows to Earth from God, to us, through Jesus.

For there is one God, and one mediator between God and men, the man Christ Jesus; 1 Timothy 2:5.

Years earlier, I had taken a bridge across Armuchee Creek with a rapist who had nearly taken me to hell; but now I had crossed a new bridge, Jesus Christ, the mediator, who is The Bridge between sinful man, and a holy God. And when I crossed that bridge a whole new world of healing and blessings opened up to me.

When we accept Jesus as our Savior, he picks us up, cleans us up, and lifts us up, into the presence of our Papa.

When I accepted Christ, his shed blood cleansed me of all my sins, and he set me free from the devil's power. Jesus took me straight into God's heart, and gave me a seat at the Family table, where there is joy, and laughter, and peace. I no longer had to climb a maple tree, or go to my bridge at Armuchee, or to Emerald Bay, to have my safe haven, God and Jesus would be with me *everywhere* I went, from now throughout eternity. Like Papa says to us in 2 Corinthians: *"I heard your call in the nick of time; in the day you needed me, I was there to help."* 2 Corinthians 6:2 MSSG.

Thankfully, God heard my call 'in the nick of time.' I was trying to sell my soul to the devil, through the Church of Satan, and instead, I ended up in a Bible fellowship in Rome, Georgia, and soon in Bible college, and then a trip to the Holy Land. Now, that's miraculous.

I looked at all the wonderful things that were taking place in my life since I came to God through Christ, and could sum them up in one word—*Awesome*.

Those early years of lie-based thinking: I am a victim, I am no good, and I'll never be able to do that had taken a heavy toll on my life. But after that marvelous trip to Israel, I saw the light at the end of the tunnel; I really could trust God. I *could* be restored from the inside out. I could become a *good* person. I *could* leave this world better off for my having been here. I had hope! And hope is a powerful thing.

Like The Doobie Brothers said, Jesus was just alright with me. He was changing my life in the most phenomenal ways.

This is the part of this book that excites me the most, sharing my own experience, strength, and hope with you; sharing my own journey of <u>deliverance,</u> and how much better my life is in every way, because of Jesus' presence in it.

Here is a rock-solid promise that Jesus made to all mankind, "When he (Jesus) ascended up on high, he led captivity captive, and gave gifts unto men." Ephesians 4:8. I was living that in Technicolor. I had been set free from the devil's captivity. What a gift. And he was giving me gifts I hadn't even asked for, just like Ephesians said he would.

Now unto him that is able to do exceeding abundantly above all that we ask or think, according to the power that worketh in us... Ephesians 3:20.

Emmett Fox wrote, "Jesus Christ is easily the most important figure that has ever appeared in the history of mankind. It makes no difference how you regard him, you will have to concede that... the life and death of Jesus, and the teachings attributed to him have influenced the course of human history more than those of any other man who has ever lived: more than Alexander the Great, or Caesar, or Charlemagne, or Napoleon, or George Washington. More people's lives are influenced by his doctrines: more books are written and read and bought concerning him... than all the other names mentioned put together."

Yes, Jesus was just all right with me, and Jesus' love is for *real*.

When I returned from Israel to the states, I did some research and found out that Flavius Josephus, Pliney the Younger, and Tacitus, all non-Christian historians who lived between 37 AD–117 AD, recorded the amazing effect that Jesus of Nazareth had on his own times and culture. They were particularly impressed with how quickly Jesus' followers multiplied all over the ancient known world.

Josephus wrote, "*Pilate...condemned him [Jesus] to be crucified... On the third day he appeared restored to life... And the tribe of Christians has not disappeared to this day.*" That was two thousand years ago, and the 'tribe' of Christians is still very much alive and well today.

Whether historians had backed Jesus history up or not, I had come to a position of faith in my own heart that he is real because I was witnessing the *power* of the living Christ daily. I was experiencing signs, miracles, and wonders first hand. The Lord was confirming His Word with quantifiable results. I wasn't the only one seeing these miracles, all those around me were witnessing the miracles in my life too. I felt like a living lighthouse, drawing others to Christ; and it felt good.

Jesus said, "If you don't believe my words, believe me for my works sake." Walking in power is a good thing, something to be desired to further God's Kingdom. "And they went forth, and preached everywhere, the Lord working with them, and confirming the word with signs following." Mark 16:20.

All those questions I had asked back in Lake Tahoe, if Jesus was for real, if he was a man or a myth, were answered. Jesus is real, and he is the true Son of God, the Messiah. I was now his little sister, a member of the family of God and a joint-heir with Christ. God loves me as much as He loves Jesus. That is some amazing grace.

The Spirit itself beareth witness with our spirit, that we are the children of God: And if children, then heirs; heirs of God, and joint-heirs with Christ... Romans 8:16, 17

Yes, Jesus is just alright with me. He is my savior, my hero, and my big brother.

From that day back in Savannah, on Tybee, when I had admitted my life had become unmanageable, and turned it over to God, answers kept coming, and I kept growing. Day by day, and year after year, I got mentally healthier as I established new thought patterns; learning how to think about life from the perspective of the One who created it, my Father, the King Eternal. Learning to soar like an eagle, and not grovel like a worm.

One day I realized I had a new feeling inside, it was joy.

Joy is an inner sense of happiness and satisfaction that things are going to work out; even if it's not apparent at that moment *how*. Joy is a very empowering emotion. It's the joy of the Lord that *is* our strength. Joy enables us to expect the best, even in a negative situation. Incredibly, Jesus experienced joy while hanging on the cross. Now that's a powerful statement.

As my broken soul continued to heal, it became easier for me to love and forgive others. I went from loathing people, to *actually* caring about them. I went from a hair trigger temper, to patient and compassionate. I let go of the constant anxiety that ate at my guts day and night, and began to live with a more peaceful heart. I was developing a deep trust in my Father, which engendered a feeling of over-all well being. All this because I invited Jesus into my heart.

You could call this book my Jesus Journey, and I am still walking it out today.

Jesus stood at the door of my heart knocking, but I was the one who had to let him in. And when I threw the door open, that was the best decision I've ever made.

I have heard people say they are afraid that if they give themselves to Jesus, they will lose their 'real *me*.' Here's a reality check: most people don't even know who their 'real me' is. It has been buried so deeply under false masks and insecurities for so long, *they* don't even know who they are, but God does. And He says you were born to be as fearless and powerful as His firstborn son, Jesus.

Do you know what you will lose when you invite Jesus into your heart? You will lose worry, you will lose doubt, and you will lose a host of other negative emotions that tie you up in knots all day. Most of all, you will lose your intimidation of God.

As I continued to have an intimate relationship with my *Abba*, to hear His still small voice and apply it, our hearts knit together as one. Jesus said he came so that we could be one, as He and the Father are one. I was starting to grasp that reality. John 17:20,23.

First Jesus sanctifies us, fills us with Holy Spirit, and then he heals us from the inside out. The Father anointed him to do that for us:

The Spirit of the Lord is upon me [Jesus], because he hath anointed me to preach the gospel to the poor; he hath sent me to heal the brokenhearted, to preach deliverance to the captives, and recovering of sight to the blind, to set at liberty them that are bruised, To preach the acceptable year of the Lord. Luke 4:18

Then Jesus said, "This very day this scripture is *fulfilled* in your ears." Hallelujah! Jesus came to provide everything we need to be fully restored, in this life and in the world to come.

To paraphrase Luke 4, Jesus said to the crowd that day, "I am here! Standing right before you, fulfilling the words of your own prophets. **I AM the Messiah** that Isaiah saw coming seven hundred years ago." Believe that and begin your journey to freedom.

Standing in the synagogue that day, Jesus ushered in a new epoch, a time when the Lord's favor would be upon 'whosoever' would call upon the namesake of the Lord.

Jesus ushered in a new age, a period of grace, and the Lord's favor, in a way the world had never seen before. The miracles that took place in the gospels and the book of Acts were just the beginning of his ministry. And Jesus continues his ministry today through us, born again believers who dare to walk like he walked, and do the works God.

When Jesus said he came to heal the broken-hearted, I am a living testimony to that promise. Through him, I have experienced a personal resurrection, a restoration in my heart and soul. And it was noticeable to those around me. I felt like shouting I was so happy.

When it comes to a broken heart, I know I am not the Lone Ranger. To everyone reading this book: you all have your own story to tell, times when you, too, have been bruised or traumatized by life. The fact is, we **all need healing**. Otherwise, why would we need a Savior? Whose heart has not been stepped on? Who has not suffered rejection? Who has not been lied to, or disappointed?

Like I said earlier, all birth certificates should come with a label: **WARNING!** Life is going to leave a mark. And Jesus' ministry is geared to heal you from those broken places, and restore your broken soul.

Jesus' ministry continues today through those of us who serve him with a humble heart, he empowered us to continue his work; so the restoration keeps right on flowing.

*"I tell you the truth, **anyone who believes in me will do the same works I have done**, and even greater works, because I am going to be with the Father." John 14:12*

Most folks go through life trying to change their physical surroundings, trying to make themselves happy with money, power, sex, or drugs. News flash! Unhappiness comes from the inside out, and so does joy and fulfillment.

If we don't get our inside straightened out, we will never ever be truly, deeply, happy; no matter how much stuff we amass on the surface. We will always feel like something is missing. And that 'thing,' of course, is God.

The whole reason of our existence, from God's point of view, is His desire to become part of His family. For a long time I thought God was the grand Pooh-Bah, some turban-headed potentate, who wanted me to fawn before him, groveling in His presence like a worm; but you have seen in these pages, nothing could be further from the truth. God wants children, not puppets. He wants us to feel free to run to Him and jump into His loving arms, and hug His neck. He wants us to find joy and friendship in His presence.

Giving to US makes God happy. The Bible says that it is God's good pleasure to give us the riches of His Kingdom. His nature is Love, His nature is Giving, and He can never get enough of it. Having a relationship with us makes *Him* happy. We bless God by receiving His abundance in our lives.

Then, when we turn around and bless one another, we keep the circle of Life going. That's the big picture, and what has been lost in translation. The healing power of God's love has been so watered down, that people are surprised when they see a miracle. I am surprised when I don't see miracles.

Man-made religion does everything it can to keep people under *their* rules and regulations, but does nothing to bring us home to God's heart, where we truly belong. A genuine relationship with God is what makes us better, loving people, and true disciples of the lord Jesus Christ.

By this shall all men know that ye are my disciples, if ye have love one to another. John 13:35

The first and great commandment is to love God with all that you are. The second is on par with the first, to love your neighbor as yourself. Can you imagine how the world would change overnight if we started loving one another with God's pure, unselfish love; a love that had no hidden agenda, just a desire to be kind to our fellow man.

And be ye kind one to another, tenderhearted, forgiving one another, even as God for Christ's sake hath forgiven you. Ephesians 4:32

When you boil it all down, the whole point of Christianity is that God would have a bunch of kids who would emulate Him; who would be kind and tenderhearted, starting today. And Jesus own life gives us the perfect template to carry that out.

Agape love. That's true Christianity. It's not rocket science. It's pretty darn straightforward. Formal religion has missed this simple message by a mile—the answer to all of life's problems is

God's love. If Jesus showed up at most churches today, he'd be asked to leave. He wouldn't fit their mold.

The genuine Jesus, the one who was ridiculed by the Pharisees for hanging out with publicans and sinners, that's the one who's all right with me. He is my role model. That's the Jesus I want to introduce to others.

Jesus *is* just all right with me. And praise God, I'm all right with him, too.

When I look in the mirror, I see God's greatest miracle staring back—*me*. Only God can make a silk purse out of a sow's ear. Only He could take a sad, broken down wretch from Georgia, and turn her into the wholesome, loving woman I am today.

My own life is empirical evidence that the Father's love is real.

Try it. You'll like it!

Chapter 21

God and Greta Garbo

Here is the good, good news: You may be a mess, but you don't have to stay a mess. God can heal you from the inside out. —Peg Y. Rhone

This book is all about the spiritual fight: the Kingdom of Light versus the kingdom of darkness.

For we are not fighting against flesh-and-blood enemies, but against evil rulers and authorities of the unseen world, against mighty powers in this dark world, and against evil spirits in the heavenly places. Ephesians 6:12

This is a book about honesty, with God and with ourselves. In the interest of full disclosure, I have to tell you something that I was really ashamed of for a long time. By the time I was living in College Park, Maryland, I had been living the Christian lifestyle to the best of my ability for about six years, but I still had a huge monkey on my back—alcohol.

The trip to Israel had most definitely put me on a Holy Spirit high. In many ways I was feeling terrific. There I was, in the holy land, the home of Jesus Christ. I had to pinch myself. I was ecstatic, feeling like God and I could do anything together. What a team!

But here's how wily our spiritual adversary is: when I departed for Israel I had been clean and sober for over a year, but a couple of nights before we came back to the States, a fellow Christian begged me to have just *one* drink with her. Her argument was, now you are spiritually strong enough to take just *one* drink. Uh, oh. Epic fail.

Don't ever let *anyone* tell you what you can or cannot do. And definitely don't do it without asking GOD. They may be well intentioned, but it could spell catastrophe for you. Sincerity is no guarantee for truth.

Nobody is accountable for your life, but you. I didn't *have* to take that drink, I *chose* to take it. I was, spiritually at the high point of my life, but going right back down the rabbit hole. Before we even got back to the States I had gotten completely wasted on the layover between London and New York. On the airplane, while sitting on the Heathrow tarmac in a snowstorm I indulged in a quart of duty-free something, and made a complete ass out of myself in front of a jumbo-jet full of passengers, mostly Christians, who were coming back from the same Bible Land trip that I had been on. What a witness. And how humiliating. All hail the conquering hero!

There's a sobering verse (pun intended) that says, *"Let him that thinks he stands take heed lest he fall."* 1 Corinthians 10:12. It was both prideful and delusional on my part to think that I could take that drink, because alcoholics can't take just one! Some people say alcoholism is genetic, some say otherwise, all I know is that an alcoholic may be able to take one or two drinks for a period of time, but at some point it happens—the 'stop' switch just isn't there—and you just keep on drinking until you drink yourself silly.

So, the bottom-line is: alcoholics cannot take that first drink. If you are not an alcoholic, I can't make you understand this; if you are one, you already have first-hand experience.

Alcoholism is not something to be ashamed of. It's something to recognize and deal with, like pulling a splinter out before it gets infected. There is great misunderstanding about alcoholism in the Christian community. Many preachers say you can be healed of it. They are wrong. **The only healing is for God to give you the strength NOT to take another drink.** Why is that so hard to understand?

At this writing, I have not had a drink for over thirty-four years, and I haven't missed a thing. In fact, it has brought me peace of mind, and the satisfaction of not losing my self control. I don't have to wake up in the morning wondering what humiliating thing I did the night before.

But, back to the airplane in London: in hindsight, I'm not really surprised that after such a tremendous miracle, one that so many had witnessed, the devil was just salivating for his moment to take the wind out of my sails. He wanted to ruin my Holy Spirit high, and make me look foolish, and with my help, he succeeded.

I'm certain that if I had asked God if I should take that drink, He would have told me an unequivocal, NO! maybe something along these lines… **"Be sober, be vigilant;** *because your adversary the devil, as a roaring lion,* **walketh about, seeking whom he may devour"** 1 Peter 5:8. I allowed the devil to entrap me while still in Israel. Sadly, that was my free-will choice. He baited the trap, but I walked right into it.

Life is spiritual. On the surface, it appears like we are challenged by flesh and blood, but in reality there are evil spirits just looking for opportunities to steal, kill and destroy, our happiness, our self-esteem, our joy, and even take our life.

Life with Jesus is called the Christian *walk*. It's learning how to put one foot in front of the other, and to stay on the straight and narrow path. It is learning to rise above the powers of darkness, and to walk in the Light. To stay put on what you know is right, and walk away from things that will mess your life up again. And we will keep learning and growing until the day we die.

When we were beginning to walk as toddlers we fell down, but we got back up and had at it again. We didn't quit. If Christians are brutally honest, that is our walk too, we fall and we get back up. Some days we do better than others, but that day on the plane was an unmitigated disaster.

Today, when I make decisions I ask myself one simple question, will this thought or action bring me closer to God? If the answer is '**no**' then I let it go, and move on.

And so my shining Israel miracle may have been tarnished, but it was still amazing nonetheless.

Shortly after I returned from Israel, in 1982, I moved to Minneapolis, Minnesota and became part of a Christian artists' group. And later, that August, I went back for my second year at *The Way Bible College*, in Emporia, Kansas.

Once there, I was given a tremendous amount of responsibility, and my drinking intensified. Somehow I kept it hidden from others, but my shame was eating me alive inside. Why couldn't I overcome this one obstacle? I had seen so much of God's glorious deliverance, and yet this one thing still caused me so much pain and shame.

Here's a brutal honesty moment, in my heart I knew the truth: it was ME, O, Lord. **I was not READY to change.** I had not hit my bottom yet.

At Bible College, I was a leader of leaders. I was asked to be the coordinator of the whole College Division, a great honor. I was a big fish in a small pond. Many students and faculty had heard of the miraculous events surrounding my life, and looked up to me as a role model. But I felt like the biggest hypocrite on the campus, because I was hiding a dirty little secret: I was leaning on alcohol instead of totally leaning on God. Others may lean on drugs, or anger, or shopping, or pornography, but these are all just crutches used to numb us out. They will always stand between you and genuine *intimacy* with God. He's not pulling away from you; you are pulling away from Him, by relying on such devilish addictions to numb your pain, or give you 'liquid courage.' Rather, you should take your addiction to the Lord, and ask Him to give you the strength to change. Otherwise, you are just spinning your wheels, and will get stuck in a spiritual rut.

If you had cancer, would you rather not *feel* the cancer, and slowly die, or be *healed* of the cancer? I think we would all choose the latter, healing. So, I *knew* the alcohol was just covering my inner-pain that was eating me up, but I had not yet decided to get help.

I was a hypocrite, and my drinking caused me great anguish and confusion.

The word 'hypocrite' comes from the ancient Greek tragedies, and means 'to hide behind a mask.' The actor wore a mask on stage to conceal his true identity. That was me, I looked supremely confident on the outside, even walking in great spiritual power, but that was masking my inner shame.

My dependence on alcohol was still causing me to self-sabotage. In some respects I was still living from one crisis to the next; crises which I brought on myself. The bottom-line was, I was sick and tired of being sick and tired. I wanted to change, and I needed to change—but HOW? I was feeling pretty desperate.

These verses jumped out at me: "Wherefore lift up the hands which hang down, and the feeble knees; And make straight paths for your feet, lest that which is lame be turned out of the way; **but let it rather be healed.**" Hebrews 12:12,13. The Lord was encouraging me not to give up, but to get healed.

I remember thinking, "Will I ever live just one whole day that is not filled with guilt, shame, and mental chaos? Will I ever have just one normal day?" Obviously this was the childhood thinking pattern that was forced upon me; chaos, pain, and shame.

I remember crying out to God, "What is normal anyway?"

I went to visit a wonderful Christian family that December during Christmas break. As I drove my little red sports car up I-35 on that long eight hours from Emporia, Kansas to Minneapolis, Minnesota, the bleak gray winter day only added to my despondency.

My mind drifted back to a time when I lived in California. I was about twenty years old, living in San Francisco. One day I decided to take the trolley car down to Fisherman's Wharf. At the second stop two older women got on the crowded car, and there was a certain electricity in the air. The older one squeezed in, and sat right next to me. I kept glancing over at her because there was something familiar about her face.

When I got a good look at her I was gobsmacked! It was Greta Garbo, in the flesh! I almost fainted at the realization. She was older now, in her late sixties, but there was no mistaking "the face," the cheekbones, the eyes, the regal mannerisms.

I had idolized this enigmatic movie star all my life. I don't know what it was about Garbo, perhaps her mystery, or her strength, or her self-assurance. She seemed to embody everything I wasn't; I was scared, lonely, and ashamed. If there was one human I wanted to meet in this world, it was Greta Garbo. And here I was, sitting right next to her.

There were a thousand things I wanted to ask her, but I couldn't force my mouth to open. I just sat there in frozen silence. She communicated with her assistant, sitting in another section, with hand signals and finger clicks. I suppose, even at sixty-eight, there was no disguising her famous, throaty voice.

Here was Greta Garbo; our bodies were touching. I sat jammed next to her for almost twenty minutes, and yet I couldn't open my stupid mouth to speak one word. I couldn't even make normal 'stranger conversation' like, 'Nice day, isn't it?' I was paralyzed with fear.

When Garbo got off the street car, just one stop before mine, I had a feeling of agony in the pit of my stomach. Good Lord! How could I be such a coward? Here I was, sitting next to my idol, the one person I most wanted to talk to in the world, Garbo, and I couldn't say *one stinking* word. A feeling of utter despair washed over me.

So, driving up I-35 on that grey wintery day, I vowed not to repeat the same mistake with God that I had made with Garbo. I knew He was right there next to me, but I was too scared to ask the really important question: how do I stop drinking?

Remember, my upbringing had taught me to be afraid of God, that He was angry and unsafe. Obviously, even after all I had seen to the contrary, I still had some more unlearning to do. Toxic emotions never die, we just bury them alive; until we dig them up and get them healed.

I mentally assented that God loved me, I had read it, I had experienced it, but I had a blockage in my soul that kept me from truly accepting it. He was still more intimidating to me than Garbo. What gave me the right to talk to *Yahweh* like the saints of old did, when even after all he had done for me, I was still a closet drunk? As a matter of fact, I had a pint of Jack Daniel's under my front seat as I drove North, 'In case of emergency.' I figured despite all the good I was doing for others, I must still be a disappointment to Him.

The Bible teaches that God wants to be both our Father and our friend, that's why Jesus called Him, *Abba* Father. But we are blind until we see. And I still had spiritual blinders on my heart in not understanding His unconditional love for me.

It's one thing to know *about* God, but it's a whole other thing to actually *know* God.

Luke 15:11-32, is commonly known as the parable of the Prodigal Son, but it should be called the parable of the Forgiving Father. Jesus himself taught this parable to show us the true nature of God. In it the father gives his two sons a huge inheritance, and the younger son takes off and squanders his with harlots and riotous living (okay, I could relate to that one). But when the younger son lost all his inheritance, and was reduced to feeding swine, he realized how foolish he had been. He mentally woke up, and had a 'Snap-out-of-it!' moment. He realized, "I need to go home, to my Father." And that's where we all need to go, back home to our Father, to His love, His friendship, and His protection.

As the younger son was making his way home, do you know where the father was? He was not sitting at home angry with his son, sulking, and thinking of ways to punish him. No! The father was out in the fields searching for his LOST child. He couldn't wait to bring him back home and restore him to his former place of honor, the heir to a great fortune. While the son was yet a great way off, his father spotted him, and ran to him, and threw his arms around the errant boy's neck, and hugged him and kissed him, sobbing with joy.

And the father couldn't wait to get his son home to give him, what? A whuppin'? No! A great big party.

That was the polar opposite of what I had been taught by the nuns, but the description in Luke came right from the lips of Jesus Christ, and I trust him to describe the *true* nature of our Father.

Religion taught me that when I misbehaved God couldn't stand to look at me. Jesus said when I blew it, God was out looking for me, to heal my pain, and fully restore me. What a difference the truth makes.

Jesus described a Father I didn't have to be afraid of, but one I could run to in times of trouble; headlong into his embrace, knowing that He loves me and understands me like no one else on this Earth can. Jesus said when any wayward child comes home, all the angels in heaven rejoice. Cool picture, huh?

The old Southern preacher Rufus Mosley put it this way, "God is the homeland of the soul. When we are lost, there is nothing to do but come home and be full of Him again." Amen. I just love that statement.

That's why when we are out in hog country, wallowing with the pigs, we feel lost and alone. There is something missing when we are not living in our Father's presence. And the only way to remedy that feeling is to pick ourselves up, and run back into Papa's arms, and hear Him say, "Welcome home, child. I love you, and I always will."

God wants to live at the center of our consciousness, in the depths of our heart all the time; He alone is the anchor of our soul. Our mind will wander from Him, from time to time, but the question is how far we will allow it to wander? When our thoughts drift too far away from God, that's when seasoned Christians get ensnared in the web of Satan's endless suggestions. So the key is to stay close to Him, by keeping God in the center of our thoughts and actions as much as possible.

On I-35 that winter's day, I could tell I was very close to having my own prodigal 'Snap-out-of-it!' moment. Alcohol was ruining my sweet harmony with Papa. I was still out messing with the pigs, embarrassed by my actions, and I needed to ask for His help, and be willing to receive it however He chose to respond. It's sort of terrifying when you really put yourself out there like that.

This was all going through my mind as I was driving my freezing Fiat 124 sports car on that brutally cold winter's day. I thought,

"If I could change just one thing about myself, what would it be?" No question—it was my drinking.

I had never heard of AA, or I probably would have gone there for help, so I was in unchartered waters. I was clueless how God could help me as I drove on in despair, but I was sure hoping that He *would* help me. The *how* would be up to Him.

The second day I was there, it happened. I was standing in my friend's kitchen around four o'clock in the afternoon, pouring myself 'three fingers' of Jack, when she came up to me and said, "Do you remember hurting Anna's feelings last night, when you were drunk?"

Oh, my goodness. Anna was her four-year-old daughter. How could I possibly hurt a child's feelings? Shaken to the core, I set the glass down on the counter. My God, how could I be so heartless? How could I do such a thing to an innocent child? No sooner had I thought that, than the phone rang. It was my good friend, V. P. Wierwille, who told me about something he heard I had done when I was drunk in Emporia. He said, "Peg, if you don't stop drinking, I'll never speak to you again."

That was a one-two gut punch! And the timing was from God. I was still reeling from hurting Anna's feelings, when V.P. called. This all happened within a matter of seconds. I know God gave me that phone call just to help me hit my bottom with an unmistakable 'Thud!' And boy, did it work. I felt lower than a snake's belly in a wagon wheel rut.

I looked at the glass of Jack. Then I looked at the bottle, and asked myself, "How can I let a circular opening smaller than a quarter ruin my life?" That was the size of the opening in the top of the liquor bottle, through which I poured its poison into my glass.

My heart cried out, "Why can't I have dominion over my battle with booze?"

And I heard a voice whisper to my heart, "Peg, *you* can't, but **WE** can; you and I together." And I knew that voice was Jesus.

I had struggled with alcohol from the time I was nine years old until I was thirty-one, and that day, December twenty first, 1982, at 4:41 in the afternoon, I poured out my drink in the kitchen sink, along with the bottle of Jack Daniel's. I looked up to heaven and prayed, "Lord Jesus, if YOU will help me stop drinking, I'll never touch another drop."

I asked him to be my strength and my partner. And without any outside help, other than Christ, I have never touched a drop of alcohol to this day.

You can never understand what a big deal this was if you, yourself have never been an alcoholic. Overcoming any addiction is something that grabs a hold of you on such a deep level, that a person cannot truly change without the power of the living God. I know, I had tried multiple times *on my own*, and failed miserably. On some level God *has* to be involved, or the change doesn't last. Even in AA, the first step is to admit that you are powerless over your addiction; and then to turn your life and will over to God (your Higher Power).

I don't recommend my method of quitting to anyone. Knowing what I know now about alcoholism, I realize that it was a **phenomenon to quit without a support group**. I believe that AA has done tremendous work in this area. But I couldn't avail myself to that program because I had never heard of it. I call what happened to me mercy upon mercy; a *bona fide* miracle, because God delivered me then and there, that day. Yes, the next few months were extremely hard, the temptation to drink overwhelming at times, but that very day, the Lord gave me the strength to resist 'just one drink.' And He told me to get myself an accountability partner, which I did.

In the car, on the way to Minnesota, I had cried out for His help from a heart that was genuinely ready to change, and He put me in the *exact* circumstances I needed to set me free. What a gift.

By God's grace and mercy I got clean and sober that day, and I learned how to depend on Him to heal my hurts, and quit hiding in a bottle.

Here's the real clincher, if I had not listened to and trusted God to go to Israel, I would not have moved to Minnesota. If I had not moved to Minnesota, I wouldn't have been standing there in that particular kitchen on that particular day, with a family that I had grown to think of as my own, and a friend whom I loved and respected. I marvel at how things work out when we let Jesus take the reins. Who could have seen all these chess pieces, fifty moves in advance, except our omniscient Father?

The greatest thing that ever happened to me was accepting Christ. But the second greatest thing was getting clean and sober. That was over thirty years ago. And if I hadn't gotten sober, I am convinced my life would still be in shambles today; that is—if I was still alive.

My friends, Jesus did not come to condemn the world, but that the world through him might be healed. Jesus came to put us back together, and to restore us to the family of God.

Our Father is full of grace and compassion. His mercies are new every morning. He casts our sins as far as the East is from the West, and He remembers them no more. That is true love. That's genuine forgiveness. And that's a Father worth knowing.

To all my fellow travelers on this journey called Life: You may be a mess, but you don't have to stay a mess. God is longing to heal you from the inside out. You can count on Him. Just ask.

"And so I tell you, keep on asking, and you will receive what you ask for. Keep on seeking, and you will find. Keep on knocking, and the door will be opened to you. For **everyone** *who asks, receives. Everyone who seeks, finds. And to everyone who knocks, the door will be opened". Luke 11:9,10*

The squeaky wheel gets the grease. I asked, and I got delivered from alcohol, and it changed my life. It gave me back my self-esteem. It gave me the confidence to come boldly before God's throne of grace and to hang out with my heavenly Father any time I chose.

Finally, I *felt* 'worthy' to draw nigh to God. I was a long way from perfect, but I had gotten rid of the elephant in the room. And the great thing about this life is that God is not looking for perfection, He's looking for participation.

The shame barrier was now broken; and I felt like I *deserved* to be part of God's family, I felt worthy to take a seat at the table. I was no longer going to be a shrinking violet when it came to reaching out to God for personal help. After all, that's why I was born, to know Him and have a relationship with Him. And I would now be bold in sharing my true feelings with Him. I realized the need to be totally honest with my Abba, and trust Him with the deepest secrets of my heart.

Shall not God search this out? for he knoweth the secrets of the heart. Psalm 44:21

Why am I making such a big point about intimacy with God? Because it is crucial to a happy and fulfilled life. From my experience, most Christians are still afraid of God, just like I was. They just sit there, mute, like I did next to Greta Garbo, and never really talk to Him, or tell Him how they feel on the deepest level. Which is sad, because He alone is our safest refuge.

Trust in him at all times; ye people, **<u>pour out your heart before him:</u>** *God is a refuge for us. Selah. Psalm 62:8*

King David got this right; we can pour out our hearts before God. He is our refuge: not the world, not alcohol, not drugs, but our gentle, loving, ever forgiving *Abba* Father. He is our refuge and our very present help in time of trouble.

Even after we are mature believers, the snares of the devil still trip us up from time to time. But, as we keep getting up, and turning our thoughts back to Christ, our walk gets stronger, and the falls get fewer and farther between. The main thing is: when you fall, get back up!

For a just man falleth seven times, and riseth up again: but the wicked shall fall into mischief. Proverbs 24:16

Notice that verse says, "a just man." Very few Christians will be completely honest on this subject. They act like once they are born again, everything is hunky-dory. If they do mess up, or fall into wrong behavior, the organized church usually kicks them out, rather than healing their own wounded. The majority of Christendom still buries their inner heartache under a mask of platitudes, fake smiles, and bumper stickers, while secretly dying on the inside.

The goal is to take the mask off your heart, and get honest with God. His ear is always open. Here is His promise: *"Call unto me, and I will answer thee, and shew thee great and mighty things, which thou knowest not."* Jeremiah 33:3. God wants to show us great and mighty things.

Prayer was never meant to be a monologue, but a DIALOGUE.

I had to learn that one too, to be still and listen for God to talk back. He said, "Call on me and I will *answer*." Duh! And after I trained myself to still my mind and listen, I began to hear His voice on a regular basis. It's not that He wasn't talking to me all along; I just couldn't hear Him through the cacophony of noise in my own head.

When I put down the booze, and gave up my worldly crutch along with my shame, the floodgates opened up between my Father and me. God didn't draw closer to me; I drew closer to Him. Funny thing, He'd never left me in the first place.

Acts 17:27 exhorts us to, "seek the Lord, if haply they might feel after him, and find him, though he be not far from every one of us."

Unlike Garbo, I did not *"vant to be alone..."* I wanted to be God's best friend, and hang out with Him. That's what healthy families do. I wanted to tell Him my deepest secrets—and I wanted Him to reveal the mysteries of life to me. So far, so good.

But it was to us that God revealed these things by his Spirit. For his Spirit searches out everything and shows us God's deep secrets. 1 Corinthians 2:10

Behold, I stand at the door, and knock: if any man hear my voice, and open the door, I will come in to him, and will sup with him, and he with me. Revelation 3:20

Jesus stands at the door of our heart and knocks; but he's waiting for us to invite him in. Jesus says that if we open the door, he will come in and "sup" with us. It doesn't say he will come in and lecture us, browbeat us, or tear us down, but he'll come in and be our most intimate friend.

In the Eastern culture you only sat down to sup with your most trusted and beloved friends. Once again, the Lord uses terms of intimacy, endearment, and understanding, encouraging us to pour out the contents of our heart to him without fear of judgment or reprisal. That's not to say the Lord won't set you straight. I have learned that God loves me just the way I am... but He loves me too much to let me stay that way. And His correction is so gentle, even that leaves me feeling uplifted and refreshed.

All the problems of this world; lying, addiction, murder, theft, and so on, stem from fear, loneliness, and lack of love. When you sit down and sup with Jesus, you lose those aspects of your personality, and they're replaced with a sense of love, confidence, and belonging. When you spend 'hang-out time' with the Lord, you yourself become more loving, more forgiving, more selfless, and more generous. The best qualities of the human spirit blossom under fellowship with Jesus Christ. He is such a wonderful tutor, and gracious counselor.

The counsel of the LORD standeth for ever, the thoughts of his heart to all generations. Psalm 33:11.

What a day of freedom it is when you realize that you are God's child, and that He is your Papa. And you awake to a healthy parent-child relationship. Many of you know that as you grow up you can become best friends with your parents. That's why we're here: To have that kind of relationship with God, and with His son.

As close as Chris J and I were, I found out that my friend Jesus is even more understanding, more compassionate, and more loving. I thank God for sending Chris J into my life, to show me the way home, to my spiritual family. And I thank Him for filling that void of her loss, with His Son's love.

Friendship with God is NOT too good to be true. In fact it is the essence of eternal life.

And we know that the Son of God has come, and he has given us understanding so that we can know the true God. And now we live in fellowship with the true God because we live in fellowship with his Son, Jesus Christ. He is the only true God, and this is eternal life. 1 John 5:20 NLT

We have sort of missed the point, that the moment we are born again, eternal life starts immediately, that's why it's called 'newness of life' and putting on 'the new man.' If we could see with spiritual eyes just how different we become in a moment of time, we would be astonished! The rest of our days on this Earth are spent learning how to change our mentality from that of a slave, to a royal heir of the Kingdom, God's child by seed. Jesus never came to start a religion; he came to bring us home to Abba, to give us a place at the family table, and to make us joint-heirs of the grace of God.

*And this is life eternal, that they might **know** thee the only true God, and Jesus Christ, whom thou hast sent. John 17:3*

Getting to intimately know God and Jesus, is eternal life, and that is what healed my life.

But be well assured of this, today, if someone tries to tell me, "Oh, Peg, you're a believer now, you can have just *one* more drink," I tell them to go jump in the lake! I love my new-found freedom too much to jeopardize it.

I once was a mess, *but I didn't have to stay a mess.* God's love healed me from the inside out.

So, don't sit there frozen, with your mouth closed, like I did on the street car with Greta Garbo; open your mouth wide and say, "Father, help me. I am a mess." Don't ever be afraid to cry out to God, and tell Him how you really feel, or ask Him the tough questions. Papa doesn't want to condemn you; He is out looking for you—to restore you. He is your refuge and very present help in time of need.

I wake up every morning expecting to have intimacy with God. And I do. He's my best friend, and He walks with me and talks with me throughout the day.

I realize that in my darkest moments, God was right beside me, just waiting for me to reach out to Him, and ask for His help.

Thank you, Father, for being so patient with me. And thank you Garbo, for that invaluable life lesson; don't be afraid to talk to those who can teach you something about life—starting with Life's Creator.

Chapter 22

He Restoreth My Soul

He leads me beside the still waters.
He restoreth my soul...
Psalm 23

Fast forward thirty years, and today my husband Chris and I live in the beautiful North Georgia mountains, overlooking Lake Lanier. I wake up thankful, every day. I am happy. I am clean and sober. I am blessed. I appreciate so many things that I took for granted in my 30's. As the challenges of physically aging come into play, the joy of wisdom that comes with age, takes center stage. I've come to realize that the greatest tragedy in life is not death, but a life lived without purpose.

I used to march to the beat of my own insane drummer, but now I march to the beat of Jesus heart: his love, his wisdom, and his forgiveness. The goal of my life is still: to leave this Earth a better place than I found it; to die empty, having left it all on the field. Every day I endeavor to use my talents, energy, and abilities for heaven's work; to run my course, and to finish my race with purpose and determination. I strive to do the good work that my Father called me to do before the foundation of the world. (Ephesians 2:10) In short, I love the life I'm living, and I owe it all to God's amazing grace. Thank you, Father!

My life has taken on a whole new depth, vibrancy and meaning because I latched on to one simple verse, "He restoreth my soul." Psalm 23:3. That simple truth has been the focus of my life and ministry for the last two decades.

In spite of all the great things I learned at Bible college, that particular ministry had a very strong aversion to counseling of any kind. All of our emotional problems were supposed to be magically resolved by the phrase "renew your mind." We were supposed to ignore the blackness deep inside and just soldier on. Thanks to the help of one man, I learned there was more to emotional healing than 'white knuckling' the pain.

And, when you know better you do better. So I would be remiss if I did not include some in-depth information about wonderful avenues of counseling available to the church today. In this chapter, we will delve into the deeper truths regarding Christian counseling, deliverance, and restoration. We will dive right into the 'chewy caramel center' of God's desire to heal the broken hearted. This is the 'how-to' chapter; the nuts-and-bolts about healing one's deepest emotional wounds from their past.

The first half of this chapter deals with the heart, and the second half delves into inner healing, or soul restoration.

I am currently a Christian counselor, and pastor of Light of Christ Ministries. I see lives changed every day in ways I could never have imagined. For those who dare to take God at His word and renew their mind, I see their joy and confidence in a Spirit filled life flourish.

For those who dig even deeper, into soul restoration, I see an even more profound *transformation* as they are miraculously healed from the wounds of their past. Inner healing brings up the deep issues of the heart so that they may be healed, and those who avail themselves to this type of counseling find themselves rid of anxiety, panic attacks, chronic disease, generational curses, and a host of other life sucking debilitations. The results are nothing short of miraculous.

As I mentioned earlier, I would not be doing what I am today without the help of one man, Dr. Henry J. Wade, and the paradigm shift I had under his tutelage.

Back in the 1990's, before moving here to Georgia, Chris and I had built and co-pastored a church in Northern Virginia. It was situated on a bucolic thirteen acre property in Catharpin, Virginia, which we called Sonlight Farm.

When I say built, I mean we, the whole congregation, literally built our church building with our own hands. What a joy that project was. It was a small church, but it was filled with love. I have such fond memories of that phase of Light of Christ Ministries out there on Sonlight Farm.

I thought of it as our 'rainbow church,' because our folks came from so many different nations, and backgrounds. Chris and I were blessed to have had the privilege to minister to this amiable and diverse congregation for many years.

It was during that time that Chris and I began having some marital challenges, and we knew that if we couldn't get our own house in order, we couldn't do our best for God's people. It was Chris who found us the most tender and understanding Christian marriage counselor one could ever hope for, Dr. Henry J. Wade.

I already had a solid foundation of biblical truth, but when it came to helping folks (including myself) get out of *emotional* bondage I was sorely lacking. I'm talking Luke 4:18 stuff here, like

Jesus said, healing the broken-hearted, those with damaged psyches, like my own.

That's where Dr. Wade had a profound affect upon my life. It was Henry, an ex-Army chaplain, who introduced us to the idea of childhood wounds, and inner healing. I'm not talking about blaming your parents for everything, I'm talking about isolating traumatic events that occurred, which left us scarred and broken. Henry showed us how to invite Jesus in to heal those 'wounds in our soul.' Dr. Wade was the conduit for transformative healing for both me and my husband (who also came from a very damaging past). In my own counseling practice today, I often think back with deep gratitude on lessons learned from this gentle healer.

During our time with Dr. Wade, my eyes were opened to a new level of efficacy in Christian counseling called inner healing. I learned that certain self-destructive attitudes, even illnesses, as well as sinful behavior *patterns* that kept raising their ugly head in my life, were tied to childhood wounds, and the lie-based thinking that *attached* itself to those events. When something would happen to 'trigger' those buried, lie-based emotions, I'd go into 'fight or flight' mode. I would feel my life threatened in an unthreatening situation. That's why I would overreact to certain everyday events; like the time I fled the movie theater when I heard the line about a child being worth "a carton of cigarettes and Chinese takeout." That statement triggered a deeply buried wound in my soul, and I took flight like a scalded cat; it was a knee-jerk reaction.

The traumatic events of my childhood had left a very dark residue in my psyche that came from lie-based thinking. And LIE-based thinking is poison, to both your body and your soul. It will run your life into the ground, if left unchecked.

To be sure, this toxic thinking does *not* come from God, but from the devil, who is the father of lies, and the great accuser. One day, while speaking to the Pharisees Jesus said: *Ye are of your father **the devil**, and the lusts of your father ye will do. He was a murderer from the beginning, and abode not in the truth, because there is no truth in him. When he speaketh a lie, he speaketh of his own: **for he is a liar, and the father of it**. John 8:44*

When traumatic events take place in our lives, the devil is right there to attach a lie to that event. The more we 'peeled the onion,' in sessions with Henry and took those incidents, and the lies attached to them to Christ for healing, the more I was able to let Jesus into my heart to carry *all* of my burdens. (You see, when you have *heart* issues, you have *trust* issues with everyone, even Jesus.) I invited the Lord in to heal the places in my heart where I had been so badly damaged. What joy and peace that brought to my soul. Each session was like having a festering thorn removed from my insides.

Henry taught us a deeper way of ministering, not just to the physical needs of an individual, but to the emotional needs as well. We learned to minister, not just to the mind, but to the inner sanctums of the heart, like Jesus proclaimed in Luke 4:18.

He [God] *hath anointed me* [Jesus] *to preach the gospel* [the truth that sets us free] *to the poor* [the humble in heart]; *he hath sent me to **heal the brokenhearted*** [that one's pretty plain], *to preach deliverance to the captives* [to deliver us from lie-based thinking that has held us captive], *and recovering of sight to the blind* [to reveal the devilish lies show us the truth], *to set at liberty them that are bruised* [only God's truth sets us free]. *Luke 4:18.*

Jesus said he came to 'set at liberty them that are bruised.' Bruising is internal damage. Jesus came to set us free from the internal pain of our past which lingers in our heart. What a promise. This verse is all about inner healing, the deeper healing of the heart that Jesus came to make available to us. Like it says in Isaiah 53, Jesus carried our **griefs** and **sorrows** over two thousand years ago. How had I missed that all those years? Jesus can and will heal our heart, which is the center of our whole life. For out of the **heart** issues life... really!

It was during our time with Henry that this truth gelled in *my* heart. The light bulb went on. Ding! Ding! Ding! The life I was currently living really did issue from *my* heartfelt beliefs, buried deep inside. Time and time again that internal pain had caused me to self-sabotage my own success and happiness.

Even though I had heard that phrase 'out of the heart issues life' a million times, I had never grasped its fullness until we were getting counseled by that wonderful ex-Army chaplain, a man who, I am sure, had seen more damaged hearts in the Armed Services than I could imagine. Men and women coming back from the horrors of war, long separation from loved ones, PTSD, and more. Yes, Henry knew his way around healing the human heart, just like Jesus said he could.

Now, Jesus is not just going to come bounding in and heal your heart, you have to invite him in. *Asking* is your job. "*Keep* [guard] *thy heart with all diligence; for out of it are the issues of life.*" Proverbs 4:23. Our heart determines our course in life.

The Hebrew word for 'issues' means 'boundaries, borders, or source.' We are told to guard our heart because it sets the course of our life, as well as the boundaries, the parameters, of *what* we will attract into our life. Our heart filters what we perceive to be true. The heart holds our personal belief system about... everything. This is huge!

There is a much deeper head and heart connection than I had ever fathomed. The mind houses the intellect, where we reason and compute facts. It is the conscious work space. But the heart, our subconscious, is where we believe; it is the place charged with emotion, and where we hold our personal truth. When is comes to the mind vs. the heart, the heart will win out every time, for out of the heart issues life. It's the heart that acts like a magnet for what we will attract into our lives; for good or for ill.

As powerful as the mind is, it will bend to the beliefs in our heart every time.

'Heart' is used over 800 times in the Bible, and only about a dozen of those uses refer to the physical organ; the rest refer to that inner place, the seat of our personal life, our subconscious, from whence **both believing** and **doubt** emanate. God gives this subject, the heart, a lot of ink, and rightfully so. You can renew your mind and spout scripture until you are blue in the face, but if your heart doesn't line up with your words, you will slide back into the same old negative habits. Ouch!

As a psychological term, the heart is our subconscious: it stores all the effects about of the things we have ever experienced; and from that input, forms our most **deeply held beliefs**. Sort of like a computer operating program, it sets the parameters that will ultimately determine what our computer can do. The beliefs stored in our subconscious determine how we will 'operate,' how we will behave, and how we will respond to various situations in life.

Heartfelt beliefs are our core ideas: our self-image; what we accept to be true. Therefore, the heart affects all our behavior patterns. Simply put, we are what we believe to be true about ourselves in our heart.

It makes me think of the Wizard of Oz. All of these things were happening in Dorothy's world (the conscious), but they were being manipulated by a little man behind the curtain (the heart, the subconscious). Dorothy did not get to the truth about her situation until she came face to face with the man behind the curtain. That's inner healing.

For instance, if a person holds true the subconscious belief that they are a winner, they will attract situations that cause them to succeed in life. How do you think that person would behave? Obviously, with an easy confidence, no matter what problem they are confronted with.

On the other hand, if a person holds the heartfelt belief that they will always be poor, then no matter how much money they have, they will lose it. How many multi-million dollar lottery winners are still wealthy after a few years? That poverty mentality issues from the heart, and no matter how much money they acquire, it will pass through their fingers like a sieve.

You and I will *always* act in accordance with our heart, our core belief system. Therefore, understanding how to get our heart in alignment with God's way is of paramount importance. What we hold in our hearts is much more powerful than the decisions we consciously make in our mind. Heart trumps head every time.

Before I met Dr. Wade, I knew plenty about renewing my mind, but literally nothing about dealing with my heart. And I realized that was the biggest piece of the puzzle needed to get my life back on an upward spiritual glide path.

Jesus taught this truth in Mark 11:

Whosoever shall say unto this mountain, Be thou removed, and be thou cast into the sea; and **shall not doubt in his heart***, but* **shall believe** *[in his <u>heart</u>] that those things which he saith shall come to pass; he shall have whatsoever he saith. Mark 11:23*

This one verse expresses the greatest law in the universe: **the law of believing**. And it can only work to our benefit when our head and our heart are in sync.

Both our conscious and our subconscious, must be in agreement to receive things from God. Jesus taught that doubt will put on the brakes. And doubt comes from the heart.

James 1:6 says that when we ask the Lord for something, *"let him ask in faith* [which issues from the heart], *nothing wavering. For he that wavereth is like a wave of the sea driven with the wind and tossed."*

Once a lie gets its hooks into your heart/subconscious, your mind can claim something, based on the truth of God's word, but if your heart disagrees, you are not in harmony internally. This is what the Bible calls being double-minded, and "A double minded man is unstable in <u>all</u> his ways." James 1:8

I don't want to be unstable in all my ways. Do you?

When I am double minded, James 1:7 says, "Let not that man think that he shall receive *any* thing of the Lord." That's a heavy truth. That's why we need to take care of our heart, as well as our mind.

For example, you may think in your head, "I have come a long way. I have lived a good life. I am not the same messed up person I used to be twenty years ago." But IF you doubt that new image in your heart, and subconsciously think, "Oh, no. You haven't really changed all that much, and you will *never* be good enough" then that's what you will manifest in your life: failure and low self-esteem. The **negative belief** in your heart will cancel out the **positive confession** in your mind; that's being double minded.

This is why a person may have 'unanswered' prayers. They don't believe in their heart that God will do what He promised He will do, which is 'doubt.' Or they believe, "He'll do it for *them*, but not for *me*." Which is still doubt.

A negative, heartfelt belief could come from something as simple as your grade school teacher making an offhanded remark that you would never amount to anything, or as egregious as sexual abuse. Then you subconsciously believed the lie, that you would never amount to much, or that you were a 'thing' to be used by others, this all became part of your core self-image. No matter how much you renew your mind, where the heart goes the mind follows. And as we get older, if these heartfelt beliefs aren't changed, we are doomed to a life of self-sabotage, sickness, and frustration.

Recent scientific studies have proven that given the right input, the heart can change, and our inner dialogue can be rewired.

Once again, science is catching up with the Bible. Like David said in Psalm 51, *"Create in me a clean heart, O God; and renew a right spirit* [attitude] *within me."* Wrong attitudes come from the heart, from lie-based thinking, like that teacher who told you that you would never amount to anything.

I have Christians who come to me and say, "Peg, I know what God's word says, and I believe it, but I am just not getting the results He promised." The problem is they *think* they believe it, but they harbor doubt in their heart/subconscious. How frustrating that can be.

Whosoever shall say unto this mountain, Be thou removed, and be thou cast into the sea; and shall not doubt in his heart, but shall believe [in his heart] *that those things which he saith shall come to pass;* Mark 11:23

I recognize the problem right away: They are double minded. They may "say to the mountain," or confess the promise, but if they doubt in their heart, no dice. This was the lesson Jesus taught his disciples in Mark 11:23. Heart and head must be in harmony, in synch, to receive the promises of God. And when they are not, there is no end to one's frustration.

That is also why one person may have great faith in one area of their life, but lack faith in another area. Each one's heart is different.

But, when our heart (subconscious) and our head (mind) are in agreement, *Kapow*! We are single-minded, unified within ourselves. Then we get answers to prayers. Then 'Whatsoever' we ask according to His word shall come to pass. And that, my friends, is the more abundant life.

There's a cute drawing of a heart and a brain walking hand-in-hand, and the heart says to the brain, "You and I need to go someplace quiet where we can talk, and agree on things." There is tremendous wisdom to that little picture. And the best way to get your head and heart in synch is to still your mind, and listen to God.

Be still and know that I am God. Psalm 46:10.

I spend at least thirty minutes every morning getting quiet, and staying my mind on God: God's love, God's power, God's majesty, His trustworthiness. I allow His peace to permeate my whole being. That's what prayer is, just thinking deeply about God. I don't let the day's schedule interfere with my quiet time, during that time I do not dwell on the problems of the day. I just think about the beauty of my heavenly Father, and the love I have for my Savior, and they have for me. I can't tell you how much good this quiet time does for my heart. I am totally relaxed. I can *feel* God's presence. I listen to His voice. He tells me things that change my heart to become more like His. He encourages me, He gives me guidance. This is the most precious time of my day, being still and knowing that He is God. It is healing, on every level.

Time spent with God was never meant to be a monologue, but a dialogue.

You and I were created for intimacy with God. The Bible is full of people who talked to God. Think about it, that's how we *got* the Bible, because people talked to God. So, **why shouldn't you and I talk to God, and hear from God?** God has not changed, we have.

Your life issues out of your heart. Your heart is what makes you, you; your likes, your dreams, and your personality. If you look at your life today, right now, this minute, you are living out what is in your heart: what you believe about yourself, about God, and about life. Are you generally happy or miserable, giving or selfish, courageous or fearful? It's a spiritual law—"As within so without." Your physical life is merely a reflection of your inner heart life, for good or for ill.

Here are a few things the Bible says about the heart:

Keep [watch over, guard] *thy <u>heart</u> with all <u>diligence</u>; for out of it are the issues* [borders, boundaries, the source] *of* [what we will manifest in] *life. Proverbs 4:23*

Guard your heart, with all diligence. Treat your heart as you would a family garden upon which your very lives depends: watch over it, water it, pull the weeds of doubt and worry, and feed it the proper nutrients (thoughts). When your heart gets right, you will reap a harvest of good fruit. *Then* you can be your best self: an overcomer, a success, the victor that God designed you to be, as well as more caring and compassionate.

Here's another illuminating scripture.

*A good man out of the **good** treasure of his **heart** bringeth forth that which is good; and an **evil** man out of the evil treasure of his heart bringeth forth that which is evil. Luke 6:45.*

That is why there is so much evil in the world. An evil heart produces evil deeds. And you can't have a good heart without asking God in to clean yours up.

I'm astonished when someone perpetrates an evil deed, and people say, "Well, he did a bad thing, but he really does have a good heart." Really? That contradicts Jesus, who said if you have a good heart, you will do good; you won't be hurting and taking advantage of others. Don't buy into man's stupidity, trust Jesus for the 411.

Here's another one:

And GOD saw that the wickedness of man was great in the earth, and that every imagination of the **thoughts** *of* **his** <u>**heart**</u> *was only evil continually. Genesis 6:5.* Not good.

The earth also was corrupt before God, and the earth was filled with violence. And God looked upon the earth, and, behold, it was corrupt; for **all <u>flesh</u> had corrupted his way upon the earth**. *Genesis 6:11,12.*

The earth became corrupt because of mankind, who corrupted His (God's) way. This evil was not God's will, but man's. The land was filled with wickedness because men and women only imagined evil in their hearts continually. That's quite a state of affairs. But please take note here: God did not send this wickedness, they brought it upon themselves. God did not arbitrarily decide to harm them; *they* hurt themsleves because *they* had evil hearts. Just like Jesus said in Luke 6:45, evil hearts produce evil deeds.

In Genesis, the intense wickedness in their hearts almost brought about the annihilation of the human race. Only eight souls survived the great flood that covered the earth. And they survived because of one man, Noah, who had a righteous heart.

*Noah was a **righteous** man, the only **blameless** person living on earth at the time, and he walked in close fellowship with God. Genesis 6:9 NLT.*

Noah had a good heart, a godly heart. Because he was a righteous man, he found grace in the midst of that horrific situation. God honored His own spiritual law of sowing and reaping; He delivered Noah and his family because Noah did not partake in man's wickedness, but honored the true God in his heart. And Noah's love for God brought about his deliverance, and that of his whole family.

Most people don't think about how practical God is. He sets spiritual laws into motion, and we can either use them to our benefit, or to our destruction. Hosea 4:6 puts it this way, "My people are destroyed for lack of knowledge." Even God's people, believers, have to know what His spiritual laws are in order to benefit from them.

The spirit world, by definition, is supernatural; it supersedes the natural realm of our five senses. Life is not 'Mind over matter.' Life is Spirit over matter, God's Truth over matter, God's Love over matter.

The physical world will literally change its molecular structure when we trust in God's power; hence the blind see, lepers are healed, the Red Sea parts, Jesus and Peter walk on water, and hearts are healed. The more we learn to apply spiritual laws to our daily situations, the more we will open the floodgate through which God's blessings can flow into our lives.

And that floodgate is—the heart. So let's keep ours in tune with God's.

Trust in the LORD with all thine heart; and lean not unto thine own understanding. Proverbs 3:5

Trusting in God is the right way to live. Those who trust in the Lord with all their heart; and lean not unto their own understanding (five senses) are the most happy, wholesome people you will ever meet. They produce good things both in their own lives, and in the lives of those around them, just like Noah did.

A good and merry heart will even produce better health.

A merry heart doeth good like a medicine: but a broken spirit [attitude] *drieth the bones. Proverbs 17:22.*

A happy heart (subconscious) produces a healthy body. God told this to Solomon some three thousand years ago, 'a merry heart does good like a **medicine**.' Finally, twenty-first century doctors are starting to catch up with what the Lord told us way back then, a merry heart produces glowing physical and mental health.

Here are a few facts about the heart (subconscious):

- The heart (*kardia*) is not synonymous with the mind (*noema*)
- The heart and mind need to be in sync, otherwise we are 'double minded'
- The heart/subconscious is basically programmed before the age of six. This emotional patterning is set in the heart, and it subconsciously drives our most basic decisions in life
- We are a product of our past, but we are not a *prisoner* of our past. Because …

- Our heart/subconscious **can be fully restored** by Jesus' love, and we can move forward to a better life

- We are never too old to change our heart, or to be healed, for God to create in us a clean heart. (Psalm 51:10)

Some folks who needed a clean heart were the religious leaders in Jesus' day. Christ rebuked them because of the hardness of their hearts.

Woe unto you, scribes and Pharisees, hypocrites! for ye are like unto whited sepulchres, which indeed appear beautiful outward, but are within full of dead men's bones, and of all uncleanness. Matthew 23:27

Jesus rightly called them whited sepulchers: whitewashed tombs with death inside. They may have *looked* good, but spiritually they stunk. That's no compliment, but it certainly described them to a tee. They were vile inside, and so they, in turn, hurt people. They did not treat others with respect and the love of God because they themselves did not *know* the love of God. They did not care one whit about anyone, except themselves. They professed to love God, but were full of envy, greed, and self-righteousness. Those attributes are the fruit of a very damaged heart.

The Pharisees tried to look all 'holy' on the outside, but inside they were toxic waste dumps; negative, negative, negative. They had no genuine love for God or humanity. They were just *using* people, to extort money and praise. Sound familiar? They despised Jesus because he came to help "whosoever" would believe in him. (That's about a simple as you can get.) And they went crazy when he *healed* people. Can you imagine that kind of evil heart? The very men who should have been healers, hated the one who actually carried out God's mandate to heal.

Out of their hearts issued their life, their true nature flowed out, that of the devil. In John 8:44 Jesus said, "Ye are of **your father the devil**, and the lusts of your father ye will do. He was a murderer from the beginning, and abode not in the truth, because there is no truth in him. When he speaks a lie, he speaks of his own: for he is a liar, and the father of it." These religious leaders despised the son of God, and all they could think of was how to get rid of 'the competition.'

Sure enough, Jesus was right; these self-centered men were the ones who eventually demanded Jesus' crucifixion, and got it. But, God raised him from the dead—so, *epic* fail on their part!

This egocentric pattern holds true for anyone in a position of power. One must have a strong and good heart to resist the temptation to abuse their power: from pastors, to doctors, to politicians. This takes humility, and submission to God, or else the ego will win every time.

Never forget this: Things are to be used, people are to be loved.

Sadly, *using* people is an unhealthy response by someone who has been used by people. This is how I was living before I came to Christ. I had been hurt and used by so many people, that I was starting to follow this devilish pattern; hurt others before they hurt you. But, praise God, He healed my heart, and has shown me a better way—the love way.

Jesus came to save a dying world from itself, to save us from our own lust, and greed, and sick thinking.

Inner healing is a gift to the body of Christ.

The world is such a mess, because so many of us are a mess. We are broken inside, and need to call on the Great Physician to restore our souls.

Emmett Fox tells a story about a film being shown in a rough mining town, back in the days of silent films. When the screen villain strangled the heroine in the movie, a miner on the front row jumped up and fired six shots into the screen at the 'villain.' But all he did was put six holes in the screen; the movie kept right on playing. If the miner wanted to change the outcome of what was happening to the damsel, the miner should have gone into the **projection booth** and **changed the reel**.

> **All life issues from the heart, not just the head.**
> **The mind is the screen, but the heart is the projection booth.**
> **If you want lasting change, you must change the reel.**
> **Change your inner beliefs.**

Many sincere Christians will get temporary results by shooting the screen (renewing their mind), but what they need to do is change the reel (change their heart). You do that by pulling out the *roots* of bitterness, unforgiveness, low-self esteem, and other lie-based toxic self-beliefs. That's when you will get lasting results—when you change the reel.

Inner healing is the way to change the reel.

*Behold, thou desirest truth in the **inward parts:** and in the hidden part thou shalt make me to know wisdom. Psalm 51:6*

How do we get "truth in the inward parts"?

For unto us a child is born, unto us a son is given: and the government shall be upon his shoulder: and his name shall be called Wonderful Counsellor... Isaiah 9:6

In Isaiah 9:6 Jesus is called the 'Wonderful Counselor.' Inner healing is a method of counseling, that when done properly, invites the Lord himself into the counseling session. That is part of his multifaceted continuing ministry to the church today, since Christ the head of the body. Through Jesus, God will reveal to us truth in our inward parts, His truth that sets us free.

When it comes to the promises of God, Jesus Christ is still the mediator between God and man. That's why we pray in Jesus' name. God has put all power and authority under Christ's feet until a time in the future, when God shall be 'all in all.' 1 Corinthians 15:24,25.

For Christ must reign until he humbles all his enemies beneath his feet. 1 Corinthians 15:25

Inner healing is a gift to the body of Christ.

In Luke 4:18 Jesus said that God anointed him to carry out this ministry of healing for the body of Christ. To set us free from the prisons of our past.

Everything that you and I receive from God flows through Jesus Christ. In Luke 4:18, Jesus gave us a laundry list of things that are currently available to God's children: the gospel truth, healing our broken hearts, deliverance from those secret prisons in our heart that hold us captive, opening our eyes to the truth, and setting at liberty those of us who have been bruised (hurt inside). All of these are part of our 'freedom package,' setting us free from the devil's power, and a demonstration of God's Son 'humbling his enemies beneath his feet.'

Christ is the mediator, the gateway to all of these blessings. As head of the body, Christ loves us with a love unspeakable, it can't be explained, it is so lovely and so pure. Part or his ministry is to **help us claim** all that God wants us to have in this life, to the end that we "Stand fast in the liberty, wherewith Christ has made us free, and be not entangled again with the yoke of bondage." Galatians. 5:1. Hallelujah!

We talked earlier about lie-based thinking, and heartfelt negative beliefs that block the blessings of God in our lives. Jesus wants to remove those lies and replace them with our Father's truth, to the end that he creates in us a clean heart and renews in us a right attitude, putting the enemy under *our* feet. (See Appendix 2)

That is 'changing the reel.'

Create in me a clean heart, O God; and renew a right spirit **[attitude]** *within me. Psalm 51:10.*

Criticism, resentment, anger and guilt: these are four horsemen of the Apocalypse to the soul. They are the fruit of lie-based, devilish thinking. They are all fear based patterns in our heart that need to go. They will poison your health, your heart, and your home. Until and unless you deal with their roots, these toxic weeds (subconscious beliefs) will keep coming back and sabotaging your life. The way to pull out the roots, to change the reel, is through inner healing.

God is Love and you were created in His image.

You were made to love, by the Author of Love Himself. He created you, not because He had to, but because He *wanted* to. God wanted kids whom He could love and bless. Unfortunately, all of us have been in some unloving situations that have scarred our souls, and brought emotional pain to our lives which have become barriers to receiving the fullness of His love for us. That does not have to continue.

Your heavenly Father does not want you to suffer even one more day. Your heart can be healed. In inner healing, we invite the Lord into the counseling session, to lead the counselee to specific hurtful memories that caused a lie to take root in their psyche. Lies such as: I'm no good, I'll never succeed, or, I can't trust God.

Once the lie is exposed (lies love to hide in the recesses of the heart), the Lord heals that area, and Jesus talks directly to the counselee, and replaces the lie with God's truth, which is awesome, because it is His truth that makes us free.

Inner healing is an exchange: God's truth for the devil's lies. He gives us His peace for our pain. It is a time of enlightenment, forgiveness and healing, a time of restoration. Inner healing is how we 'change the reel.'

All of this happens Spirit to spirit, by revelation: word of knowledge, word of wisdom, discerning of spirits, and gifts of healing. The human counselor is only the *facilitator*; it is Jesus who does the actual counseling; via the holy spirit of Christ in you.

You may be thinking, "What? Has this girl gone crazy? Jesus wouldn't talk to me!"

My response is, "Why not?"

In the old testament the Lord talked to Balaam through an ass! In the new testament Jesus spoke directly to Saul, Ananias, Peter, James, John and others. The Lord can talk to whoever he wants, through any means he wants, even a donkey. But you have to ask yourself, why do *we* keep limiting him in our own lives? Jesus said his sheep hear his voice? Do you love Jesus? If so, then you should hear his voice, too.

Think about the times you have sung the song, *In the Garden*. The words you sing are: "He walks with me, and he talks with me, and he tells me I am his own." Who tells you that you are 'his own'? Jesus! "And the words I hear, falling on my ear, the Son of God discloses." It's the Son of God, speaking to you. So why don't you practice what you sing?

Jesus said the Kingdom of God is within you. And the King of kings is closer than your very breath. He talks to you, Spirit to spirit. That's how you tap into it the wisdom of God's Kingdom, spirit to Spirit. That's how you come boldly before the throne of God to find grace to help in time of need.

And the great thing is—the Wonderful Counselor is always in. We have a hotline to heaven, and when we call, the Lord always picks up and answers.

It's one thing for me to tell a person in a counseling session that Jesus loves them, but it's a whole other ball of wax when Jesus *himself* tells them that he loves them. And His words always hit the mark, usually prompting tears of joy and deep relief. If you can talk to someone who has participated in inner healing, they will tell you what an electrifying and life-changing experience it is.

Without a doubt, you and I can still hear from the Lord today, like folks have for centuries. We sing it, so let's believe it, and practice it. As I mentioned earlier, God has talked to man since Genesis 2. God has not changed, but we have, to our own detriment. It's not too late to wake up and get with the program, and return to the intimacy and communion with God that we were born to enjoy.

For unto us a child is born, unto us a son is given: and the government shall be upon his shoulder: and his name shall be called Wonderful Counsellor... Isaiah 9:6

I had read that passage in Isaiah many times, that Jesus would be the Wonderful Counselor, but until Henry Wade showed it to me in practical application, I missed its full meaning. I did not understand that it is *only* the Lord who can give us truth in the *inward* parts. No one knows our hearts except the Lord, and He desires to give us truth in the inward parts so that we can be healed.

Behold, thou desirest truth in the inward parts: and in the hidden part thou shalt make me to know wisdom. Psalm 51:6

"In the hidden part, Thou shalt make me to know wisdom." It is very clear Who makes us to know wisdom, the LORD; not a 'well trained' counselor making an educated guess. And I'll trust God's revelation (*rhema*) over the five senses any day of the week.

God shines His light in those dark places, and heals us.

I remember my mama pulling mattresses and other household items out into the sun during spring cleaning. She always said, "Honey, sunshine is the best disinfectant." And she was right.

Sunlight is a great disinfectant, and so is Son light. The key to healing your heart is to expose underlying negative emotions to the light of God's wisdom, and let the Wonderful Counselor, Jesus Christ, come in and heal your heart.

God's not in the hiding business, He's in the healing business.

In AA there's a saying, "You are only as sick as your darkest secret." That's a great truth.

Have you ever been feeling guilty and said, "This thing is eating me up *inside*" or "If I don't tell someone, I'll explode?" Then you've experienced some of the negative power of secret sins. The Bible puts it this way, "Confess your faults one to another, and pray one for another, that ye may be healed." James 5:16. We confess, we get stuff up and out, into the Son's light, so that we can be healed.

There is just something cathartic about speaking your problem out loud to a trusted person. You don't need a priest, but it helps if you have a spirit-filled counselor to show you the way.

That's why I am laying my heart bare before you in this book, so that you can see the struggles I've been through, and how, with the Lord's guidance, and with good counseling, I have come through my own life traumas better, and not bitter. Not just surviving, but thriving. And, I am thoroughly convinced that since God has done that for me, He can do it for anyone. You are never so far gone that God can't restore your soul.

All the things I went through in my life, both good and bad, have made me who I am today. And I love the person I am now, so I wouldn't change a thing. But I had a choice to make when the after effects were still eating me up, to *deal with* my pain, or keep it buried and them and let it fester. It was my decision to face it head on, so that I could be restored; rather than ignore the mess in my own heart. I chose to make my own inner restoration a priority. You can't give what you don't have. If I wanted to help others on a deeper level, I had to first help myself. And through Dr. Wade's wise counseling, I did.

I thank God for good Christian counselors. One saved my life.

Our negative emotions don't die, we just bury them alive.

At some point we have to do a little digging, and get rid of the poison of our past. Hey, I could have ignored my mess, and kept doing okay for a while, and then smashing my head into a brick wall again, but that would not have been very smart.

Through inner healing, I dealt with my own lie-based thinking and started living in the now. I stopped living in the rear view mirror, a prisoner of my past. I finally stopped blaming other people and circumstances for what was currently going wrong in my own life. Instead, I took ownership, full responsibility for my current mental and physical situations. I learned to harbor life-giving thoughts and beliefs, instead of debilitating lie-based thinking; and better health, and decision making followed like a tail on a dog.

Thankfully, many Christian's do believe in physical healing, but not as many have embraced the reality that Jesus came to heal our broken hearts, when he took our griefs and sorrows to his cross, too.

Isaiah 53:4, "Surely he hath borne our **griefs**, and carried our **sorrows**." These words in the Hebrew are 'griefs, and sorrows.' Those are emotions: internal sickness, the bruised or broken heart.

Even though I had been physically healed many times, that day when reading those verses in Isaiah the full impact of those two simple words hit me like a jackhammer. Jesus took my griefs and sorrows to his cross. What a revelation! I broke down in tears of anguish because I had missed that truth for decades.

I mourned my lack of understanding. Jesus came not only to heal my body, but to heal my soul, my **griefs**, and my **sorrows**. To heal all those negative emotions that were eating my lunch every day. All that secret pain that had torn me up for decades; Jesus took all of that to his cross. I wailed like a baby, at this newfound understanding. It was a primal cry of relief. He took my griefs and sorrows, so I could finally allow my healing to take hold in earnest.

When longstanding grief, sorrow, and resentment are taking up space in our heart, they are toxic to our relationship with God, and others. The Bible calls them 'strongholds.' Our mission is not just embracing God's love, but identifying those things that are blocking that love from flowing freely through our lives. The 13th century poet, Rumi said, "Your task is not to seek for love, but merely to seek and find the barriers within yourself that you have built against it." That is a powerful statement, but it cannot be achieved by our flesh, our five senses.

For though we walk in the flesh, we do not war after the flesh: (For the weapons of our warfare are not carnal, but mighty through God [spiritual] to the pulling down of strong holds;) Casting down imaginations, and every high thing that exalteth itself against the knowledge of God, and bringing into captivity every thought to the obedience of Christ; 2 Corinthians 10:3-5.

We do not war after the flesh, and the weapons of our warfare are not carnal, but spiritual. There is no fleshly or carnal way to accomplish pulling down these inner strongholds; it can only be done Spirit to spirit, by inviting the Lord in to do the job.

The New Living Translation puts it this way, "We use God's mighty weapons, not worldly weapons, to knock down the strongholds of human reasoning, and to destroy false arguments (lie-based thinking lodged in our hearts)."

Thoughts are things, in that they become tangible reality.

The 'false arguments' in this verse, refer to lie-based thinking that contradicts the truth of who God made us to be in Christ. God says we are wonderful, important, loved, and courageous. But lie-based thinking tells us that we are worthless, weak, scared, and a failure. Can you see why you might want to get some inner healing? After all, as a man thinks, so is he.

We do not war after the flesh, our warfare is spiritual. The only one who can reveal truth to the inward parts, and tear down strongholds is the Lord. When we stop fighting with God (in that area, for we can have more than one stronghold), then we can lead our thoughts in obedience to Christ, and receive God's blessings. The blockage, the stronghold, is removed. The flow is restored. The truth sets us free.

It is our emotional damage that blocks us from receiving God's best.

He Restoreth My Soul

I am convinced that we need inner healing even more than we need physical healing, because out of our heart issues our life. If we don't remove the roots, the sickness or situation will just reoccur.

Statistics show that 95% of all disease comes from the mind. The physical toxins produced by stress, anger, resentment and guilt, can turn into cancer, heart disease, arthritis, and more. Can you see how cleaning up your heart life would affect your health, in both the short and the long-term?

Jesus pointedly addressed man's need for inner healing in Luke 4:18, and said, "This day is this scripture fulfilled in your ears." Luke 4:21. That very day he lovingly gave us the means to deal with our bruised souls; some of it is conscious, but much of it is subconscious, that's why we need the holy spirit to guide us into all truth. These strongholds keep us from living the fullness of our new life in Christ.

The renewed mind will take us far, but inner healing deals with your long-standing 'griefs and sorrows,' those stubborn places that have taken deep root in your heart. And that's when we call out to the Wonderful Counselor, "Lord, help me."

And the great news is—the Counselor is always IN.

Toxic memories cause us to act out in ways that we can't even explain. We might freak out over some minor issue, and wonder, "Where on earth did that come from?" Like the time I ran out of the movie theater when I heard the line about a man killing a child for a carton of cigarettes and some Chinese take-out. A long-buried grief, of worthlessness, got triggered in my subconscious, which set off my internal fight-or-flight defense mechanism; and I fled the theater without even thinking. It was a visceral reaction. It came from toxic, lie-based thinking, which the Bible calls our 'old man' nature; that's the part the Lord tells us to 'put off.' And if God asks us to do something, He's has supplied the means to carry it out, in this case, inner healing.

The basics of our personality are, for the most part, formed in childhood, where we experienced events that molded us on the inside. And yet it is not the event, per se, that took root in our hearts; it is how we responded to the event, and the negative emotions, the lies, that attached themselves to the event, that causes us problems in the future.

The old saying, "Sticks and stones may break my bones, but words will never hurt me." is a big fat lie from hell. Words can leave wounds deeper than any knife, especially the words we speak to ourselves. Words can hurt us for years, until we decide to get help.

I have counseled people who went through, what would appear on the surface, to be a relatively 'easy' childhood; food, family and a good support system, and yet they might be more messed up than someone who was repeatedly raped by a relative. It's all in how each individual reacted to their circumstances, and how deeply they took on the 'victim' mentality.

All this happens on the subconscious level, and so it is not consciously known to the person until the Lord reveals it to them. As Jeremiah says, "I the LORD search the heart, I try the reins (inner thoughts)." Jeremiah 17:10. We need the Lord's help to get rid of strongholds, the roots of emotional damage hidden in the recesses of our hearts, and the synapses of our brain. Remember, our mind and our heart are supposed to work together, we are not supposed to be double minded.

Here's the good news:

You may be a product of your past, but you are not a prisoner of it. Hallelujah!

Inner healing (soul restoration) is literally the spiritual, emotional, and physical healing, of one's heart and mind.

Dr. Caroline Leaf is a cognitive neuroscientist, with a PhD in Communication Pathology, and specializes in Neuropsychology. Dr. Leaf has put forth empirical evidence that toxic thoughts in the heart kill brains cells and produce toxins in the body and emotions. Therefore, when we heal the heart we clear the body of that constant release of toxins (poison).

Brain scans show that where a person has held long-term toxic thinking, or long time drug use, there is literally a dark hole there. The synapses and dendrites suffer tremendous damage. On the brain scan that area looks like a black hole. But when the same person's brain is scanned *after* they change their heart to godly thoughts for a period of time, that area in the brain 'fills in' and blossoms with new life. The before brain scan looks like a barren, emaciated, withered tree, with a dark hole in the center; but the after scan looks like a flourishing oak; like a tree of life.

[The Lord's] Wisdom is a tree of life to those who embrace her; happy are those who hold her tightly. Proverbs 3:18

The old wasted places in the heart and brain can be healed and fully restored by replacing toxic, lie-based thought patterns with positive godly patterns, through inner healing.

And they that shall be of thee shall **build the old waste places:** *thou shalt raise up the foundations of many generations; and thou shalt be called,* **The repairer of the breach, The restorer of paths to dwell in.** Isaiah 58:12.

Today, Spirit filled believer's carry out the ministry of Jesus. (John 14:12) We are now the facilitators, the repairers of the old waste places as we lead others into the Lord's presence. And as those 'waste places' are healed, the breach is repaired, and godly neural pathways are restored in the brain. How cool is that?

As a matter of fact, when the heart and mind are healed at this deep level the brain begins to produce enzymes that **heal the cells** in your body. No wonder God said a merry heart does good like medicine. He taught man three thousand years ago that a healthy *heart*-life translates into vigorous physical health. Now that verse can be proven scientifically. Again, science is playing catch up with God.

On the other hand, the person who chooses not to deal with their inner pain inevitably becomes hard-hearted, or uses some other form of addiction, in a futile attempt to block their pain. It's called 'numbing out.' The sad reality is, these avenues offer only a temporary 'fix' because it wears off like novocaine, while leaving the rotten tooth. The pain is still in there, festering like a toxic dump.

Here's the deal, both pain and **joy** come in through the same door. So, if you numb yourself out to your pain, you have also closed the door to life's joy. It is only by confronting the pain head on, and getting rid of it, that you can once again *feel* joy, as well as other **positive** emotions.

If a downed tree is blocking the road, you have to remove it before your car can move forward. Those who never removed the 'tree' caused by trauma are blocked from moving forward past the time when the inner damage occurred. That's why so many grown ups continue to manifest emotional adolescent behavior well into adulthood, their emotional growth is, in essence, frozen in time.

Since Chris and I moved to North Georgia, the Lord has taken my inner healing ministry to a whole new level. He showed me that after pulling out the lie-based roots, Jesus could speak very specific and personal truths to an individual, to counter those lies. **And he taught me to <u>never leave the 'old waste' place empty</u>, but to fill it with truth.**

Never end a session until you have filled the 'old waste place' with *rhema*, divine revelation, truth from Jesus' lips. This is what keeps the demons from coming back in and reinhabiting their old homestead. (See Luke 11:25,26)

This method of counseling gets to the nub of people's problems. It doesn't just cut the weed off at the surface; it pulls it out by the roots, and then fills the hole with God's love and truth.

And the results are astounding. Using this method, I have helped hundreds of others find the peace they have long been seeking. I have seen dramatic personality changes, addictions healed, and families restored.

He Restoreth My Soul

I believe that the prophets of old understood inner healing, and it is now coming back to the forefront in the body of Christ. Why? Because we need it.

King David understood this foundational truth when he penned: **Create in me a clean heart, O God; and renew a right spirit within me.** Psalm 51:19,12.

David was a great man of God, but when he got off the ball, he made some catastrophic mistakes. But he understood that only the Spirit of the living God could heal his heart, and renew a right attitude within him; to get him to the place where he could once again feel the joy of the Lord's presence in his life, and get back on the good foot. That is why David invited the Lord in, to reveal truth in his inward parts.

Behold, thou (God) desirest **truth** *in the* **inward parts:** *and in the* **hidden part** *thou shalt make me to know* **wisdom**. *Psalm 51:6.*

Hey! The LORD desires truth in our inward parts, and we should too; because the result is the restoration of our soul, and our relationship with Him.

Restore unto me the **joy** *of thy salvation (wholeness); and uphold me with thy free spirit. Psalm 51:12.*

The result of receiving 'truth in the inward parts' was joy. David felt whole again, and on his game. David and the Lord were in sync again. This set him back on the path of life, of right living, the breach was repaired. Who wouldn't want that?

Friends, David wrote about inner healing in 950 BC. And he must have taught this to his son, Solomon, because he used inner healing to help the Queen of Sheba:

And when the queen of Sheba heard of the fame of Solomon, she came to prove Solomon with hard questions at Jerusalem... and when she was come to Solomon, **she communed with him of all that was in her heart.** *And Solomon told her (answered) all her questions* [How? By revelation]: *and there was* **nothing hid from Solomon** [word of knowledge, word of wisdom] *which he told her not. And when the queen of Sheba had seen the wisdom of Solomon... there was no more spirit* [ungodly attitude] *in her. 2 Chronicles 9:1-4.*

Solomon *facilitated* as God's human representative, but only the Lord can reveal truth in the inward parts of a person's soul. God sees, we speak it forth. And God does the healing.

And the queen's healing must have been a doozy, because Luke 11:31 tells us that this once pagan queen will be in the resurrection of the Just. Now that's some kind of healing! She received emotional healing in the here-and-now, and gained eternal life in the process.

The queen of the south (Sheba) shall rise up in the judgment with the men of this generation, and condemn them: for she came from the utmost parts of the earth to hear the wisdom of Solomon; and, behold, a greater than Solomon is here. Luke 11:31

That's quite a record of what inner healing can do. In Luke 11 Jesus was upbraiding those religious folks standing right before him, because all of them could have had their hearts healed too, but they chose not to. And to put a fine point on it, he said they would be judged by the once pagan Queen of Sheba, in the future, for turning their backs on his message.

Too many of us are still missing out on Father's blessings today. God has tried His best to show us that He still talks to His children all through the Bible, but we are the ones who refuse to believe it. God wants intimacy; a relationship with us, not religious rituals.

Tragically, the simple truth of how God interacts with the body of Christ through His Son, is shunned my many Christians. Nothing could make Satan happier, he is, after all, the thief. And don't underestimate him, he wants to steal your truth, your joy, your health, and your future.

Time spent with God was never meant to be a monologue, but a dialogue.

Hearing from God is supposed to be an every day normal occurrence. It is called walking by the spirit. It's what God's kids are designed to do. *Not* hearing from Him should be the anomaly.

For as many as are led by the Spirit of God, they are the sons of God. Romans 8:14.

How can God lead us daily if He doesn't talk to us? Where did we ever get the idea that God *stopped* talking to His children? I have just spent most of this chapter describing how Jesus talks to us during inner healing. Well, where is he getting *his* information from? God! 1 John says that we fellowship with both the Father and the Son. (1 John 1:3) Jesus walked and talked with God all the time. He only did those things he saw and heard the Father do. And that's what he's still doing today. As believers, right now, you and I are 'as he is' in this world. We are God's offspring, and have His divine nature within us. We are supposed to be getting the 411 from God all through the day, too.

The Messiah, the mighty, spirit-filled Jesus said without God, HE could do nothing. So shouldn't you and I have the same attitude? What an electrifying truth. Jesus invited God in, he opened his heart fully to the Father, and they had an intimate Father and child relationship. They were best friends. Jesus trusted God implicitly, in both his head and in his heart. That's how he did those mighty miracles, by living in concert with the Father's will, being led by the Spirit. There's the pattern for us to follow, how you and I are supposed to live as well. Then we will be those who heal, and do no harm.

The five senses feed our mind information, but so does our 'sixth' sense, our spirit. We need to get a lot more attuned with the spirit that lives within us. That is our hotline to heaven.

The heart is the center, or the seat of your personal life. It is the heart/subconscious, which is the clearing house for what you ultimately will, or won't believe. Your attitudes, your habits, your life simply reflects the image you carry of yourself in your heart. If you want your life to change, your heart must change. And, thank God, we now know that this is one of the main things Jesus came to do, to heal our damaged hearts.

There is great wisdom in the old saying, "Let's get to the heart of the matter." I wish more folks understood the depth of that statement.

God's wisdom comes from our heart. Sometimes people refer to this as a 'gut feeling.' They don't rationally understand why something 'feels' right or wrong, but it's coming from their 'gut,' their heart. The smart thing for them to do is pay attention to that feeling. We sometimes call it 'mother's intuition,' but all of us have it.

In the body of Christ there are many avenues to minister healing. A person with the ministry of a pastor is called to shepherd the flock. A good shepherd binds up the wounds of his flock, like Jesus would. Well, human 'sheep' don't need fly ointment for their eyes, they need healing, in body and soul. That's why Jesus always made such a deep connection between sickness and sin; mind and body, in the gospels. "Sin" is simply a separation from God's ways in our hearts. And when we are not trusting God, we end up thinking negative, toxic thoughts. Those toxins create *dis-ease* in both the body and the soul/mind.

Through the years I have experienced numerous physical healings, for which I am very grateful, but often times the same illness would return. I didn't understand why I could not maintain my healing until I understood that physical and emotional sickness comes from the heart. The reason the physical sickness would return was simple: the belief patterns in my heart had not changed. I had not 'changed the reel.' As long as the toxic roots were still in my heart, I would manifest the same kind of illness over and over.

When I received inner healing, I was able to maintain my physical healing much more efficaciously. What a relief.

Jesus said he came to heal the broken-hearted. For years I missed that simple truth and it held me back in my spiritual growth. I desperately wanted to love like Jesus loved me, and to forgive like Jesus forgave from the cross, but I still had so many roots of bitterness, resentment, fear, and shame in my heart that caused me to fall short.

Dr. Wade showed me that for years I had been clipping the weeds at ground level (renewing my mind), but never pulling up the roots (changing my heart). So, the weeds kept coming back with a vengeance. That is why I opened this book with some of my own childhood traumas, to show you how the roots, even though formed in our early years, will last and last, until we ask the Lord to <u>pull out those **roots**</u>, and replace them with His **truth**.

Renewing our mind is something we need to do all the time, it's like breathing, we need to think thoughtfully and on purpose all through the day. On the other hand, inner healing is needed only on occasions, when the Lord reveals to you a **stronghold** that needs to be 'cast down.'

Renewed mind is like putting gas in your car, you need it all the time for it to run, but inner healing is like changing the oil. It is needful, but on a much less frequent basis.

I think of inner healing as a resurrection of the soul, for the parts of our subconscious that have been shattered, or deadened, by lie-based thinking. Those dead areas can be resurrected to newness of life. During these sessions a miracle of healing happens, and produces immediate results for the counselee. (See Appendix 2).

Negative emotions never die; we just bury them alive.

Like Lazarus who stunk after he had been dead for four days, after a time, toxic emotions will stink up your life. With the help of a Spirit-led counselor, who can assist you, and bring you to a place of peace where you can hear the voice of Jesus for yourself, you, too, can be restored. Like when Jesus called forth his friend Lazarus from the dead, Jesus will speak life into those damaged places in your soul. He will even show you where you need healing; he will expose the lie-based thinking. And *then* comes the resurrection. Jesus replaces the lie with words of Truth and life that he himself will give you. This is an amazing thing to experience. Then it's up to them to hang on to it.

With inner healing comes new attitudes that change us for the better. Where we had hate, we now have love and forgiveness. Where we had anxiety, we now have trust in the Lord. The renewed mind is the key to power, but without inner healing you will find your mind continually filling up with weeds.

Don't let the thief steal your prize! Which is why I encourage the counselee to sit quietly and journal as soon as possible after a counseling session. The Lord will continue to inspire them to write down thoughts that will inspire and encourage them to retain their healing.

Keep [guard] *thy heart with all diligence*; *for out of it are the issues of life. Proverbs 4:23.*

Thousands of years ago Job asked, "Who hath put wisdom in the inward parts? Or who gives understanding to the heart?" Job 38:36. Only God can give us that kind of wisdom, no one else knows our heart, except the Father. And He reveals that to us through His son. Jesus can do for you and in you what no human counselor could ever do because he's not limited by the five senses. He is getting his information straight from God, our

Father, the Creator and Maker of all life. The One who knows our innermost secrets. And he has no agenda except to heal you.

Our hearts didn't get messed up overnight, and they are not going to get straightened out overnight. Inner healing is a journey, like peeling an onion, it has layers. It may take a lifetime of getting help from time to time. Only when Christ returns, we will be fully perfected. In the meantime, God's not looking for perfection; He's looking for participation. And we can all do that—participate.

Here's a tip, I realized early on that I can't force anyone to get help. The only person I can change is myself. And with the help of others I have become the person I longed to be: good, loving, and kind and I will be there to help anyone who hungers for the same things. But none of us can make someone else want to get well. Only they can make that decision.

The more we allow God to tear down those strongholds in our heart, the more like Him we become. Jesus said, "I and the Father are one." And that is the goal, for all of God's children to be in sync, to be of one heart and one mind, with our Father.

*Holy Father, keep through thine own name those whom thou hast given me, that they **may be one, as** we are [one]. John 17:11.*

The Lord is ready, willing and able to help you achieve that oneness. Two thousand years ago, in the garden of Gethsemane, Christ prayed for us, here in the twenty-first century, who would reach out and respond to this invitation.

*Neither pray I for these alone (his current disciples), but for them also which <u>shall</u> believe in me through their word. **That they all may be***

one; *as thou, Father, art in me, and I in thee, that* **they also may be one in us:** *that the world may believe that thou hast sent me.* John 17:20,21.

That fateful night in the garden, when Jesus was about to be tortured and crucified, **YOU were on his mind**. He was praying for you and for me. What a gift! What joy. We can be one with the Creator of all things. Thank God he had the foresight to do that for us.

Remember, the universal cry of every child is: *love me! Care about me! Keep me safe*! God ticks all those boxes, and wants you to feel His love and safety throughout every cell of your body.

In Psalm 23 the Lord said He could "restore my soul." My response was, "Have at it Lord. Please. I made a mess of my life without You." And I still hold on to that verse.

Today, I happily say, "Lord, I am an open book. Heal me O, Lord and I shall be healed. I trust You with all my heart."

All healing begins when you start believing the Bible, but inner healing is for those of us who need more specific help with deeper issues. Why limit God? He can remove the barriers in our heart that hinder us from receiving the fullness of His love and blessings.

But unto you that fear (respect) my name shall the Sun of righteousness arise with healing in his wings; and ye shall go forth, and grow up... Malachi 4:2.

The Son of righteousness has risen with healing in his wings, and he is the one who sets us free through inner healing. He promised to restore our souls. All we have to do is open up our hearts, and let the Son shine in.

Without a doubt, inner healing is a supernatural experience. It is a miracle from God. When Jesus heals your heart and your emotions, it affects your whole life for the better.

For years I missed the promise in Psalm 23, 'He restores my *soul*' and yet there it was, set like a diamond. But I missed the importance of that verse until Dr. Wade; it's *soul* restoration that makes the rest of the good things in Psalm 23 flow freely into our lives.

I am so thankful to Dr. Wade; through his counseling ministry the Lord opened my eyes to a better way of inner healing, the Jesus way; and how to help others receive soul restoration through the power of the Living Christ.

Chapter 23

Reach Out in the Darkness and You May Find a Friend

"I think it's so groovy now that people are finally getting together ... Reach out in the darkness, and you may find a friend... Don't be afraid, don't be afraid to love."
Friend and Lover

The old song, *Reach Out in the Darkness*, had a haunting refrain, "Don't be afraid, don't be afraid to love." As a teenager I didn't know how profound those words were, and how much they spoke to my condition. One thing is for sure, until 1974 I was afraid... no, *terrified*... to love.

I had walled myself off from all feelings, both good and bad, and from getting too close to people in the hopes of never getting hurt again. Like the Pharisees, this carnal method of self-healing only made me more hard-hearted and mean.

I did not feel pain, but I also did not feel joy. I put myself in a prison of my own making. But in 1974 I reached out in the darkness, and I found a friend—his name is Jesus, the Light of the world. I turned my life over to him and through the years he has lovingly restored the pieces of my broken soul.

When you look at this world, it's plain to see that the number one problem still is people are *afraid* to love, and *be* loved. They are afraid to expose their heart, and so, they do what I did, they harden it, numb it, or distract themselves with addictive behaviors.

Since "Hurting people hurt people" you now have a crash course on why the world is in such a mess. Negative emotions don't die, we just bury them, and they fester like a rotting corpse, until the stench of our own behavior cause us to acknowledge it, and reach out for restoration.

When any of God's creatures are abused, the soul becomes fractured. Slowly but surely we lose part of ourselves, or give it away to others. Jesus came to make us whole again, to restore our soul, and make us better than before.

Aptly enough, Satan is also called the pejorative Beelzebub, the "lord of dung." He is the one laying all the crap of life on you, your family, and the world. He is indeed "Lord of the Flies" and will never rise above that humiliating position.

There are only two forces in the universe: one is Good and the other is evil. We have to consciously choose to tap into one or the other with our free will. But here's a bedrock truth to consider:

<u>All</u> bad things ultimately come from—Satan

<u>ALL</u> good things ultimately come from—God

I strongly suggest you choose to follow God.

Here's the deal: God <u>is</u> love. God is not *loving*... He is all Love. He has no hidden agenda, no ulterior motive; He is right up front. He simply loves you, and wants you to love Him in return. Then, when you begin to trust Him, He can heal your hurts and mend your broken soul. And then you can really be a force for good in this world, sharing His unconditional love with others.

When we are born again into God's family, He makes us spiritually whole; complete in Christ. He infuses us with His divine nature. He gives us all the tools to become our best selves. And we learn over time how to go to God, and trust Him with our now, and with our tomorrow. That's when Life becomes a whole new ball game for us. Finally we are in the Catbird seat; we have the upper hand. We are no longer the victim, but the victor.

As you can see, my own journey to inner freedom has been one amazing ride. Learning to trust God is the best thing that I have ever done with my life, because prior to that all I had done was make a complete mess out of it.

Looking back over the years, the three most life-altering events in my journey were: giving up my twins for adoption, the rape by Dirty Harry, and the afternoon with God at Berry College. These are the three events that constantly affected my moods, my decisions, and even my health. The first two affected me in a very toxic way, and the third one was unbelievably healing. But I am thankful for the lessons I have learned from each of these events, because they have made me who I am today; and I like me. In fact, I love me.

Perhaps one would think that the childhood molestation would be the worst; but as traumatic as that was, it merely set the stage to draw other catastrophes into my path. It flung open the door to shame-based thinking. The truth is, I never allowed myself to fully recall my childhood molestations in detail until I was an adult. The mind is an amazing thing. It can cover over things too painful to remember. But that doesn't mean they don't have an impact. Unfortunately, my low self-esteem acted like a homing beacon calling in even more demonic abuse; that is, until the Lord began healing me from the inside out.

But giving up my girls for adoption was the worst one of all. It laid a load of guilt and worry in my heart that was more than I could ever have prepared myself for. The sleepless nights filled with the gut-wrenching uncertainly, wondering one thing, were my girls *safe*? Their safety was always on my mind.

Most of the self-harm I brought into my life was a direct result of the self-loathing that overwhelmed me because of that one decision. Even though, in my heart of hearts, I believed I did the right thing for my twin's safety at that time, the guilt remained a constant drip, drip, drip, emotionally and mentally tormenting my soul.

We are free to choose, but we are not free to control the consequences of those choices. And some have life-long consequences. That one certainly did.

Even when you make the best decision you can, it is not always easy to live with.

I learned the hard way why forgiveness is such a key to good health, both mentally and physically. Especially self-forgiveness.

In bible fellowship I had learned that Jesus forgave me two-thousand years ago, but to make that an experiential reality in my own heart took years to achieve. Had I been in a church where they understood the necessity of healing the heart through Christian counseling, it may have happened a lot sooner. That is why I do my best to spread the good news that Christ came to heal all of you: body, soul, and spirit, which includes your heart. I don't want to leave others with nowhere to turn for answers; lost, and beaten down like I was for decades.

Self-forgiveness was the essential part of my own restoration. Forgiving myself was harder than forgiving any of my abusers. Forgiving 'Ronnie' the twin's father who abandoned me, was easier than forgiving myself.

I remember running into 'Ronnie' about a year after the girls were born. I was with my dad, Papa Joe, in a crowded diner when my ex saw me; he was leaving as we were coming in. He looked like he wanted to crawl under a table. We ended up almost smacking into one other. My dad had gone on ahead to get us a table, and I was a just few inches from 'Ronnie's' face. I looked straight into his eyes, and before I could even think about it three words literally flew out of my mouth—"I forgive you."

Wow! That surprised even me.

As raw, and deeply hurt as I still was, those words leapt from somewhere deep inside. I shocked myself when I blurted them out, but *intuitively* I knew I spoke the right thing.

Here was the guy who had betrayed me, abandoned both me and his babies. He was as responsible for my plight as I was; and yet he had zero sympathy for my predicament. This was the jerk that refused to marry me, but wanted to screw me because I was already pregnant. This was the guy I saw after I had given birth to his daughters, and he never once asked me how I was doing, or how his own children were doing. Unbelievable.

As Jennifer Aniston said regarding Brad Pitt's betrayal, 'Ronnie' was missing a sensitivity chip. He was a totally self-absorbed, narcissist. I remember thinking, "How pathetic it must be to be him. What a contemptible human being." And yet, I still forgave him.

When I uttered those words, he looked stunned, more like I had slapped him in the face than forgiven him. He quickly looked down at his shoes, never said a word, and scurried like a rat out of the restaurant. Thank God, I have never seen him again.

I reckon something beyond my conscious mind knew that if I didn't forgive him, I would suffer even more. And that unseen force pushed those words right out of my mouth that morning. Here's an odd thing, we don't forgive people for *their* sake, we forgive them for *our* sake.

Unforgiveness is like drinking poison and expecting the other person to die. It only kills the carrier.

We must cut off the root of bitterness before it gets a chance to take hold. That doesn't mean we have to like the person, or rationalize that what they did was okay. It was not okay. But forgiveness means that we release them, and turn them over to God, and let Him sort it out.

Forgiving myself was much more difficult. My decision to give my girls up for adoption had not just left a small hole in my heart; it had left a gaping wound as big as the Grand Canyon. The only thing big enough to fill that void was God's love. Through years of counseling, prayer, and trying to live right, I have forgiven myself to a great degree. I would be lying if I said it doesn't bother me anymore, but it doesn't consume me. My soul and I have reached *détente*.

The second big event, the rape by Dirty Harry when I was twenty, only compounded my sense of degradation and powerlessness. I felt like a used-up rag doll all through my childhood, then by 'Ronnie' in high school, and Dirty Harry fit my inner profile. I'm not saying I somehow made 'Harry' rape me, but I am saying we will attract people and situations into our lives that will line up with our inner script; what we think we deserve in our *subconscious*.

Because my grandfather molested me, my inner script said, "Peg, you need to be punished. You have been a bad girl." This is a perfect example of lie-based thinking. Of course I had not been bad. I had been a child, victimized by an adult. But this is how insidious the devil is. He will take the victim and mess them up inside, too, leaving them feeling as though they deserved the evil that was perpetrated upon them. Which is crazy! No one deserves to be victimized and brutalized, especially a child.

I didn't even know how deeply I felt that way until years later.

Short of death, rape is the most horrific thing that can happen to anyone. It is not even about sex, it is about power and control. Rape is a sick desire to play god, albeit a satanic god, over another human being. There is no greater loss of a sense of safety than captivity, and rape.

And in my case I also had a loaded gun, cocked, and held to my temple, not knowing if I was going to live or die that night. If you have never been in this kind of life and death situation, let me tell you, it changes you on the deepest level. I suffered from Post-Traumatic Stress Disorder for years, before I was a formally diagnosed with it. For decades I had night sweats, and unfounded anxieties. That whole ordeal altered my perception about... *every*thing. My ability to trust people, even to trust God, was hamstrung for a long, long time.

Unfortunately, I know that I am only one of millions of the walking wounded, due to rape and abuse, and my heart bleeds for every one of them.

This kind of abuse causes fears that we can't even name. Everyone has some kind of irrational fears and insecurities that come from somewhere. But the good news is they can all be healed through the power of the Holy Spirit, through inner healing.

Believe it or not, there was a silver lining to that horrible rape, and that was what I learned about the kingdom of darkness. In just one night I had a crash course in supernatural realities. I felt, saw, and heard, more than I could have ever learned from years of Bible study about the devil's wiles and methods. I saw firsthand how he used fear, intimidation, and manipulation to bring me into his snare.

The Dirty Harry experience actually opened doors that later on, helped me understand how to help others who have been through, well... just about anything. It gave me firsthand spiritual wisdom and insight regarding *how* demons operate, and how truly evil they are. It also gave me a compassion, and understanding for other victims of violent crimes that I would not otherwise have had.

I don't sympathize I empathize with the hurting. I've been there.

My eyes were opened to the stark reality that there IS a kingdom of darkness that feeds on human weakness, in sick and depraved ways.

I saw first-hand that people can get so infiltrated with demons that they can literally shape shift, using ectoplasm, which is water molecules from their own body. That's how Dirty Harry 'grew' fangs, and transformed into a werewolf. (I'm sure many others have seen this type of demonic manifestation over the centuries, hence all the folklore about werewolves and vampires.) When the wind and snow assailed our car that night; it was big Ju-Ju from a bunch of pissed off demons because Harry did not kill me that night as planned—thanks to Jesus' intervention.

The Harry experience brought home the reality that we all exist in two kingdoms simultaneously; one is visible, and the other one invisible, but it is every bit as real as the one we can see, smell, hear, taste, and touch. I dare say, it is even more real, for the things that are 'not seen' are eternal.

In spite of how it was gained, I am truly grateful for that knowledge because when it came time to learn about the kingdom of God, and the manifestations of the Holy Spirit, I took to it like a duck to water. I had already seen some astounding supernatural power from the dark side. So, when I learned that the true God had given His children supernatural powers, too, that just seemed normal. And I figured God's must be way better than anything the devil could ever cook up, and I started performing miracles right out of the box. Easy peasy. After all, God is a zillion times more powerful than Satan.

The third life changing event was 100% positive, there was no down side at all. That October afternoon, by the lake at Berry College, when the Lord revealed His love to me in glorious Technicolor. That day is still the most life changing event that has ever happened to me. It fundamentally changed my wiring because it broke through my heart of stone, and showed me that I could have a tender heart, like Christ.

That spectacular fall afternoon by the lake, the Lord God Almighty filled my need to be loved on the deepest level. I knew, in the depth of my soul, that I mattered, that Someone cared if I lived or died, and that Someone was my heavenly Father.

Knowing that you are loved is essential to a healthy emotional and physical life. I'm talking about *agape* love, pure spiritual love which wants only to give to another, and asks nothing in return. That day by the lake, I got a supercharged dose of it, and it changed me for the better forever.

That was the day I knew beyond a shadow of a doubt that my heavenly Father had been looking out for me all those years. Through all my pain and sorrow, He had been there, keeping me alive, sustaining me, and guiding me home to His Kingdom life.

Sitting there, by the lake, in my car, with my Bible open to Galatians, for the first time in my life I experienced genuine hope that I could be a good and decent person, and perhaps even help others along the way. And He showed me a vision of myself standing on a stage and teaching others. I can't tell you how many times I have clung to that vision, and it has carried me through many other storms in life when I wanted to quit the ministry because it just got too hard.

That day the Lord took a dagger out of my heart that had been plunged in deeper than Excalibur into the stone of my heart, and caused me years of heartache and madness.

And, lo and behold, I *have* changed into the woman I am proud of. I am a giver, not a taker, a forgiver, not filled with bitterness. I do all I can to treat everyone I meet with kindness, and respect. And that's a track record worth something; one that will be rewarded by our Lord at the resurrection.

I am living proof that with the Lord's help, you can live through hell and get better, not bitter. And that's what I have done these last forty-plus years: I've gotten better, and better. More whole, and less stressed. Success is a journey, not a destination. With God by my side, my journey has been more exhilarating than anything I could ever have imagined.

Which brings me back to my girls. Countless nights I cried myself to sleep, asking God to just let me know one thing, that the twins were *safe*. I worried for over forty years if they were okay. Had their adoptive parents protected them?

In spite of my own pain, I was so thankful I had not opted for an abortion. At least I knew that I gave two women a chance at life. And I prayed fervently that they were enjoying happy and productive lives... somewhere.

Due to the positive changes in my life, I felt like I finally had something to offer my girls besides chaos. Mine was a closed adoption, but I still began to look for them in earnest in my mid-twenties. The question was, would I ever find them? My husband helped me comb through records at the courthouse in Bartow County, where they were born, looking for their birth certificates.

I called the doctor who delivered them and pumped him for information. I went online, did people searches, and talked to attorneys. We left no stone unturned in our search. The older I got, the more concerned I became about their welfare. After forty years, was it just too much to hope for, that we could ever be reunited?

In December of 2012, I had been through my latest bout of frustration in looking for the twins. They were now in their mid-forties. I figured if I hadn't found them by now, maybe I should just let it go, and quit tormenting myself. After all, they had my name on their birth certificates, so I figured they just didn't want to know who their birth mother was, and I had to accept that bitter pill.

But a couple of days later on December 4th, 2012, I received this email on my laptop:

Dear Mrs. Rhone,

You artwork is lovely. This question may seem out of left field, but I was wondering if you might be Margaret Anne Yarbrough from Cartersville? I have been looking for her for some time and happened across your website today.

If you are and want to contact me, my name is V—. My sister and I were born on March 27, 1969.

Sorry if this seems weird. Personal quests often are. It would be pretty amazing if your artwork led me to the right person.

If not, God Bless.
Sincerely,
V—.

What?! Adrenaline shot through me like a bolt of lightning. I thought I was going to pass out. I was hyperventilating. I immediately called my husband Chris, crying and trying to talk. I wondered if this could be some kind of cruel hoax. Was someone out there playing with my emotions, or was this the real deal?

But I figured, what did I have to lose? Excited and apprehensive beyond words, I emailed her back:

Dear V—,

I can hardly type... I have been waiting for this moment for 43 years! You have no idea how many ways I have tried to find you both. I just prayed about it again yesterday. I can hardly believe it. I am shaking like a leaf, and filled with joy.

Yes, I want to get to know you. Thank you from the bottom of my heart for contacting me. You are loved, and wanted!

I live in GA. Where do we go from here?
Love, Peg

Yes, yes, yes! My birth daughter had found me on the internet. Yay! Yippee! Hurrah! Hallelujah! Jump for joy! Confetti and music!

I was stunned and amazed—but most of all, I was relieved. I cried most of the night from a mixture of relief and joy.

As we corresponded, I found out my girls were just fine, in fact, they were better than fine. Apparently, due to recent health issues they had pursued finding me. — went on line, and found me on the internet under my married name, which is a miracle in itself. I no longer go by Margaret, but Peg, and thank God, I had kept a hyphenated last name all these years... *just in case.*

Reach Out in the Darkness and You May Find a Friend

It may have been my artwork that caught her attention, but it was my heavenly Father who brought us together. As it turned out, I was the *first* person she contacted when she started looking online. I don't know about you, but I call that another *bona fide* miracle.

A few months later, we all met up for the first time in Georgia, including their mom, and my adorable grandson. We all got along like a bunch of long lost cousins. I know not all birth reunions go this way, but ours did. And for that I was even more thankful. Who could ask for more? What a gift! What a blessing! My girls were not only safe, but they are well-adjusted, happy, loving women. I thank God, and their wonderful adoptive, parents for that blessing.

I cannot replace the years that we lost, but I revel in the years we have left. I am so proud of both of them. After forty-three years, I saw first-hand how God had placed them in the most loving, and nurturing home I could have imagined. No pedophiles, no abusers, just good, salt-of-the-earth people, who had prayed to God for more children. What a blessing for all our lives.

My girls were fine the whole time I was driving myself crazy with worry. The hand of God was on their lives, just like it was on mine. My greatest fear was put to rest.

Even though it took a long time for this to come to pass, I realized that you can reach out in the darkness, and there's a friend named Jesus, just waiting to love you, and put you back together again. He heals the broken-hearted, and sometimes that might include reuniting families, even children you haven't seen for 43 years.

Reach Out in the Darkness and You May Find a Friend

In short, life is a contact sport. We all have our trials and tribulation, but be of good cheer, Jesus says he will put us back together and help us overcome the pain of this world.

These things I (Jesus) have spoken unto you, that in me ye might have peace. In the world ye shall have tribulation: but be of good cheer; I have overcome the world. John 16:33.

Reach out in your darkness, and you too can find a friend named Jesus, who will love you, comfort you, and heal you.

"I think it's so groovy now that people are finally getting together ... Reach out in the darkness, and you may find a friend

Chapter 24

A *Living* Sacrifice Can Burn With *Life*!

*I beseech you therefore, brethren, by the mercies of God,
that ye present your bodies a living sacrifice, holy, acceptable unto God.
Romans 12:1.*

Living here, in the beauty of the North Georgia mountains, I consider myself the most blessed woman on earth.

I wish everyone could know how liberating it is to live in Christ; and how it feels to be loved unconditionally. There is so much solace in knowing I have a Helper, an Aid in life who will never leave me nor forsake me. And I know that I know, I never have to face any of life's problems alone. I know that no matter what gets thrown at me, I can thrive. I can do all things through Christ who strengthens me. Philippians 4:13.

Over the last fifteen years of living in this spectacular place of peace and beauty a lot has happened: I have made new friends, buried two parents, beaten cancer, and witnessed countless miracles. Life goes on. And through it all, my heavenly Father has been with me, in jubilation and in sorrow. And He is longing to be there for you too.

That's why I say, victims survive, but victors *thrive*.

I am a victor! I am thriving. Jesus freed me from the shackles of my past. That is true freedom. And I want to help others experience the same.

That's what this book is all about, your freedom. And once you have been set free, you have the ability to help others get set free, too. You can show them the way. But you can only give what you have. And, you can't fake soul restoration. You have to want it, and it takes work. But when we hit our stride, life takes on a whole new dimension.

Why not give God's way a try? What have you got to lose?

Let's face it, millions of people today can't stand themselves, and so they turn to addictive behaviors, whether it is drugs, alcohol, pornography, sadism, lust for power, or the less obvious addictions such as anger, lying, gossip, or bullying. These all stem from people who do not feel loved, people trying to fill that dark hole in their hearts—with even more darkness. And that never works, only light dispels darkness.

All God's waiting for is for us to reach out and ask Him for help. One of my favorite prayers is simply, "Lord, Help me." To which He always answers, "I am happy to oblige." He even beseeches us, or lovingly begs us, to accept this gift of liberation, not for His sake, but for ours.

*I beseech you therefore, brethren, by the mercies of God, that ye present your bodies **a living sacrifice**, holy, acceptable unto God... And be not conformed to this world: but be ye transformed by the renewing of your mind, Romans 12;1,2.*

God is not looking for reformation, a Band-Aid, He's looking for *transformation*. He is longing to overhaul your life from the inside out, from your heart, from whence joy and peace emanate.

I was in so much inner pain, back in San Francisco, that I was willing to crawl onto a filthy satanic altar, and die in search of truth—really? Could some deluded devil worshipper have ever given me that? Absolutely not! I would've ended up being even more at the mercy of the demonic forces that had already taken such a toll on my life. I am so incredibly thankful to God, who sent His angel to get me out of there. Once again, He literally saved my life.

The Satanists did not have the truth, but the Bible does.

Only the Truth can set you free.

Strangely enough, I did end up becoming a sacrifice, albeit a living one. (Romans 12:1.2) And God did not abuse me, or cut my heart out; rather He gave me a new heart, a better one, a tender one. He gave me wholeness, and restored my sanity. And He continues to restore my soul in every area that I choose to turn over to Him. He healed me big league, and asked nothing of me in return. That is genuine love.

And, He wants to do the same thing for you.

Transformation starts when you look to God, and realize that His way is the better way, it is the total opposite of the world's insanity. He already sees you as lovely and acceptable, and He wants you to see yourself the same way. He knows the secret to radiant living is when you feel good about yourself. So He fills you up with His own divine nature, and makes you lovely and acceptable. What a change! And then you start treating others with more respect and dignity, too.

A Living Sacrifice Can Burn With Life!

When you 'let go and let God' you let go of fear of the future. You don't wake up every day full of nervous frustration. You acquire a deep sense of inner peace. You are released from living 'beneath the wheel' that Hermann Hesse wrote about. 'Stuff' becomes less important, and building loving relationships with God and people takes top priority in your life. You let go of selfishness, and genuinely care about the welfare of others, regardless of their personal beliefs. And that, my friend, is transformation.

Here's a truth a lot of Christian's would disagree with: The true God doesn't ask us to die for Him, He asks us to LIVE for Him!

The true God never asked us to die for Him, but wants us to LIVE for Him. Why? For our own sake. Because that is how we will be the most blessed. God doesn't want us to 'suffer for Jesus' he wants us to glorify Jesus. We don't glorify him through our pain, but through our power: power to love, power to heal, power to inspire others with hope.

The things God wants us to 'die' to are selfishness and fear. Let them go. And replace them with warmth, love, humility and service to our fellow man. That's how to live an abundant life, and bring glory to God. Have an open door to tell others how they can have the same blessings. Share the message that it is our Father's good pleasure to give us the Kingdom, which is rich in love, peace, joy, health and a happy heart. Those are true riches.

Fear not, little flock; for it is your Father's good pleasure to give you the kingdom. Luke 12:32.

Today, I choose, by my own free will, to be a living sacrifice, daily turning my life over to my Father, asking Him to lead the way.

And in return, He gives me soundness of mind and a cornucopia of blessings.

The only way to truly heal on an emotional level is to get the Maker of man's emotions involved. Only the Lord can put broken people back together. Like the old nursery rhyme, Humpty Dumpty took a great fall, and all the King's horses and all the King's men could not put one little *egg* back together again; let alone a human heart. Only the Creator of the human heart can do that.

Life is not rocket science; you are either embracing God's healing love or you are hiding from it, but you can't do both. A double-minded man is unstable in all his ways.

Today, I am on fire *inside* for Him, because I realize I have His DNA coursing through my veins. And He has shown me the path to peace and joy.

I believe that I have survived this long because, unbeknownst to me, the fire within me burned hotter than the fire around me. I loved God as a very small child, but became a POW of the demonic kingdom for a period of time. Christ removed my shackles and set me free again. Now I want to be a beacon of light, guiding others into the safe harbor of God's love.

Since I have taken God up on His offer to take care of me, my life has changed 180 degrees. He has done for, and in me, what I could never have done for myself. Lord knows, I tried without Him, and failed miserably. Through the healing love of Jesus, the patience of God, and the power of the Holy Spirit, I am living a life that once seemed impossible. All of this happened because I chose to invite the Savior into my heart.

It cost me nothing but time and effort, but it cost Jesus everything to give me the life of my dreams. Astonishingly, this gift of deliverance is there for the taking for anyone who will wake up and take it.

Wake up, for our salvation is nearer now than when we first believed. Romans 13:11 NLT

When you confess Jesus as your Lord, you become God's child by seed. God is the Creator of all mankind, but He is the Father of those who call on His Son, in faith.

And just what is a father? He is someone who nourishes, and provides for his children. A father protects his children; he fights for his own. He stands up for his family. Well, God is all of that… and more. One wonders how Christianity could have ever gotten so far away from such healing truth and replaced it with judgmentalism and dead rituals.

Every day I grow more deeply in love with my heavenly Father, who has literally taken me from death unto life. The words often come to my mind of the old hymn *Amazing Grace*:

> *Amazing grace how sweet the sound that saved a wretch like me.*
> *I once was lost but now I'm found. Was blind but now I see.*

We don't need God because we are perfect; we need Him because we are broken, and His love is the only cure. God is not looking for perfection, but He is looking for love.

Some folks accuse me, "Peg, you just see the world through rose-colored glasses." I can assure you, nothing could be further from the truth. I have my own personal challenges from the everyday craziness that we all deal with; like the day I got my cancer diagnosis. So, no, I don't see through rose-colored glasses, I see the problems of the world clearly, but what I DO is trust God to get through them. He is always by my side and in my heart. I believe He has my back.

*These things I have spoken unto you, that **in me** ye might have **peace**. In the world ye shall have tribulation: but be of good cheer; I have **overcome** the world. John 16:33.*

Jesus said we shall have tribulation in this world, but he gave us the antidote, "be of good cheer," because through him we can overcome anything the world throws at us.

Knowing that he has my back gives me peace in my heart. And that's why I can be ebullient in the midst of situations that used to drive me into a panic. Jesus promised that I am more than a conqueror in every situation when Jesus and I tackle it together.

I have very rough days, where I am heartbroken by the pain, the humiliation, and the deprivation that man inflicts upon his fellow man. I am, after all, a Christian counselor. I have seen and heard it all. And some of the things are just heart-wrenching. It is difficult to witness the pain men and women inflict upon each other when I know there is a better way — the love way.

But I never feel powerless against the darkness of life, because I am an overcomer. And I can show others, who want real change, the way to get out of the messes they are in if they really want to. And they too, can and walk in newness of life.

There are still some days when I become a bit unmoored myself, and this is what I do, I encourage myself in the Lord. I read something like Psalm 91 which says, "He that dwells in the secret place of the most High shall abide under the shadow of the Almighty. He shall cover thee with his feathers, and under his wings shalt thou trust: his truth shall be thy shield and buckler." Then I move under the cozy, warm shelter of my Daddy's wings, and release my problems to Him; I focus on His peace and presence in the midst of the day's insanity.

No matter how long you know God, you will still have good days and bad. The world keeps churning. But, after a while, the good times become more frequent, and the bad times don't freeze you up with fear.

Thankfully, God doesn't call the qualified, He qualifies the called.

I will admit, even with all that I have seen God do in my life, some days I still get hit right smack in the 'self-esteem.' It is that place near my solar plexus that can cause the wind to go out of my sails, and my stomach to hurt. I become a sitting duck for waves of negativity to roll over the sides of my mind. And even today if I'm not careful, those days can cause me to sink into an ocean of despair. At times like that, I know that I am not thinking about myself the way my Father thinks about me. I am looking at my flesh, which is never going to be perfect. And that's when I am tempted to wallow in disappointment and self-pity; which is never a good place to be. Then I have two choices: stay negative or change my mind. I'll choose door number two. I renew my mind and think about myself according to my new nature, my spirit man, which is perfect. I remember that God thinks I am awesome! Not because of what I have accomplished, but because of what Christ has accomplished *for me*. And the spirit of Christ in me is the part of me that is holy and without blame. I do what King David did, I encourage myself in the LORD.

And David was greatly distressed; for the people spake of stoning him, because the soul of all the people was grieved, every man for his sons and for his daughters: but David **encouraged himself** *in the LORD his God.* 1 Samuel 30:6.

Recently, during one of those dark moments, I got quiet and turned my attention to the Lord to help me get out of my funk. Here's what he said to me: "Peg, the most Enlightened, Holy, Perfect Being in the universe loves you. Why don't you love yourself?"

Since I didn't have a good comeback for that, I said, "Yeah! I do love myself." I thought, "Who am I not to love what God loves? After all, He's a lot smarter than I am." And when I focused on what God thinks of me, my day turned around.

Right away things started to change. My mood got lighter. Answers started coming, and all day I nursed the thought, "The most Enlightened, Holy, Perfect Being in the universe loves me." And that put a great big smile on my face. What we focus on we become. And the more I focus on the Christ inside, the more I become like him: happy, light-hearted, kind, fearless. Nothing gets me down for long, and no problem is too big for me to handle knowing that God and Christ are flanking me with their power.

The Lord may use other words to communicate His Love to you, but I am certain if you ask Him, He will respond to you in a way that touches your heart. Then hide those words deep inside, believe them, repeat them over and over to yourself with feeling, and soon you too, will once again be sailing victoriously on the ocean of God's love.

This is just one example of how the Lord is my helper all day, every day. And as you have seen through these pages, He has helped me countless times in the most unexpected and supernatural ways. Many have been fantastical, miraculous, and seemingly beyond belief; and yet they all actually happened to me.

I have no idea why I have been exposed to so many supernatural experiences. But, Lord knows, I've had a front row seat to Crazy Town as well as the Throne Room of God. And today, I am a living testimony to God's goodness. Therefore, I am happy to bare my soul, and to share some insight into the spirit realm, where there is an ongoing battle for the hearts and souls of men and women. Satan never sleeps—but neither does God! Our Father's out in the fields of life, looking for ways to help us twenty-four hours a day.

I know that my life has been atypical, in the amount of supernatural encounters I have experienced. So what. Or, perhaps I have just been more aware of them than others who tried to slough them off. The point is, God's love is not dependent on how much phenomenon you have experienced in your life, it is dependent on your acceptance of *His unconditional love for YOU*. He will reach out to each of us in different ways, because each one of us is on our own unique journey.

Obviously, you and I have not been on the exact same kind of spiritual journey, we are all blessedly unique. But we are also all the same, in that all of us have been hurt, and we need Christ's help to restore us, to help us reach our full potential.

Life leaves a mark; all the unkind or violent things that have happened to you along the way require healing. And Jesus came to heal all your wounds, whether old or new, from the inside out.

Perhaps my path unfolded the way it did just so I could write this book, and give you some hope. Or to reach others who have witnessed bizarre supernatural events in their own lives, and did not know how to process them.

Perhaps sharing my own experience, strength and hope will encourage someone to realize that terrible things can happen to you in life, and you can fully recover.

Perhaps I wrote this book to open blind eyes, and expose the spiritual battle that rages around all of us every day.

Perhaps I wrote it as a love letter to my Papa, *Jehovah Rapha*, the Lord who Heals, to tell the whole world what a loving God we have.

All I know is that I was compelled to write it, and I pray that it has helped you in some small way. The Father is no respecter of persons; only of one condition—do you believe Him? The door to God's heart is always open.

Because I have had so many harrowing, near-death, experiences, I may value the gift of life more than the average person, who just takes it for granted. Joni Mitchell sang, 'You don't know what you've got 'til it's gone.' But sometimes you don't *appreciate* what you've got, all of life's blessings, unless there was a time you did not have them. That's where I'm at. Simple things, like being able to think clearly, or make good decisions, just thrill my soul. And every day I wake up six feet above the dirt, I am so very thankful, thankful, thankful to be alive, and filled with God's hope for today.

Here's a reality sandwich: if you walk through a graveyard, every corpse is equally dead. None of them are deader than others, no matter how they met their demise. The point is, you may not have had the close brushes with death and demons that I did, but if you don't have Christ in your life, you are just as dead on the inside as I was without him.

This book was written to show the dramatic change that can happen when anyone lets go of the bitter hand life may have dealt them, and puts themselves in God's sweet hands. He is the potter, we are the clay.

There is a good life waiting for you on the other side of the storm.

Today I have a sunny mind in spite of the darkness in this world. Things that used to drive me to drink don't even ruffle my feathers. People who used to push all my buttons are just a slight challenge; I call on Jesus, to fill my heart with his compassion for them.

The truth shall make you free, but there's no one moment, where you have a certain insight and say, "Bingo! Now, I'm done! I can coast for the rest of my life, and I'll be trouble-free. I'll never have another problem." Life doesn't work that way because we have an adversary, the enemy of God and His people.

A Living Sacrifice Can Burn With Life!

Stay alert! Watch out for your great enemy, the devil. He prowls around like a roaring lion, looking for someone to devour. 1 Peter 5:8 NLT.

And here's the solution, "Humble yourselves under the mighty power of God, and at the right time he will lift you up in honor." 1 Peter 5:6. There you have it again, teamwork!

Life is dynamic, it is fluid. We are constantly either growing or dying on the vine. I wish there *was* an *aha!* moment, or a one-time fix, but that won't happen until the Lord returns. I am thankful to understand this truth, it keeps me grounded; it guides my way, and stops me from banging my head against the wall. This is how life works, we have good days and bad days, ebb and flow. The point is, no matter how our day goes, God is right there with us to make it better.

Once you are born again, you will spend the rest of your days putting off the old thoughts, and putting on the mind of Christ. It's like breathing. I am breathing right now, and I'll need to keep breathing tomorrow, and the next day. I'll never say, "I've taken in enough oxygen to last me a lifetime, and I don't need to breathe any more." The same thing goes for seeking God's presence. Like oxygen, we need Him all the time.

For God is working in you, giving you the desire and the power to do what pleases him. Philippians 2:13.

The Bible is an instruction manual; written in the form of a love letter. It contains all things that pertain to both life and godliness, and we just have to read and practice what it says to get the results.

But the Bible's main purpose, which has been all but forgotten, is to **lead us to its Author.** That's the point of the Bible, intimacy with its Author, God. Without that Father-child relationship, I am sorry to say, the Bible is just another book of nice platitudes. It's the *relationship* with us that God is after.

Life is kind of like tag-team wrestling, only my teammate is the One who made heaven and earth: "In this corner, height ... *unknown*, weight ... *unknown*, reach *unknown*, is The Heavyweight Champion of the Universe, *Elohim!*" And that's one heck of partner to have in life.

On the other side of the ring is the devil, and on his best day, he's no match for my teammate, the Creator of heaven and earth.

With God all things are possible. Stuff that used to knock me for a loop is now a little hurdle to jump over, because I am confident that God is working with me, and in me. I get to invite Him into all my tough times; we are a team, with Him doing the heavy lifting. And because of that attitude, I keep racking up victory after victory.

> *For God sent not his Son into the world to condemn the world;*
> *but that the world through him might be saved (made whole, healed).*
> *John 3:17.*

Praise the Lord! God is all about making things better. Salvation. Wholeness. Restoration. Reconciliation. He didn't send His son into this world to condemn us, but to save us, to make our lives whole in every way. I know, I've been there, done that, brought back the T-shirt–*God's Way Works!* I am a living testimony to His power to put a broken life back together.

A Living Sacrifice Can Burn With Life!

Every day when I brush my teeth, I see a *miracle* staring back in the mirror—me!

What He did for me, He will do for you. That's what happens when you become a living sacrifice, and decide to be on fire, to burn with life for Him.

Chapter 25

Don't Quit!

The key to recovery and wholeness is simply: Don't give up.
—Peg Y. Rhone

I am an overcomer! I am a victor, not a victim!

And I am here to tell you, just because your past was a mess, doesn't mean you have to stay a mess. Your future can be better than you ever imagined!

As I said in Chapter One, life is messy, none of us had a perfect childhood. The true story of everyone's childhood is, "Oops. That's going to leave a mark!" It just varies by how big and how deep your marks are. The good news is there is no damage that Jesus cannot heal. We just have to hang in there, and keep pressing into his Love.

The book of Hebrews addresses what to do when you have that feeling of being utterly worn out and wanting to throw in the towel.

*So take a new grip with your tired hands and strengthen your weak knees. Mark out a straight path for your feet so that **those who are weak** and lame will not **fall but become strong**. Hebrews 12:12,13.*

In other words, Hebrews says, "Get a grip! Don't quit!" Yes, you feel tired and weak and lame, but don't give up! Take that which was weak, and become strong. Just keep moving, no matter what, don't give up. Life is not always about the strongest, or the smartest, or the wealthiest; it is about the most **persistent**.

Don't Quit!

As you have seen, from my own harrowing testimony, I made it through childhood wounds, abandonment, rape, attempted murder, Satanists, a brutal first husband, and by God's grace, I'm still standing. In fact, I'm not just surviving—I'm thriving.

The key is simple: **Do NOT Give Up**, but keep putting one foot in front of the other, and keep looking for the Light.

There is a story that goes something like this, in 1905, Trudy Ederle had a lifelong goal to swim the English Channel; a feat accomplished by only a couple of dozen people. This twenty-one mile swim is considered by many to be the ultimate challenge in long-distance swims. The water is extremely cold, so you have to cover your body with thick grease. The Channel is filled with jellyfish that constantly sting you, along with other dangerous obstacles. On top of all that, it is one of the busiest shipping lanes in the world, so the water is always choppy. The winds and the traffic often generate seven-foot swells. The English Channel is inhospitable to swimmers, to say the least. Sounds a lot like life itself, doesn't it?

This determined woman trained for years, month after month of grueling practice, greasing up her body for the frigid waters, and swimming for hours at a time along side of her spotters in a row boat. Then, doing the same thing the next day, and the next, and the next.... all in preparation for the daunting twenty-one mile challenge.

Finally the day arrived for the big event, to make the swim. The fog was so thick you could cut it with a knife. She could not see her hand in front of her face. Twenty-plus hours into her endeavor, exhausted, cold, covered in jelly fish stings, she'd finally had enough. Tired and dejected, she swam over, and they hauled her worn out body into the spotter boat that had been faithfully by her side throughout the trip.

Shivering, cast down, and despondent, she climbed into the boat. But she was utterly stunned by what happened next. When the men pulled on the oars two more strokes—*thunk*! They hit land.

Can you imagine her heartbreak? After swimming more than twenty-one miles, **she was only a few yards away from her goal when she quit**. Another minute in the water, and she would have accomplished what few have ever dared to attempt.

I heard that story over forty years ago and decided then and there, that I did not want to be Trudy, who, after so much pain, snatched defeat from the jaws of victory.

Sometimes the trick to life is just staying in the game. Don't give up.

So, here's the rest of the story... even after that bitter experience, Trudy went back the next year. She not only became the first woman to swim the English Channel, but beat the men's time by two hours. She returned to America, to a ticker-tape parade, and was touted as "Queen of the Waves."

That's what can happen if we persist.

There's a trend going around these days where people tattoo a semicolon on their body. It's called *Project Semicolon*, which describes itself as "a faith-based non-profit movement dedicated to presenting *hope* and love to those who are struggling with depression, suicide, addiction and self-injury."

Though it is a Christian organization, *Project Semicolon* is quick to clarify that they do *not* exclude those who follow any other beliefs or religions.

As to the significance of the symbol itself, the organization writes on its website, "a semicolon is used when an author could've chosen to end a sentence, but instead chose not to. The author is *you* and the sentence is your life." Don't end it early.

The semicolon tattoo is a physical representation of personal strength in the face of internal struggle. It is choosing life over suicide, perseverance over quitting, moving forward over giving up.

There's a great old poem called *"Don't Quit"* which I committed to memory forty years ago, and it still keeps me going when things get tough:

> **Don't Quit**
> *Often the goal is nearer than*
> *It seems to a faint and faltering man;*
> *Often the struggler has given up*
> *When he might have captured the victor's cup;*
> *And he learned too late when the night came down,*
> *How close he was to the golden crown.*
> *Success is failure turned inside out,*
> *The silver tint in the clouds of doubt,*
> *And you never can tell how close you are,*
> *It might be near when it seems afar:*
> *So stick to the fight when you're hardest hit*
> *It's when things seem worst that you must not quit.*
> *—Edgar A Guest*

I want to encourage everyone reading this book—DON'T QUIT! Your story isn't over. The best is yet to come.

Stick around long enough not just to find out *who* you are, but *whose* you are.

Through all of my personal trials, there was Jesus, calling me to the safe harbor of his protection. And he gave me heaps of love, wholeness, restoration, and forgiveness. That's the real Christ message; he came not to condemn you but to save you, to make you whole in every way. To heal the hurts of your past, and give you a brighter tomorrow.

You may not even realize it, but there is a longing in every human heart for this spiritual food; the 'Bread of Life' is Jesus Christ.

As much as I love my earthly father, Papa Joe, my heavenly Father is the one with whom I truly identify; He is the one to whom my deep sense of self is tied. He is the one who has known me since before the foundation of the world. He is the one who is with me twenty-four seven. He's the one who knows the secrets of my heart. He's the one I look to as my constant source of strength, encouragement, and inspiration.

I encourage any of you who are struggling, to hang in there. Reach out in the darkness, and you will find there is help for the weary and real answers to life.

No matter what your age, you can put off the old habits, and make a new start with God's help. Spiritual growth is a learning process, just like a child learns to walk. You will stumble and fall sometimes, but don't stay down, pick yourself up and keep growing.

For years I mourned the fact that maybe, if I had known more about healing at the time, I might've been able to save Chris J. Or, maybe I should have insisted that she leave "Death Mountain." But I had to come to terms with the fact that we cannot save everyone, each of us has free will. And, just as important, we cannot change the past. Holding on to a could-a-would-a-should-a attitude only makes you sick in your own soul. I finally took all of this baggage to the Lord, and let it go. Maybe you have heard of *The Serenity Prayer*:

> *The Serenity Prayer*
> *God grant me the serenity*
> *To accept the things I cannot change;*
> *Courage to change the things I can;*
> *And the wisdom to know the difference.*

That pretty well sums up how I live day to day now, in His serenity.

On the positive side, I used Chris' death to fuel my own passion to stay alive and live a godly life. I see Chris J in every person I meet. I understand that even a perfect stranger is *special* to someone's life, just like Chris J was to mine, and rich or poor, I value them.

In the early days of my Christian walk, when I would feel like giving up and going back to my old rotten ways, I would think about Chris J, and I would keep going for *her sake*. I believe in the resurrection, and that one day I will see my friend Chris J again. When I do I want to give her a giant hug, and a good report of how her life touched thousands of others through mine. Love is the only thing that lasts.

After all these years of walking with God, there are still days when I just don't want to renew my mind, I can get tired and crabby, like the rest of the teeming masses. That's when I take a deep breath, stand up tall, and put on my 'big girl' pants; I keep-on-keepin' on, and just do the next right thing, in honor of Chris J, or my Granny, they are my invisible accountability partners. These two women modeled unconditional love for me. For all the crap that has happened to me in life, I had these two loving, courageous women to show me the love way. How grateful I am for that. I'll bet if you really think about it, you have one or two special people like that in your own life, who cared enough to show you a better way, too. Maybe even a stranger.

Jesus didn't just open the prison doors of my heart; he blew them off the hinges!

The strongest prisons in our lives are not what's around us, but what's inside of us, those secret prisons in our hearts that hold us back, or encase us in fear. The greatest moments in our lives come when we let go of that fear, guilt, resentment, or condemnation; the times when we break through the chains of adversity by embracing courage and hope.

Since inviting Jesus in, my life has not been perfect, but it has been better in every way. The guilt and shame took a while to let go of, but shame is removed through love, understanding, and absolution; Jesus gave me all three.

Shame keeps us trapped in the past, reliving the stupidity of our mistakes over, and over, and over, again. Shame is a great prison warden, it tells your mind, "There is nothing you can do about me. I'll be with you forever!" And it will, until you take the upper hand, and cast it out in Jesus' name.

And I am even more in love with the Lord than I was that day back on Tybee Island. How could I not love someone who took me from the depths of despair, and gave me a life worth living?

My love for the Lord, for myself, and for others has grown with each passing year.

I encourage you to let Jesus take you by the hand, and to walk out of your own prisons: out of self-loathing, and away from hatred, and jealousy. Instead, let the love of God fill your heart and mind. Then you move past the semi-colon, and on to the rest of the story. If you are still breathing, there is hope for you. Just because your past was a mess, doesn't mean you have to stay a mess. Your future can be as bright as the promises of God.

Oh, what glorious freedom awaits those who call on the name of the Lord in sincerity; those who reach out to Him *expecting* to receive. He hears your cry, and responds with abundant deliverance.

Jesus told the apostle Paul that he came to set us free from Satan's power once and for all.

To open their eyes, and to turn them from darkness to light, and from the power of Satan unto God, that they may receive forgiveness of sins, and inheritance among them which are sanctified by faith that is in me. Acts 26:18.

And Jesus did just that, he set us free from the power of Satan, and showed us the way to liberty. He forgave our sins and gave us, an inheritance in God's Kingdom. An inheritance that we can cash in on now: a new spirit, a new kind of love, and a boatload of supernatural power. What a gift. What a savior.

We cannot change the bad things that have happened to us in the past, or the bad things we have *done* to others, but we can learn from them. Ask for forgiveness and accept it, take it all to the Lord, and he will show you valuable lessons to make you wiser and stronger for the future, just like he has done for me. The point is, let go of the past, and set your sights on a brighter today.

Whatever your motivation to seek a better life, friends, family or yourself, the bottom-line is, just do it! And when those positive changes come, hang on to them like a Texan on a pork chop.

Just don't give up! Like Trudy Ederle got back in the game and swam the English Channel, your victory will come if you just don't quit.

Chapter 26

I Saw the Light... but He Saw Me First

Then Jesus came like a stranger in the night
Praise the Lord I saw the light
–Hank Williams

That old Hank Williams song has taken on a deep meaning to me. All those years, when I was hurting and alone, the Lord was shining His Light, beckoning me to, "Come on home to Papa, child."

This verse of scripture aptly describes my 'before' life, "*He* [God] *brought me up out of a horrible pit, out of the miry clay, and set my feet upon a rock, and established my goings.*" Psalm 40:2. I was going and almost gone, but He reached out and saved me.

Until that day in 1974, when Chris J persuaded me to go to Bible fellowship, I had been living (spiritually) in a horrible pit; stuck in the miry clay of fear, self-loathing, and madness. But the Lord brought me out of the darkness, and set me upon THE Rock, Jesus Christ, who illuminates my walk to this day. He gave me a new purpose. He put a new song in my heart, and praise in my mouth.

To coin another old hymn, '*What a wonderful change in my life has been wrought since Jesus came into my life.*' My prayer is that, through this book, many will see what God has done for me, and will decide to put their trust in the Lord too. Others will blow off this opportunity, and stay stuck in the mire. That's their free will.

But, I am eternally grateful I chose God's way. He has never let me down.

Over the last four decades I have lived all over the country, grown up spiritually, and helped a lot of people find Jesus. Because of my lifestyle, they too, have been touched by the Master's hand, and laid hold to peace of mind in their own lives.

Every day we are all faced with two choices, to live life the love way or the world's way. The world's way is filled with selfishness, fear, and frustration; but the love way is filled with trust, unselfishness, and peace of mind. You would think this would be an easy choice, but the pull of the flesh is strong. That's why it takes concerted effort to choose good, over and over and over again.

My desire is simple, to be like my big brother, Jesus. To go about doing good, and healing all who are oppressed of the devil, for God is with me. I say that with no arrogance whatsoever, but with a deep humility that all of God's children have been given a unique set of supernatural powers, and we are supposed to be using them to make this world a better and more loving place. To reach out to others, one heart at a time, and show them the Light. That's our job description in God's Kingdom.

Now we are Christ's ambassadors; God is making his appeal [to you] through us. We speak for Christ when we plead, **"Come back to God!"** *2 Corinthians 5:20 NLT.*

All of God's children are called to be His ambassadors, to be representatives of the King Eternal here on Earth. And He has fully equipped us to succeed as His ambassadors. But, you can only give what you have. You can't give the measles if you don't have a case of them. You can only give God's light and love if you have a heart full of it. Otherwise, you are just pushing more darkness and religion. Our heavenly Father wants us to show others how to have a relationship with Him. I pray daily for a bigger heart, and more kindness and understanding, for that is my Father's true nature.

So let's recap some of the major points we hit on in the book.

Only Love never fails.

God is Love, and Love is real. Love is the nucleus of miracles. It's the 'stuff' they are made of.

The power of Love is greater than the power of Niagara Falls, or the atom bomb. Love is the most powerful thing in the whole universe because Love created the universe, the vast oceans, the soaring mountains, and mankind whom He made, 'in His image.' Love sent His Son to set us free from the devil's power. Love made a way for us in the wilderness of life. God's love is the *summum bonum*, the 'highest good' we can aspire to in this life.

God's love is like water, it is always seeking a place to flow into, to heal, and to bless. All of our hearts have plenty of cracks in them, and God is longing to fill them with His healing love. But the question remains, will you invite Him in, or turn off the spigot?

Before I went to fellowship in 1974, I was bankrupt in the love department. I was fed up with people. I was fed up with myself. I had become mean, surly, and vindictive. I lied to my friends, I lied to my lovers. I didn't trust anyone. Heck, I didn't trust myself, so why should they? I could have cared less if people trusted or even liked me. I was rebellious and dark on the inside; unfeeling and uncaring. I might have been as cute-as-a-button on the outside, with my All-American looks, but inside I was Grade-A damaged goods. I was full of venom; like a tightly coiled rattlesnake, just waiting to strike. I was hard-hearted, and afraid. Like a feral cat, I was unpredictable, and even dangerous. I was on a collision course with tragedy; an accident waiting to happen. People who know me now find this very hard to believe, but it's the honest truth.

Now, I am happy, whole, and free. I have become a healer, a helper, and a lover of men's souls. Like the Hippocratic Oath: if I can't heal my fellow man, then at least *I will do no harm*. And that's a darn good way to live.

Coming home to the family of God was the greatest thing I ever did in my life, and that one decision has changed everything for the better.

"God is the homeland of the soul. We are no good away from home, except to return, and once again be full of Him" said Rufus Moseley. That, my friends, is the meaning of life; that is the 'Why?' of mankind— come home to Papa.

Even though I had accepted Jesus as a young child, I was robbed of my heavenly identity by my grandfather. He put me on a glide path to shame and self-loathing, which holds true for most sexual abuse victims. Because of that psychological damage, I began to doubt God, and I definitely did not know the power I had in the heavenly realm. I grew up like a scared rabbit, a slave to Satan. I was an heir of God, being held in bondage, like it says in Galatians.

Now I say, That the heir, as long as he is a child [doesn't know their rights], differeth nothing from a servant, though he be lord of all... Even so we, when we were children, were in bondage under the elements of the world. Galatians 4:1,3.

But, Chris J loved me enough to show me the light, the way back home, so that I could claim my sonship rights, and glorious freedom has ensued. And Larkin taught me my rights and privileges as a child of God.

And I made a host of new friends, ones searching to walk in God's love, just like myself. I am blessed to know these folks, who are true and honest. They are not content to live the status quo, but are looking to emulate Christ in this world. I love and respect people of all faiths, but I depend on my Christ-filled friends to keep me honest, grounded, and on the straight and narrow. When they see me out in left field, I expect them to say, "Hey, Peg, you might want to check out how you're handling that." And I take heed to their wisdom.

As the Bible says. "Iron sharpeneth iron; so a man sharpeneth the countenance of his friend." Proverbs 27:17. My true friends help me stay sharp. They have no hidden agenda; they just love me, warts and all. But, we love each other too much to let the other one drive headlong off a cliff, and go 'splat!' (That's how Chris J loved me.) We all have skin in the game. We are part of the body of Christ, and we have each other's back. No matter how far apart we are physically, we are inextricably linked by the spirit of God. We are all more connected than we realize.

This makes for harmony among the members, so that all the members care for each other. If one part suffers, all the parts suffer with it, and if one part is honored, all the parts are glad. 1 Corinthians 12:25,26 NLT.

I am so thankful for my loving and loyal friends; you make me feel like the richest woman on earth. I cannot imagine where I would be today were it not for my friends who are there for me through thick and thin. Let's face it; good friends make life a lot more fun.

And, above all, I spend quality time with my best friends, *Abba*, and Jesus. As the apostle John said, "Truly our fellowship is with the Father, *and* with His Son, Jesus Christ." I start and end my day with them, and check-in throughout the day. This is how I live my best life, in harmony with God, who surrounds me with His favor, His goodness and His mercy. I have peace in my soul.

Love is the great healer.

One of the best things my Mama taught me as a child was, "Hatred stirs up strife, but love covers all sins." Proverbs 10:12. Love is the great healer.

God 'covered' for us through the man Jesus, whose sacrifice set us free. Getting a hold of that truth is what transforms the human soul, and frees us from the shackles of our past. The soul can rise like a bird, into the air, not feeling the barriers of man, but the beauty of Love, which is eternal. I got my dream, I got my freedom to soar in life.

Hurting people hurt people. That's another reason I wrote this book; I've been on both sides of the coin, and that's why I want to help other hurting people get set free. Hurt was all I knew before

I went to that fellowship at the Tamassee Apartments. But today I am restored. I have let go of the baggage of yesterday, forgiven my tormentors, and given them over to God. And that is what allows us to grow to our full potential.

Just like hurting people hurt people; loving people love people. Isn't that a better way to live?

Gradually the blinders came off of my own wrong thinking; then I could see life in a whole new dimension, from God's perspective. This included my own self-worth. I believe that every person reading this book is special, and unique; filled with a set of talents and abilities that no other human being possesses. You may not look in the mirror and see how great you are right off the bat, but if you keep looking at Jesus, he will show you.

You are God's greatest miracle. Why stoop to being a copycat when God made you an original? Oh, what a day it was when I could look at myself in the mirror and say, "Peg, I love you." and mean it. It is an amazing paradigm shift when you start to see yourself, and others, the way God sees you, for you truly are a thing of beauty.

There's an old saying, "What you are is God's gift to you, but what you make of it is your gift to Him." That's wisdom for the ages, and it's free.

Jesus stands at the door of your heart and knocks, he wants to come in and heal your hurts, but you must invite him in, and trust him with your heart. Even though he is the healer, and the Prince of Peace, he is also a gentleman, he will never force his way into your life: you must be open to his invitation. His love is the great healer.

Jesus took all the things that have caused you sorrow and grief, and nailed them to his cross. He bore *your* pain in his own body. "Surely he hath borne our griefs, and carried our sorrows" Isaiah 54:4. So what do you have to lose by inviting him in?

A better question is, **"What do you have to gain?"**

The answer is, *everything*!

When His love begins to settle in your heart, you will gain freedom from the pain of your past, a new self-respect, access to His wisdom and guidance, and a partner who will never fail you. Jesus didn't come to condemn you, he came to love you into loving yourself.

If you think you have done something so horrible that you dare not approach Jesus, just remember that we have all sinned and come short of the glory of God — that's why we need a savior in the first place. We are all broken. But thank God we don't have to stay that way. There is help for anyone and everyone. God is aching to heal you, and restore you to the fullness of who you were born to be.

Jesus took upon himself all the sins of the whole world. No exceptions. You just have to receive it. Even the great apostle Paul, who had once murdered Christians, was forgiven, and called to be one of Christ's greatest spokesmen. That same Jesus has already forgiven you, too.

Emotions can kill.

Here's another reality: toxic emotions never die; we just bury them alive.

God is in the resurrection business; only He can restore what the devil has harmed. When any of God's creatures are abused the soul becomes fractured. Slowly and surely we lose part of ourselves or give it away to others unknowingly. Only God can repair and replace what the thief has stolen.

While the brokenness is still in there it causes cancer, heart attacks, ulcers, and dozens of other diseases that are linked to one common factor—stress.

I was shocked when I went to the doctor for high-blood pressure, and he said, "Peg, the number one cause of your high-blood pressure is stress." Which of course stressed me out even more. I thought, "Living in this insane world, how do I get rid of all my stress?"

So I searched the scriptures on how to stay blessed? And there was the answer in the first Psalm.

Blessed is the man that walketh not in the counsel of the ungodly, nor standeth in the way of sinners, nor sitteth in the seat of the scornful. But his delight is in the law of the LORD; and in his law (words) doth he meditate day and night. Psalm 1:1,2.

There was my answer, dwell on God all day, and practice His presence. Now, I begin my day with stress relieving breathing exercises, and spend a half hour meditating to quiet music, and simply resting in the Lord's presence. I praise Him, I thank Him, I stay my mind on Him, and turn my day over to Him. I do what the good Book says, "Be still, and know that I am God." Psalm 46:10. If my mind begins to wander to problems, I gently push them away, and return to staying my mind on God. It is such a time of refreshing. That gives me quiet seas in my heart.

I may not be able to get rid of all my stress, but I have markedly tamped down my stress level by staying my mind on God, and replacing self-confidence with God-confidence, by casting my care upon Him, for He cares for me.

I have been doing this for almost seven years, and I now guard that time as my spiritual life's blood. Then I start my day sharp, in tune with the Father, and get more accomplished in the day than if I had neglected it. Did you know that just getting quiet, and thinking about God is one of the highest forms of prayer? Not asking for anything, but just thinking about Him. This is liberating and beneficial on so many levels.

Through this practice of staying my mind on God, I have attuned my spirit to hear God's voice much more clearly. He will often speak to me during this quiet worshipful time. I began to see a marked change in my stress level, I have more peace, more patience, and within the first 3 months my blood-pressure went down considerably. All good stuff.

And I availed myself to more inner healing, to get rid of more wounds that were still getting triggered. I keep peeling the onion because that's how inner healing works. And Lord knows in the toxic emotion department I had a lot to work with.

By the time I was twenty-three I had a heart of stone, surrounded by barbed-wire, ringed with land mines. I kept everyone *out*, including myself. I was the least self-aware person I have ever met. Back then my mantra was: Ignore it and it will go away. But toxic emotions don't die; we just bury them alive, where they continue to fester and infect. It's like improperly shielded radiation, we can attempt to surround our heart with a wall of stone, but the deadly off-gassing of toxic emotions will make us sick any way, until we clean out the dump.

So clearly, hard heartedness is not the answer to our problems. Pain and joy come in through the *same* door. If we close ourselves off to pain, we also close ourselves off to joy. And we don't even realize what we have been robbed of until we quit numbing out, and start to feel again. I know it's scary to open up and take down those long entrenched defenses, but the Lord will hold your hand all the way through the process.

My spirit-man within me amplified both my desire and my courage to be totally open with God. Again, that was my free will. I knew way back in Tahoe that I *needed* to change, but I did not know where to turn for truth. Once I got a hold of the truth the problem was, did I *want* to change? When I did, Papa was there to embrace me through it all, and profound changes happened.

A new heart also will I give you, and a new spirit will I put within you: and I will take away the stony heart out of your flesh, and I will give you a heart of flesh [tenderness]. Ezekiel 36:26.

The first time I read that verse I was electrified. Father wanted to give me a new and tender heart. What I didn't realize was that it didn't happen all at once, it comes in layers. It's like calling in a 'God Will' moving truck to haul away the hurt, the Lord has to make several trips to cart away all the debris buried in the attic of my psyche, and replaced it with His truth.

When Dr. Wade fist shared this idea with me, about inviting Jesus to heal my heart, I was pretty skeptical. But I figured out I had to let go and trust somebody to help me on a deep level, and it might as well be Jesus. I saw that scene from the Passion Play, when I was five years old, where all the joyful little children were running up to Jesus' lap, and how happy he was to love them and protect them. I decided to become like one of those little children.

Then he (Jesus) said, "I tell you the truth, unless you turn from your sins and become like little children, you will never get into the Kingdom of Heaven. So anyone who becomes as humble as this little child is the greatest in the Kingdom of Heaven. Matthew 18:3,4.

When I humbled myself and opened up to Christ with a childlike trust, I was not disappointed. Having an actual encounter with Jesus was so much better than the play!

When God heals our emotions, it affects our whole body.

And the very God of peace sanctify you wholly; and I pray God your whole spirit and soul and body be preserved blameless unto the coming of our Lord Jesus Christ. 1 Thessalonians 5:23.

Man is a three part being that works as a unit. Homeostasis is achieved when all three parts, spirit, soul and body, come into harmony. Since life issues from the heart, when we get spiritually healed, it has a positive effect on our whole being.

News Flash! We are not physical beings having a spiritual experience, we are spiritual beings having a physical experience.

The Spirit alone gives eternal life. Human effort accomplishes nothing. And the very words (rhema) I have spoken to you are spirit and life. John 6:63 NLT.

When Jesus speaks to you personally (*rhema*–a specific word from God directly to you), those words literally bring life to your whole being. As Solomon said, God's words are 'health to your navel and marrow to our bones.'

How does that work? I haven't got a clue. But I am living proof that it does work. There is life in the words that come from His Spirit to your spirit. These healing sessions have brought wholeness, and sanity to my own life. And I've seen it do the same for hundreds of others.

All true healing comes from God. Even if you go to the greatest doctor, he's just a facilitator. The design of the human body to heal comes from God, its Maker. (Otherwise, we would bleed to death if we cut our finger.) On an emotional level, the same holds true. The counselor is a facilitator, but it is God who brings healing to your soul and emotions. That healing affects you on a cellular level, and brings healing to your whole body as it is set to a new vibration, in tune with God, instead of the dissonance of the devil.

Only the Wonderful Counselor can do that, no earthly counselor can. Only Jesus' counsel can heal you in the inwards parts.

Who hath put wisdom in the inward parts? or who hath given understanding to the heart? Job 38:36

Only Christ can put God's wisdom and understanding in our hearts, and heal our toxic emotions. THEN life begins to flow again.

Prior to 1974, I had been a puppet on a string, dancing to Satan's endless suggestions. Then, God's Son cut the strings and set me free. But, being a disciple of Christ doesn't mean nothing bad will ever happen to you again (hey, I got cancer), it would be silly to think that. What it does mean, is that together, with Christ, you have the wherewithal to handle any situation life throws at you, which gives you great confidence to face the day.

Peace I leave with you, my peace I give unto you: not as the world giveth, give I unto you. Let not your heart be troubled, neither let it be afraid. John 14:27.

"Let not your heart be troubled." How many people are living a troubled life of fear, frustration and hopelessness? Rich, poor and in between, we all have our stuff to deal with. But the Lord is more than willing to deliver us from this torment.

The power to heal comes from God's love.

He sent his word, and healed them, and delivered them from all their destructions. Psalm 107:20.

God loved us enough to send His son, to heal us in every part of our lives. Love is the healer. Like the Dionne Warwick song, "What the world needs now is love, sweet love, that's the only thing that there's just too little of." Look around at the world, and that statement explains the evil we see every day. People all over the world need God's unconditional *agape* love. What a remarkable change that would bring to our whole planet if we would each tune our lives to the key of Love.

The power of God's pure love, that was the epiphany I had on Tybee Island in Savannah, Georgia, after the loss of my friend Chris J. To paraphrase the Twelve Step program, that day I admitted I was powerless, and that my life had become unmanageable, and that I needed a Power bigger than myself, bigger than the whole ocean, to help me.

I made a conscious decision, standing on the beach that day, to turn my will and my life over to the care of God, as I understood Him. I trusted that the same God, who raised Jesus from the dead, **could restore** me to sanity. And He has.

Did I still experience heartaches and tragedy after that day? Yes. Did I still get deeply hurt along the way? You know I did, I married a wife-beating creep. Life happens. But, after that day at Tybee, I knew I had an Ally to go through the battles with me, the Lord of heaven was my safe harbor, through both the good times and the bad.

Here's a reality sandwich: **Life was meant to be lived *with* God.**

Yann Martel wrote in the *Life of Pi*, "Life is a story... You can choose your story... A story *with* God is a better story."

Life was meant to be lived with God. Contrary to popular belief, turning your life over to God doesn't limit you, it sets you free, it opens new vistas. Obedience to God is a paradox because following God's voice is the most liberating thing you will ever do. When you do, life starts to make sense. Then you understand spiritual principles, and you can use them in your *favor*. (Who wouldn't want that?) You start going through your day as more than a conqueror. You will experience signs, miracles and wonders on a regular basis. And most importantly, you can love: fully, completely and without reservation.

Love is the greatest power in the universe.

As a person who has been on both sides of the fence, love is better than hate any day. Hate drove me to lie, to cheat, to despair, and ultimately to want to die before my time. I almost missed my 'semicolon moment' in San Francisco. Hate and bitterness were driving me crazy. I was literally losing my mind, and ready to institutionalize myself. That's how sick I was inside.

God's Love has *made* me whole. By His mercy I have gotten honest, with myself, and others. Love has set me free to live an *unselfish* life, and to experience a joy and peace that I had never known before. Love has caused me to have a zest for life. Every day I am excited to get up and see what the new day brings.

It was love that gave me the desire to help others, because I know what it feels like to be tormented in the secret prisons of your heart.

The answer to Alfie's burning question, "What's it all about?" Life—is all about LOVE. How deeply and genuinely we love is the only thing that matters in the end.

To paraphrase Rufus Moseley, "The ultimate goal, the Master's plan, is this: the utter triumph of Love over hate, of good over evil, of light over darkness, joy over sorrow, health over disease, and life over death—the utter triumph of Love over everything unlike Himself." And one day soon, that will all be accomplished. In the meantime, we have the new birth, and the gift of Holy Spirit to carry us along this rocky path called Life. *Agape* love is the great balm that continually heals the hurts that the world inflicts upon us.

Only Jesus has the cure for what ails mankind—*redemption*. Buying back man's freedom. Setting us free from the devil's oppression. Jesus paid the price for our freedom, so take it. You are never so far down that the love of God is not deeper still. He's knocking on the door of your heart right now; will you let him in?

God wants to be your Friend.

Man o' man, talk about an amazing turn of events to a very shaky beginning in my life. I hit the heavenly jackpot when I opened my heart to Jesus Christ. But there's more...

"Abraham believed God... and He was called the friend of God." James 2:23.

Most people would blow the buttons off their shirt if they were friends with the President, or some other 'important' figure. You were created to be a friend of GOD! The Creator of all things! The King Eternal! Now that's truly mind blowing. God doesn't want to be some ethereal intangible concept, but He wants to move into your heart and have an intimate relationship with you. That's what Jesus modeled for us.

I never dreamed I'd meet Greta Garbo face to face, but one day, there she was, sitting right next to me on a San Francisco trolley. Just like I never dreamed it was possible to meet a loving God, who would touch me so profoundly, and want to befriend me. But there you have it. I did. God is now my closest friend, and, believe me, that's way better than Greta Garbo.

Now, we get to share the wealth.

And then he told them, "Go into all the world and preach the Good News to everyone. Mark 16:15 NLT.

Preach what Good News? The Good News of deliverance, of reconciliation to our Father, of spiritual, mental and physical prosperity. Nothing beats the good news of eternal life, and liberation from life's oppression, found in Jesus Christ. He sets us free to be our best selves. And, it is more blessed to give than to receive. So spread the wealth.

If the Son therefore shall make you free, ye shall be free indeed. John 8:36.

Living and sharing the love of God is addictive. And that's the only addiction on earth that is a healthy one, in the best sense of the word; once you have tasted His love you will want more, and you will want to share it with others, too. Not by brow beating them or 'converting' them, like another notch on you belt, but by modeling love, and kindness, and having joy in your own life.

But now, after that ye have known God, or rather are known of God, how turn ye again to the weak and beggarly elements, whereunto ye desire again to be in bondage? Galatians 4:9.

This was the verse that began my transformation, that day by the lake at Berry College. After I got a taste of God's love, I no longer wanted to return to the weak and beggarly elements of the world that caused me to be in bondage. And by His grace, I have not returned to my old ways.

The worst kind of enslavement is the slave who thinks he is free.

I run into folks every day who are living in bondage and don't even know it. Remember, God's people are destroyed for lack of knowledge, and it's not knowledge of Wikipedia or the 6 o'clock news, it's the knowledge of the spiritual kingdom and how life really works. There is a spiritual realm comprised of the Kingdom of God/Light, and the kingdom of darkness; the latter of which will come to an end one day, and God will be all in all. (1 Corinthians 15:28).

I hope that by sharing some of my own encounters in the spirit realm, with both angels and demons, as well as the Father and His Son, I have opened your eyes to the greater part of life, that eternal part that we cannot see with our eyes. I confess it took courage to write this book, to tell my story, knowing that I could be laughed at. I'm sure some people will think my life experience is absurd, that it is inconsistent with 'reason,' or common sense. I assure you, nothing could be further from the truth.

The great battles in life are always spiritual.

For we wrestle not against flesh and blood, but against principalities, against powers, against the rulers of the darkness of this world, against spiritual wickedness in high places. Ephesians 6:12.

Job said, "Oh, that mine adversary would have written a book" which is why I wrote this one, to unmask your adversary, the devil, and show you how you can live victoriously in this world through Christ. I want to help those who have had supernatural experiences, or been oppressed, to understand that they are not alone, these things really *do* happen, even in the twenty-first century.

The only enemy you need to fear is the one you do not know.

Now you know who the real enemy is, and how the Lord can set you free. You also know how to take charge of your life, by stepping out of the devils' bondage, and into God's marvelous light. But it's up to you to seize your prize.

You may be a product of your past, but you are not a prisoner of your past.

Your past may have shaped you, but it does not have to define you. God's truth can define you.

Today, I am not just getting by; I am flourishing in every aspect of my life. I am in the Catbird seat, I have the upper hand. I have the inner awareness to forgive myself, and to let go of my past. I count my blessings and thank the Lord above for every precious moment of the new and improved me. Only God's love made this possible for me; to live through my insane childhood, and thrive.

Victims survive, but victors thrive!

I have not thought of myself as a victim for decades, instead I see myself as the victor that Christ has made me to be. I believe God cast my sins as far as the East is from the West, and remembers them no more. If He can let go of my junk, so can I. And He will do the same for you.

Forty years ago the Lord spoke to me "Peg, 'Write the vision, and make it plain upon tables, that he may run that reads it.'" Habakuk 2:2. In other words He said, "Write a book." I was not a writer, but a classical artist, a painter. So I was a bit confused. But I thought, "Well, if I ever do write my life's story, it would be called, 'From Victim to Victor.'" But I ended up calling it 'I Saw the Light—But He Saw Me First.' Different title, same story, but the first title focused on me, and the second one focused on God, my deliverer. That's why I am sharing with you my own journey, from a child of abuse, to a child of God. To plainly write the vision of deliverance for the hopeless, and for those who feel like they are almost gone, so that you can run to the light of God's love, and go from victim to victor. You are only at your semi-colon; this is not the end, there's a better life waiting for you, too.

Only God can take you from victim to victor.

The goal for me was not just to stay alive, but to have a life of peace and purpose. I wanted *quality* of life. My objective was to let all the bitterness and hatred within me go, and I have. I craved that new heart that God promised in Ezekiel, and now I have it.

The one you can always count on in life is *God*; He *always* keeps His promise.

So, grab on to your freedom package.

Salvation comes with a whole package of goodies, and learning to *forgive* is part of our freedom package. Forgiveness sets two people free, you and the person you forgive.

Now I *choose* to forgive others, not because they deserve it, but because I *deserve* peace. Hating someone only messes up my own heart; it doesn't change their life one bit. So I have relinquished all of my ill feelings of yesterday, and been set free from the devil's snare. Today, I cannot think of one person that I have any bitterness towards. I hold no grudges. And, that, my friends, is Good News.

Slowly, but surely I have shed the skin of my old man like a snake skin, the one the devil tried to smother me in; and I have put on the new man, created in Christ Jesus, the one created in righteousness and true holiness.

And let me tell you, there is still plenty of life left in this ol' girl. I feel the next chapter of my life will be the best chapter of my life. There's nothing like having some of life's wisdom under your belt, while remaining hungry for more.

When the great artist Michelangelo, was on his deathbed at the age of 87, the last thing he cried out was, "*Ancoro Imparo!*" which means, "I'm still learning!" About to take his last breath, that was his cry. He was hungry for more, he was still learning. What a way to go.

I feel that same hunger, to know God, and to know how to love and be loved more deeply. I stay teachable, I stay hungry, I stay humble to learn and better myself, and to help others, too. And my *Abba* never disappoints. "*Ancoro Imparo!*"

God is the homeland of the soul.

"God is the homeland of the soul. We are no good away from home, except to return, and once again be full of Him." —Rufus Moseley. And I am so thankful to have come home to my Papa, and the light of His love.

The people that walked in darkness have seen a great light: they that dwell in the land of the shadow of death, upon them hath the light shined. Isaiah 9:2.

I was one of those people who walked in darkness, and I have now seen great light. I now have a grasp of the "whys'" of life because I see life from a spiritual perspective. Without discerning of spirits, all one can do is guess, and go by their five senses, which are limited because they only register the surface activity, and not the deeper spiritual realities of life. Those truths only come to us via the spirit.

This illumination begins when we invite Jesus into our heart, and we study the Bible for ourselves. Then the "aha" moments start to come. All the while, we are being enlightened and healed by God, Himself.

My life's journey started out with incest, abuse, demons, fear, and shame; not a great beginning. But when I reached out to the living God, He healed me and gave me hope. He cleaned me up, He loved me up, and He filled me up, with His eternal peace, and joy, and forgiveness.

They stumble because they do not obey (choose) God's word (way)... But you (who look to God for deliverance) are not like that, ... As a result, you can show others the goodness of God, for he called you out of the darkness into his marvelous light. 1 Peter 2:8,9 NLT.

First Peter sums up the choice we all have, in a succinct and beautiful way. All of us are free to choose to go our own way, or to reach out to Christ, and go God's way. The former leads to more darkness, and stumbling blindly thought life, never seeing the greatness of why we are here; the latter, choosing God's way, moves us out of the bondage of darkness, and into the freedom of His marvelous light.

God called and I answered, stepping out of the darkness of the devil's bondage, and into God's marvelous light. And Jesus taught me how to deal with my adversary, and how to take on all comers in life, demonic or otherwise, with his help. As a result, I can now show others the way to the goodness of God, so that they, too, can be set free.

Dr. Myles Munroe put it this way, "Jesus is the light of the world. Light means knowledge. He came to show us who we really are and to expose the enemy... Jesus came to introduce us to ourselves and to call us to become the people God always knew we could be. He came to call us home."

It might have taken me a while, but in my twenties, I saw the Light. And it was through writing this book that it *really* hit me—I saw the Light, but He saw me first. Father was just waiting patiently for me to reach out to Him so He could take me home to my spiritual family—just like He's waiting for you.

I wandered so aimless life filled with sin
I wouldn't let my dear savior in
Then Jesus came like a stranger in the night,
Praise the Lord I saw the light!

Epilogue

I Will Fear No Evil!

*And lead us not into temptation, but deliver us from evil:
Amen. Matthew 6:13*

God has delivered me from evil. Praise the Lord, I never have to fear those crazy demons again. He is my Protector.

I realize in hindsight, that all the bad things that happened to me through the years could have messed me up for life, left me in a psych ward, or worse; but the Lord delivered me from them all. He delivered me from the evil one, and the emotional damage he had done to my heart.

God is all about deliverance. What a relief. He delivered us from evil (past tense). And He always makes good on that promise, when we ask.

Because of the accomplished work of Jesus Christ, Satan is toast. And Jesus passed that victory baton on to us. Satan is now under our feet whenever we walk in our supernatural God given abilities. But if we don't know our legal rights, Satan will deceive us into thinking he's still got the upper hand. No way!

The thing that terrifies the devil more than anything else is that YOU will find out how truly powerful <u>you</u> are.

He's terrified that you will believe that you have been delivered from his evil power, and that you will *take your life back*. That you will walk in the dominion and authority that was given to you through Christ Jesus!

That's why what you don't know *can* hurt you.

Epilogue

So let me clue you in, for the child of God, we need fear no evil, because the Lord is in us and with us all the time.

Yea, though I walk through the valley of the shadow of death, I will fear no evil: for thou art with me; thy rod and thy staff they comfort me. Psalm 23:4.

The Lord is my shepherd; He is your shepherd. He is with me every step I take. His rod and his staff, they comfort me. Whereas the rod conveys authority, dominion, and victory over the enemy, the staff represents his patient guarding of our lives. The staff is what the shepherd uses to pull the sheep back from harm's way. And he uses the rod to cudgel the wolf, good and proper. He beats back the enemy that would try to harm us.

From the time I was three, I walked through the valley of the shadow of death. Demons were trying to mess me up in ways only they could imagine; working through my grandpa, dragging me into the kingdom of darkness, appearing in my room at night. And later Dirty Harry informed me that Satan had sent demons on a special mission just to kill me. But through it all, the Lord was my shepherd.

I often wonder what would have happened if I had **not** called on Jesus during that brutal rape? Thank God, I'll never know. But, it gives even deeper meaning to "whosoever shall call on the name of the Lord shall be saved." I called on the Shepherd, Jesus, and he saved me, big time!

The fear the demons left in me after the rape almost destroyed me through drinking, drugging, and self-destructive choices. Of course, that was all before I learned who I am, and *whose* I am,

Epilogue

that I am a child of God. He is my Father, and He has placed me far above Satan in the spiritual pecking order.

Since I have come to Christ and been filled with Holy Spirit, I fear no evil. Over the last forty years, I have had multiple encounters with demons, and cast out scores of them, and I have no fear of them. Zero! Because I know that greater is he that is in me, Christ, than the demons that are messing with the folks I'm helping.

Ye are of God, little children, and have overcome them (devils): because greater is he that is in you, than he that is in the world. 1 John 4:4.

I now live 'under the blood,' which means I operate in the authority accomplished on the cross, and bequeathed to me by Jesus Christ. He thoroughly defeated the host of hell, for the good of all mankind, and because of Christ in me, I can defeat them, too. All I had to do was learn about my legal, God-given rights, and start *using* them. A signed check is just a piece of paper until you cash it in. We have to *use* what our Savior gave us.

*For this **purpose** the Son of God was manifested, that he might **destroy the works of the devil**. 1 John 3:8.*

"For *this purpose* the Son of God came to earth," to destroy the works of the devil. And God doesn't half-step. When He sent His son on a mission, Jesus took up the mantle and did a perfect work. All those years I had lived in fear of spirits and demons, all the moving I had done over the years, trying to outrun my fears, when all I had to do was cry out to the Lord, who delivered me from all my fears. How beautiful and how simple that is.

One of the greatest things Jesus did when he was present on this Earth was *expose* the works of the devil. Much like today, the religious leaders were blaming all of the bad stuff on God. Jesus came along and tore the manhole cover off and said, "Look into the devil's sewer. This is the one who is making you sick. This is the one who is killing your kids prematurely. This is the one who is a murderer, and the father of all lies. Take a good look at this slimy creature, and stop blaming my Father for the devil's evil works!"

Furthermore he told them, "I have come to set you FREE from the devil's power!"

Well, praise God, and pass the peanut butter. That is some fantastic news. When Christ filled me with his spirit, vicariously, I overcame everything he overcame; I got all the goodies that he accomplished in my stead. It's part of my inheritance. Jesus did in me and for me that which I could not do for myself. Through the accomplished work of Christ I had finally overcome the devil. And don't have to wear a special amulet, or use any 'magic' incantation. I just take my legal authority, and use the name of Jesus.

I've now learned to live without fear. What a day of deliverance, when I locked into that truth. I now wield tremendous supernatural power, and so can you.

And [to know] what is the exceeding greatness of his power to us who believe, *according to the working of his mighty power, Which he wrought in Christ, when he raised him from the dead, ... Far above all principality, and power, and might, and dominion, ... And hath put all things under his [Christ's] feet. Ephesians 1:19ff.*

Which means those principalities and powers are under my feet, too. God has given His children supernatural power that exceeds

Epilogue

greatness How big is that? Bigger than we can even imagine. As His heirs, we now wield the same power that *raised* Jesus from the dead; a man who had been dead for seventy-two hours. That is some mind-blowing power. We just believe it, and use it.

Some years back, I raised my mother-in-law from being brain dead after she was "Code-Blue" for fifty-five minutes. She had been taken to hospital, put on a ventilator, and declared brain dead. My husband was flying up to Connecticut to say good-bye and, presumably, pull the plug. But God put it on my heart to pray for her to be "raised from the dead" and restored to fullness of life, and I did. There are only two people on record in the United States who have come back to fully functioning mental capacity after being "Code-Blue" for fifty-five minutes, and my mother-in-law is one of them. She was in her seventies, the other guy was in his forties, whom the doctors declared "a medical miracle." So the restoration of my mother-in law was pretty spectacular. (I can guarantee you, *she* and her family were happy about it!) By the time Chris arrived, his mom was sitting up talking to the nurse—That is godly supernatural power in action.

Now, Jesus had been dead for three days and three nights when God raised him from the dead. And the apostle Paul said that same resurrection power is now at the disposal of every child of God.

I also pray that you will understand the incredible greatness of God's power in us who believe him. This is the same mighty power that raised Christ from the dead and seated him in the place of honor at God's right hand in the heavenly realms. Ephesians 1:19,20 NLT.

Epilogue

Children of God can wield the same power that raised Christ from the dead. Can you see why your enemy, Satan, would NOT want you to know that? He likes to steal, kill and destroy, and he doesn't want you to know that you have more power than he does. Just think of all the good that you can do, right now, if you just got a hold of that one truth.

For this purpose the Son of God was manifested, that he might destroy the works of the devil. 1 John 3:8.

Jesus did just that. Boom! Jesus lowered the hammer, and destroyed the works of the devil. But if you don't know your enemy is defeated, you are still living in fear of him. Sadly, Satan has a great PR campaign and has succeeded in *deceiving* most of the Christian's into thinking that he still holds power over them. Which he does not!

The best way to beat the adversary is to know who you are in Christ, to know your rights and privileges. Believe that Satan was defeated two thousand years ago. Thusly armed you can stop his wicked acts at every turn—in the name, the authority of Jesus Christ.

You have read about a lot of demonic events in this book; but you have read about many more godly encounters. The bad is far outweighed by the multitude of phenomenal, miraculous blessings from the true God. I have been blessed over the years with thousands of miracles of God's grace; I was only able to share a few of them with you here. I could write another book on those, and maybe I will some day.

I did not share with you the details of how the Lord delivered me from aggressive cancer. Or how he took care of Chris through

Epilogue

quadruple heart by-pass surgery. Nor the details of how He paid my way through Bible College, or how He sent me through four years of art school. Or, how He led me to open one of the largest classical art galleries in the United States, in Old Town Alexandria, Virginia, a gallery that changed modern culture. Or, how He blessed me with gift ministries, and ordained me to found Light of Christ Ministries, or how He miraculously blessed us with thirteen spectacular acres in Catharpin, Virginia upon which to build our church. And the list goes on and on and on, because God's goodness is infinite. He has given me a life so much better than I could ever have imagined.

For I know the plans I have for you," says the LORD. "They are plans for good and not for disaster, to give you a future and a hope. In those days when you pray, I will listen. If you look for me wholeheartedly, you will find me. I will be found by you," says the LORD. "I will end your captivity and restore your fortunes. Jeremiah 29:11-14.

I don't have enough ink to tell you all the ways He has worked with me, and through me, and given me the privilege to help thousands of others find miraculous peace through Jesus. I can relate to this verse in John 21, *"And there are also many other things which Jesus did, the which, if they should be written every one, I suppose that even the world itself could not contain the books that should be written. Amen."* John 21:25. I am certainly not Jesus, but I don't know if I could record ALL the miracles God has done for me, either. They happen every day.

If you were to look up "one blessed woman" in the dictionary, you would see my picture there.

Epilogue

But the point is not what I have done, but what God has been able to do through me, as I offered to be His hands and feet. As I gave my heart and life to Him, and believed that I could, and should, love like Jesus' loves.

Remember: Love is the nucleus of all miracles.

I could never have planned such an exciting and fulfilling life on my own; no, not in a million years. Suffice to say, God has never disappointed me, and He has never led me astray—ever. Who else can you say that about?

For the scripture saith, Whosoever believeth on him shall not be ashamed. [disappointed in his expectations]. *Romans 10:11.*

I have had many major disappointments in my life from people, even after I came to know God, but the Lord has never disappointed me. He is the best thing that has ever happened to me.

Over forty years ago I began my love affair with God, and Jesus. I studied, I prayed, I listened to tapes, I ran fellowships. I did all of this not out of religious obligation, but out of my deep hunger to know God more intimately. And the deeper I got into Him, the more I brimmed with newness of life. This is what caused genuine transformation in my life: building trust in my Creator.

The deeper I sought God, the more I experienced His peace and optimism. I believed that I could do all things through Christ who strengthens me. As I focused on His presence in me, and with me throughout the day, this slaked my longing for safety. And brought me a deep sense of inner peace, and God-confidence.

Epilogue

Once I knew that He is with me all day, it made life sing; now I trust that He is by my side, with me, all the time. I can turn to Him for wisdom, strength, and solutions, day or night. I know that I have come home, to my spiritual place in the family of God, and it is a place of safety—and not torment. I have escaped 1200 Dean Avenue, with all of its horrors, and come home to Papa's agape love.

Ho, every one that thirsteth, come ye to the waters, and he that hath no money; come ye, buy, and eat; yea, come, buy wine and milk without money and without price. Isaiah 55:1.

This verse is a figure of speech saying that you and I can't buy the things of God with money; it is a free gift of love and grace. Or, to put it another way, Jesus came to pay a debt he didn't owe, because we owed a debt we couldn't pay. Only Christ's innocent blood could pay for the sin-stain that Adam left upon mankind. But—where sin did abound, God's grace did much more abound!

I can guarantee: he that hungers and thirsts after righteousness *shall* be filled, for that is a promise from the Almighty God. Just open your heart to Him.

All of us are pilgrims, on our way to a better place, an eternal city whose builder and maker is God. This world in not our home, we are just passing through. And once you understand that life is all about eternal verities, you too, can come home to Papa, and start enjoying the Kingdom life in the here and now.

The Lord is my Shepherd, and the light of my life. Though I walk through the valley of the shadow of death, I will fear no evil, for He is always with me, His rod and His staff they do *comfort* me.

Epilogue

What a joy it is to live life unafraid; knowing that God is your Father, your provider, and your protector. And that Jesus is the friend and savior that you have longed for all along.

May God bless you on your journey.

Appendix

*Put on the whole armour of God,
that ye may be able to stand against the
wiles of the devil. For we wrestle not against
flesh and blood, but against principalities,
against powers, against the rulers of the
darkness of this world, against spiritual
wickedness in high places.*
Ephesians 6:11,12

Appendix 1

Angels and Demons

And there was war in heaven: Michael and his angels fought against the dragon (devil); and the dragon fought and his angel. Revelation 12:7.

There are two realms we deal with in life: the physical, the spiritual. One we can see, hear, smell, taste and touch, and the other is invisible to the five senses. The spiritual realm is home to *both* angels and demons. 2 Corinthians puts the importance of this invisible realm into perspective.

For the things which are seen are temporal; but the things which are not seen are eternal. 2 Corinthians 4:18.

The world which we see around us is temporal; it will 'wax old like a garment,' but that which is not seen, the spirit realm, is eternal. And in that realm, there are two kingdoms: one is Light, and the other is darkness. One is the Kingdom of God, and the other is the kingdom of 'this world' orchestrated by Satan.

The spiritual realm is bigger and more important of the two, because **the physical realm came forth from the spiritual**.

Through faith we understand that the worlds were framed by the word of God, so that things which are seen were not made of things which do appear. Hebrews 11:3.

For by him were all things created, that are in heaven, and that are in earth, visible and invisible, whether they be thrones, or dominions, or principalities, or powers: all things were created by him, and for him: And he is before all things, and by him all things consist. Colossians 1:16,17.

The supernatural, or spirit realm, is where forces operate that are far beyond scientific understanding, forces that can, at times, supersede the very laws of nature. To succeed in life, we need to

Appendix 1

understand that there is an ongoing battle between good and evil for the very hearts and souls of men and women.

Ephesians 6:12 says, "we wrestle not against flesh and blood, but against ... the rulers of the darkness of this world, against spiritual wickedness in high places."

Folks, denying the invisible realm's existence doesn't change the fact that it is real. As the famous author Mark Twain said, 'Denial is not a river in Egypt,' but it is the state of mind of the skeptic, and the unbeliever.

Both angels and demons inhabit the invisible realm, and both affect your life.

Let's start with the good side, God's Kingdom, and angels: they are good spirit beings who are wholly loyal to the one true God. They minister to God's children, heirs of God's grace. They deliver messages from heaven to earth, and they fight for God's people. They have free will, and an intellect. I will not get into angels too much here, suffice to say, they are the good guys, they wear the White Hats.

Jesus said to Nathanael, "Verily, verily, I say unto you, Hereafter ye shall see heaven open, and the angels of God ascending and descending upon the Son of man." John 1:51. In point of fact, angels ministered to Jesus on numerous occasions, so don't you think we need them too?

After Jesus was tempted in the wilderness, "Then the devil left him, and, behold, angels came and ministered unto him." Matthew 4:11. When Jesus was in agony in the Garden of Gethsemane, making a world changing decision. "And there appeared an angel unto him from heaven, strengthening him." Luke 22:43.

Appendix 1

Angels have appeared to help folks out dozens of times in both the old and new testaments, bringing messages from God, letting folks out of prison, shutting the mouth of lions, fighting battles for God's people, and so much more. God is the *Lord of Sabaoth*, the Lord of heaven's armies.

Angels are around us all the time, doing good and protecting us. I have seen them come into concretion, like the two 'men' on the bridge, who picked up my TR3 and set it back on the road that icy night in Atlanta. Or the 'man' named Michael, in the Waffle House, who told me all the things that were in my heart, and who delivered an encouraging message to me from 'our Boss.'

The book of Hebrews tells us, "Don't forget to show hospitality to strangers, for some... have entertained angels without realizing it." How right Paul was. While reading my book, you may have remembered a situation that you now recognize as an angelic encounter.

And then there was the voice I heard in San Francisco that told me to, "Go back to Georgia." Heeding that one message literally saved my life. What a tremendous blessing angels are, and how thankful we should be for their ministry.

But, my main focus in this appendix is to discuss their sinister counterparts, demons.

So, let's talk about the elephant in the room.

Lest Satan should get an advantage of us: for we are not ignorant of his devices. 2 Corinthians 2:11.

What you don't know can kill you. Therefore God does not want us ignorant of Satan's devices.

Appendix 1

All the forces of darkness cannot stop God's purpose and plan for your life, if you know your enemy. So let's roll up our sleeves and have at it.

The only enemy you need to fear is the one you **do *not* know**. So let's expose those nasty creatures. If you know how the thief operates, you can keep your house safe. If a homeowner knew exactly when a burglar was coming, he would keep watch and not permit his house to be broken into, would he? (Matthew 24:43). God wants us to know the score too.

Devils/demons have free will, and an intellect. They are not stupid, they are just mean. But they will have their day in the lake of fire. In the meantime, we must deal with them.

Satan, the devil, devils, demons, the Serpent, that old Dragon, and Lucifer, are mentioned in the Bible over 200 times! And Satan goes by many names.

And the great dragon was cast out, that old serpent, called the Devil, and Satan, which deceiveth the whole world: he was cast out into the earth, and his angels (demons) were cast out with him. Revelation 12:9.

They are busy little beavers, gnawing away at mankind's happiness and well-being. Satan is mentioned as far back as the book of Job, coming before God and taunting Him about His servant Job.

Again there was a day when the sons of God came to present themselves before the LORD, and Satan came also among them to present himself before the LORD. Job 2:1

The secret to Satan's success is the secrecy of his moves. Satan is called, "sly, wily, the serpent, the accuser, the devil, the father of lies, and the great deceiver." He loves to work through secrecy

Appendix 1

and deception. The average Joe doesn't even realize that demons are behind all the evil going on in our world today, but they are.

Demons are not just in the movies, they are actual entities that want to destroy our lives. Demons, or devils, are fallen angels who rebelled against God under Satan's leadership. They all have one thing in common: the burning desire to steal, to kill, and to destroy human lives in every way possible. They are filled with jealousy for God's crowning creation, man. They revel in chaos: inflicting pain, sickness, poverty and premature death.

Demons are masters of stealth and delusion. Demons understand that the most powerful kind of enslavement is the slave *thinks* he is free. Demons love to incite mayhem, and make the person think it's their own idea.

But the good Lord has not left us defenseless or ignorant of our enemy. The Bible declares, "These signs shall follow them that believe; In my name shall they cast out devils." Mark 16:17. Jesus himself cast out demons/devils on a number of occasions, showing how its done, as well as the disciples in the new testament.

Make no mistake, demons do not have one drop of kindness or compassion in their nature; they are stark raving evil and they will strike like a cold-blooded viper. And yet they can entrap the neophyte by coming off as something good, even religious.

And no marvel; for Satan himself is transformed into an angel of light. 2 Corinthians 11;14.

They are masters of stealth. Both angels and demons are normally invisible to the naked eye, unless they come into concretion under the certain circumstances, as previously discussed. But make no mistake, both angels and demons are all around us; sentient beings who can think, plan, and make choices.

Now before you freak out at that bit of information, here's a comforting thought: there are *twice* as many angels as there are demons. More importantly, we have God and Jesus on the side of good. So the odds are *always* in our favor if we know how to trust God, and claim His protection no demon can touch you, when you use the name of Jesus with authority.

Demons have been around a lot longer than you and me; they have been around for centuries. It was the head demon who tricked Adam and Eve. Jesus dealt with demons throughout his entire ministry. Demons, devils, and unclean spirits are discussed about one hundred times in the gospels. If delivering folks from demons was so important in Jesus' ministry, why would it not be just as needful today? Why is the church so reluctant to discuss this topic, let alone to cast them out?

Demons are like the 'third rail' of Christianity, very few pastors want to talk about them. And if someone does believe in doing the works of Jesus, like casting out devils, they are given the pejorative moniker "Oh, *they* have a *deliverance* ministry," like deliverance is something to be scorned.

Why shouldn't deliverance be a part of every godly ministry?

Satan and his minions were defeated two thousand years ago at Calvary. Deliverance should, and must be part of every ministry IF you are going to carry out the works of Jesus Christ.

*Verily, verily, I say unto you, He that believeth on me, the works that I do shall he do also; and greater works than these shall he **do**; because I go unto my Father. John 14:12.*

Appendix 1

Jesus commissioned all future disciples, just like the Father commissioned him; he sent us forth to do the works of the Father. Therefore, we are supposed to do the same works/miracles that Jesus did. Jesus has a continuing ministry in heaven on our behalf, but here on earth, we are his hands and feet. We are his 'by means of'—continuing God's gracious work of deliverance here on earth, in his stead.

*God anointed Jesus of Nazareth with the Holy Spirit and with power: who went about doing good, and healing all that **were oppressed of the devil;** for God was with him. Acts 10:38.*

Jesus healed all that were oppressed of the devil, and now WE take his place. That means that you and I have power over the devil, and we need to learn to use it. Because Jesus commissioned us, and equipped us, to do that very thing.

*Then said Jesus to them again, Peace be unto you: as my Father hath sent me, **even so send I you.** John 20:21.*

Most Christians are happy, even eager, to talk about angels, but bring up demons, and they cower with fear. Others just want to ignore the subject altogether, as if ignoring it will make them go away. They hide their heads in the sand. Epic fail!

What you don't know could kill you; because Satan is an equal opportunity destroyer. And we need to take hold of our spiritual powers, and use them to heal and deliver ourselves, our families, and others in need. (Mark 16:17,18; 1 Corinthians 12:7-11)

All of us are affected by demons either directly or indirectly; like the guy who raped me, he was taken over by their will, and through him, they affected me *very* directly.

Let's say a child is kidnapped, it can tear a family apart, even the whole community. Many lives will always be affected by that one

Appendix 1

evil deed. When President John F. Kennedy was assassinated that one demonic act destroyed the innocence of an entire nation. We were never the same after that.

Today we are faced with rampant terrorism, events like 9/11. Those terrorists were pawns of Satan, doing his bidding to kill, to put fear in people's hearts, to steal our sense of safety, and to divide and destroy our nation. It is still dividing us. We live in a world where we need to grow up and call evil what it is—EVIL. And stop coddling the perpetrators. And we need to learn how to believe God for a hedge of protection around ourselves and our loved ones.

Then Satan answered the LORD, and said, Doth Job fear God for nought? Hast not thou made an hedge about him, and about his house, and about all that he hath on every side? thou hast blessed the work of his hands, and his substance is increased in the land. Job 1:9,10.

Satan understood how God's people can have a hedge of protection around them, so we'd better get smart on that front, too. We too, can have God's hedge of protection around us by asking for it, in Jesus name.

We are also being affected by demons in less obvious ways, such as: the news media, movie messaging, ungodly music, nefarious world leaders, who are motivated by a lust for power and greed. The demons have their propaganda and enslavement baked into all of these ugly pies.

Am I saying demons are directly involved in *all* of this stuff *all* the time? No. But, their influence is pervasive in **most** of what goes on in our world today; sadly, much more than the beauty of God's truth.

The devil is ALWAYS bad, but God is ALWAYS good.

Appendix 1

Everyone is also affected by God, but His ways are much quieter, more peaceful, and sometimes harder to recognize. "For in him we live, and move, and have our being." Acts 17:28. Whether you believe in God or not, every day you breathe His air, you experience His sunshine, and the blessings of His magnificent creation. Even if you live in a crowded tenement, you can still look up and see His lovely blue sky. God's heart's desire is to bless everyone.

Be the children of your Father which is in heaven: for he maketh his sun to rise on the evil and on the good, and sendeth rain on the just and on the unjust. Matthew 5:45.

If we look for it, every day we can experience the miracles of life, in small and big ways. God is everywhere present, just in a quiet and peaceful way. Satan is a loudmouth braggart. Think Mother Theresa vs. Al Capone. That's why the Bible says, "Be still and know that I am God."

The devil is an interloper, a parasite, a loud-mouthed leach, who craves to steal the beauty of life, as God meant for it to be lived from everyone he can hoodwink.

Just as Satan's evil can poison the well of people's lives, those of us who stand for God, who work on His behalf, can spread His antidote. We heal, uplift, encourage, give hope, and offer deliverance to the hurting souls of this world. We are often the catalyst for restoring families, and making communities a better place in which to live.

Think of the joy and hope that just one tiny godly woman, Mother Teresa, brought to the whole world. She went about doing nothing but good, in a totally unselfish way, and is recognized by almost everyone as a 'saint,' a truly godly human being.

Appendix 1

Whereas, you get a hand full of demon manipulated humans, and what chaos and misery ensues. Demons are directly or indirectly, the source of all of mankind's misery, disease, and death. How much of that do you see around you every day? Frankly, way too much.

So you can see, we are all affected to one degree or another, by both angels and demons.

The way to rise above this miasma of this world is to learn to deal with the adversary, and defeat him on legal grounds, in the courtroom of heaven.

Read the Bible, get informed, and learn how to counter demonic influence in your life. Satan won't go away by wishful thinking or ignoring him. Let me spell it out for you in simple, King Jimmy English.

Be sober, be vigilant*; because **your adversary the devil**, as a roaring lion, walketh about, seeking whom he may devour;* ***Whom resist steadfast*** *in the faith, knowing that the same afflictions are accomplished in your brethren that are in the world. 1 Peter 5:8,9.*

The New Living Translation says, "Stay alert! Watch out for your great enemy, the devil. He prowls around like a roaring lion, looking for someone to devour." We need to wake up and be vigilant!

From the President of the United States on down to your best friend, Satan can get a foothold in people's lives; and pain, misery, and destruction will always ensue. No one is immune to his ruthlessness. Not even you.

So, know your enemy, but even more importantly, know your Savior. You can learn the Truth, and get set free from the power

Appendix 1

of Satan and sin today. (For more on this topic go to: http://locm.org/angels-demons/)

Ye are of God, little children, and have overcome them [demons and those under their influence]: *because greater is he that is in you, than he that is in the world (Satan). 1 John 4:4.*

What a comforting verse. **If you are a child of God, greater is Christ in you, than any demon in the universe that operates on this earthly plane.** Demons are under your feet; you just have to become aware of your rightful position in Christ. This puts you in the Catbird seat and makes you an overcomer in any situation.

When I was being raped, I didn't even know if I still believed in Jesus, but just thinking that one thought, "Jesus, IF you are real, this would be a great time to show up..." and he did! Which saved my life. That is how merciful God's love is.

Like I said earlier, what you don't know can kill you. I am not writing any of this to depress you, or to frighten you, but to show you **how to get set free** from demonic oppression. How to get control of your life back, by realizing that for the child of God, greater is he (Christ) that is in you than the he (the devil) who is in the world.

Jesus said, "If I cast out demons by the Spirit of God, surely the Kingdom of God has come upon you." Matthew 12:28. Jesus brought the Kingdom of God with him, and gave us a place at the table through the new birth. Now, he is King of kings. We are joint heirs with Christ. Through him we have regained the power and dominion that Adam lost.

When Jesus got up from the dead, he took Satan to the eternal woodshed, and gave him a whoopin'! At that moment all principalities and powers were put under Jesus' feet. Which means they are now under your feet too, when you believe in the accomplished work of Christ, and **use his name with authority**.

Paul exhorts us to stand fast in the liberty wherewith Christ has made us free, and be not entangled again with the yoke of bondage. Jesus freed all of us captives, and it is our job and privilege to appropriate that freedom in our day-to-day living.

Thank God, Jesus came to destroy the works of the devil. He came to heal all who are oppressed by the devil, because one of those folks used to be me. And as far as I have come in my own deliverance, I still need Jesus' love and guidance every day to remain free from the devil's tangled web of deception. I need the Savior's gentle voice to guide me in the paths of right living.

The events that I have described in this book have highlighted just a few of the many encounters I have had with both angels and demons. And yes, the angelic encounters are much more edifying. But I am convinced that both kinds of spiritual encounters are more mainstream than anyone would care to admit. *No one* gets through this life without dealing with both angels and demons. It's just that the average Joe is usually unaware of the source of their miracle, or their misery, whichever the case may be.

But, <u>if you don't know you have a question, you don't know you need an answer</u>. We all need more spiritual understanding.

Be assured that from the first day we heard of you, we haven't stopped praying for you, asking God to give you wise minds and spirits attuned to his will, and so acquire a thorough understanding of the ways in which God works. Colossians 1:9-12 (MSSG)

What an informative section of scripture. God wants you to have a wise mind, and a spirit attuned to His will, so that you can

Appendix 1

understand the way God works. God's desire is to bless you and set you free.

The Bible says there are two Gods: the God and Father of our Lord Jesus Christ, *Jehovah*, and the god of this world, Satan. And God does not want us blind to this truth.

In whom the god of this world hath blinded the minds of them which believe not, lest the light of the glorious gospel of Christ, who is the image of God, should shine unto them. 2 Corinthians 4:4.

When people say that God and Satan are on equal footing, they are dead wrong. Satan is a created being, and God is the Creator. He has the devil on a leash.

Satan was once a beautiful spirit being who, lifted up with pride, rebelled against God, and tried to steal His glory. That's how he became Satan. One of the reasons God wrote the Bible was to show mankind how to live free of the devil and his torment. But Satan is a deceiver, and has made powerful inroads into this world.

When one accepts Christ, they are enlightened by the gospel, and set free from Satan's power. Satan has no more legal right in our lives. However, we can still give the devil access to our lives through our own ungodly thoughts and actions, to rack-and-ruin God's children. In essence, we are the ones who put out the "Welcome" mat for the thief to come back in.

Satan is the god of this world. He feeds off the weakness of your flesh and mind. The goal of Satan and his minions is to make life as miserable as possible for anyone they can get their grimy fangs into.

Christ came to set you free from the devil's bondage by introducing God's love and light into the world. I'm talking about the truth, not half-truths. For centuries Satan and his cohorts have been free to promulgate their lies through the occult, philosophy, and now the media, the internet, music and advertising. But the most dangerous avenue of all is still through religion.

Satan is the great deceiver. He struck a masterful public relations *coup* when he got the world at large to believe that the true God was the one who brings sickness and death. That one trick freed him to blame his death-dealing ways on the wrong party, God. But, Satan is a liar, and the father of lies. Jesus exposed that lie because he did nothing but heal. He never made anyone sick to bring them closer to the Father. God is never the one putting problems on us to 'test' us, we can pin all of those terrible things on their true author, the devil. (James 1:13)

Jesus came **to "destroy him** that had the power of death, that is, the devil." Hebrews 2:14. That statement is crystal clear. The true God never harms or kills anyone, especially an innocent little child. But preachers preach that God lays this stuff on people to 'make them humble.' Really? Is that what *any* loving father would do? Absolutely not. You really have to be taught to be that stupid! That's why the traditions of men are as deadly today as they were in the time of Christ, when he upbraided Israel's religious leaders for, "Making the word of God of none effect (null and void) through *their* traditions." (Mark 7:13)

God is love. And love is real. Perfect love casts out fear. God doesn't **bring** fear into your life; He casts it out. God is the Author of peace, joy, safety, good health, prosperity—all those things come from God. And only God's power can cast out demons, or cast out fear, and relieve your torment. (James 1:17)

Satan wants to keep you ignorant, like he did to me when I was a child. I was already born again, and loved the Lord, but he kept attacking me with fear and distrust; he eventually tricked me into doubting the very existence of God.

Fear is toxic, and habitual toxic thinking is what demons feed on. Toxic thoughts produce over 90% of all physical disease, and 100% of mental health issues. Toxic thinking literally excretes toxic enzymes, and sickness, into the cells of your body.

When the Lord cursed Satan in the Garden of Eden, he said, "On thy belly shalt thou go, and dust shalt thou eat all the days of thy life." Adam's body was made from dust. (Genesis 2:7; 3:19) Satan's curse limited him to feeding on the *weakness* of man's *flesh*, man's senses, which are all connected to the mind/heart. **The devil was limited to feeding off man's toxic thinking; that's his inroad to wrecking a life.**

So the smartest thing for us humans to do is learn to feed and dwell upon wholesome, godly thoughts; which will quench the fiery darts of the wicked one every time.

Feed your faith and starve your fear.

Satan runs the other way when a person starts praising God, and embracing the power of faith in Jesus Christ. Jesus taught his disciples that faith, or trusting God, can move mountains.

For verily I say unto you, That whosoever shall say unto this mountain, Be thou removed, and be thou cast into the sea; and shall not doubt in his heart, but shall believe that those things which he saith shall come to pass; he shall have whatsoever he saith. Mark 11:23.

But to have faith you have to be taught rightly, and the foundation is God's love for humanity.

Appendix 1

Sadly, very often, the ones who should be teaching us to trust in God, defending His honor and reputation, are dragging His name through the mud; right alongside the God rejectors and the Satanists. That's why God says to check it out for yourself.

Prove all things; hold fast that which is good. 1 Thessalonians 5:21

We are supposed to prove or test all things against the Truth of the bible. Don't take Reverend So-and-So at face value, see if their teaching lines up with God's.

To top it all off, many of our so-called spiritual leaders are living secret lives of lust and debauchery themselves. They rail about sin, while judging others for doing the same things *they* are doing. Like a peacock, they proudly strut their stuff on TV, in the name of a 'Jesus' I don't recognize, in search of the almighty dollar. Who's got the biggest jet? Who's got the biggest buildings? It's a disgrace to my *Abba* and His son.

I turn them over to the Lord, and he will deal with them in due time, for we must all stand before the judgment seat of Christ one day, to give an account of what we did in this life, including those slimy 'pastors,' who fleece the flock. Shame on them.

They are not my concern. But to *refute* their lies is my concern. Only the truth makes us free; not man's opinion.

Here's what God is: God is Love, God is truth, His word is true. Only He can be trusted to the uttermost, for God is not a man that He should lie.

God is not a man, that he should lie; neither the son of man, that he should repent: hath he said, and shall he not do it? or hath he spoken, and shall he not make it good? Numbers 23:19.

Appendix 1

God never lies to us. He is not behind those phony preachers. He is not behind ripping-off widows and orphans. That is the devil's handiwork, and he skillfully uses it to give the true God a black eye. I can't tell you how many broken people I counsel who have turned away from God because they have been hurt by 'the church,' or by judgmental hypocritical congregants, or a false pastor, or priest. Wolves in sheep's clothing. Fleecing the flock.

On the other hand, there are many wonderful, honest, spirit-filled ministers who genuinely love people from a pure heart, and want to help them, but you must choose carefully, and be spiritually sharp. That's why we must learn to tell the difference between truth and error: to discern spirits, and see whether a thing is coming from God or the devil. And we can only do that by being born again and filled with the Spirit of God, and studying His word. Then we can tap into information from heaven, and find out what is going on spiritually. (2 Corinthians 12: 8-11).

All through life people have failed me, disappointed me, and at times abused me, but God has always been faithful to me, and He always will be. Don't get me wrong, I have often disappointed myself. But God is the One who has never disappointed me. He has always helped me, cleansed me, and delivered me. By His grace and mercy, I have become more and more Christ-like, through His work of grace in my life.

So many things about life become crystal clear when you begin to acknowledge the spirit realm.

Unfortunately, most of what we read, or see in the movies about spirits only shows the scary side of things. People go see "The Exorcist" and they sleep with their lights on for a couple of weeks, but they gain no useful information. Here's the deal. Many of the events in "The Exorcist" were based on true facts. But how do

Appendix 1

you separate the facts from the fiction? Where do you go to find answers about what's really going on 'out there,' beyond the veil? The psychic hotline? No!

All the answers we need are in the Bible; if one will just take the time to read and understand the book. It contains everything we need to know about life and godliness. That pretty much covers the subject.

According as his divine power hath given unto us all things that pertain unto life and godliness, through the knowledge of him that hath called us to glory and virtue: 2 Peter 1:3.

How do we get truth? We find it through the knowledge of Jesus Christ. Not what someone *says* about the Jesus, but what does the Bible say?

And for those Christians who deny Satan's existence, why hasn't it occurred to them that Satan, the Serpent, is introduced in the third chapter of the Genesis? He and his demons are recurring characters, right up until the end of the book of Revelation, when finally, in the end, they are cast into the lake of fire by the Lord himself.

Casting out demons was a huge part of Jesus's ministry. This topic must be made clear so that people can know the score. Hosea 4:6 says, "My people are destroyed for lack of knowledge."

The worst kind of enslavement is the slave who *thinks* he is free.

By sharing some of my firsthand dealings with both angels and demons, I hope I have opened your eyes to the truth—fear not! Greater is he that is in you, than he that is in the world.

Appendix 1

Job said, "Oh, that mine adversary would have written a book." And that's why I wrote this one, to answer questions about your adversary, and to show you the way to freedom in Christ Jesus.

The only enemy you need to fear is the one you <u>do *not* know</u>.

Now you know better, so you can do better. This book is designed to shine a light in the dark places, and to expose how human beings have been enslaved by these parasitic spirit beings since Genesis chapter 3. Like a thief, Satan and his minions come only to steal, kill and destroy. But, demons have *no legal right* to even one cell, not one scintilla, of your life, your thoughts, or your dreams, once you know the truth. But if you don't know you have a leech on your back, you can't pour salt on it. We cannot afford to be ignorant of Satan's devices.

Demons are not something to fear—they are something to <u>cast out</u>!

How? They are cast out in the name (authority) of Jesus Christ, and by the power of his blood. By *understanding* the accomplished work of Christ, and being schooled in the power of the blood. Satan may have bruised Jesus' heel, but Jesus crushed the Serpent's head. We win, but only if we claim our freedom.

Wherefore he saith, When he ascended up on high, he led captivity captive, and gave gifts unto men. Ephesians 4:8.

Jesus came to set the captives free and give us gifts. One of the gifts he gave his Church was freedom from demonic oppression. But if you don't know you are a captive, how do you look for a way out of your prison?

And ye shall know the truth, and the truth shall make you free. John 8:32.

Appendix 1

The word that best describes the works of the devil is–bondage, the opposite of freedom. Moses may be dead and buried, but nothing has changed since those days in Egypt. My heart is still crying out to God, "Let my people go, that they may serve You!"

Spiritual truth has not changed over the centuries; it has just been buried—for a long, long time. It's high time to dig up the answers, walk out of bondage, and into His marvelous light. Isaiah tells us the payoff for pressing into God:

THEN shall thy light break forth as the morning, and thine health shall spring forth speedily: and thy righteousness shall go before thee; the glory of the LORD shall be thy rear guard. Then shalt thou call, and the LORD shall answer; thou shalt cry, and he shall say, Here I am Isaiah 58:8,9

Now that's one powerful relationship between you and your Father; the Creator of heaven and earth.

Appendix 2

Inner Healing

Inner healing is a gift to the body of Christ.

Inner healing is one of the many gifts that Christ has given to his followers. It is just one of many ways he sets the captives free.

Wherefore he saith, When he ascended up on high, he led captivity captive, and gave gifts unto men. Ephesians 4:8.

When any of God's creatures are abused the soul becomes fractured. Slowly and surely we lose part of ourselves or give it away to others, unknowingly. That is why inner healing is all about restoration, giving us back that which was stolen.

I have spoken at length about inner healing earlier, but I felt it was important enough to restate some key points, and **give you a truncated version of Chapter 22**, along with a few additional insights.

Here are some signs that you may need inner healing: constant criticism, resentment, anger or guilt, these are four horsemen of the Apocalypse to the soul. Are you carrying any of those in abundance? Their fruit is doubt, unworthiness, and unbelief; all fear based-emotions that will rack and ruin your life. They will poison your health, your heart, and your home. Until and unless you deal with their roots, the weeds will keep coming back; choking the garden of your heart.

When I first got involved in inner healing, almost two decades ago, it was considered kind of 'out there,' but today it is fairly mainstream. And thank God for that, because inner healing is such a powerful and effective way to restore the broken souls of men and women, and to carry out the promise of Psalm 23, "He restores my soul." Inner healing is one of the most effective ways

Appendix 2

I know of to remove deeply rooted fears, and phobias, hidden in the recesses of one's subconscious. It is a gift of healing to the body of Christ. And boy, do we need it.

In Isaiah 9, Jesus is called the "Wonderful, Counselor." How did I miss that truth all those years? Before Dr. Wade showed me its significance, it never occurred to me that Jesus Christ himself could be this personal, this intimate with us. Or frankly, that interested in my life. I hadn't yet grasped the truth that he knows each *and every one of us* (intimately), and calls us all by name, "He calls his own sheep by name, and leads them out." John 10:3. Leads us out of what? Bondage, pain and misery. That is intimacy. The shepherds in the old testament knew every sheep by name, knew their weaknesses, their strengths, and their individual needs. Jesus used that imagery to describe how much we matter to our Father, and to him.

Are not two sparrows sold for a farthing? and one of them shall not fall on the ground without your Father. But the very hairs of your head are all numbered. Fear ye not therefore, ye are of more value than many sparrows. Matthew 10:29-31.

I remember asking God if this kind of intimacy could actually be true, and He said—"Why not? I am God. I know all things at all times, and I can do anything!" And Jesus loves us with the same love that God has for us. Cool.

When the Lord told me how much He loved me, I had a paradigm shift. My perception of God, Jesus, life... *everything*... took on a whole new light. I had an epiphany about the depth of God's love for mankind, and it is a beautiful thing.

When I started renewing my mind, phenomenal change and deliverance came into my life. And yet, at some point, I knew I needed something more. There were certain mental patterns I just could not seem to shake; specific phobias and thought patterns, going back to my childhood that kept sabotaging my prayers and actions. As I found out through Dr. Wade, those were the places where I needed inner healing.

Inner healing takes place when you invite the Lord Jesus into a counseling session, and ask him to do the healing. He will show the counselee, by revelation, the lie-based thoughts that have kept them all twisted up inside. He will reveal the lie, what they need to see, and then tell them how to deal with it through the *rhema*, specific words from the Lord that heal a specific hurt in your heart. He removes the lies that have caused strongholds of unbelief to harden in their heart, and replaces it with the balm of truth.

The lie-based event could be as 'insignificant' as a teacher embarrassing you at school, or as traumatic as rape and abuse. But lie-based thoughts are the strongholds of darkness, and invite in spirits of fear and insecurity which *blocks* us from receiving God's best.

The lie that was attached to the event could be any negative belief such as, "You're no good. You'll never amount to anything. You'll always be sick. No one will ever love you," and so on. But once the Lord reveals the lie to your heart, and you can renounce it, then Jesus does the most marvelous thing, he fills that black void in your psyche (the human heart, the subconscious) with the light of God's life affirming truth.

For example, if the lie was "You are worthless!" the Lord might say to you something like, "I loved you in your mother's womb. I looked forward to your birth. You mean everything to me. You are so special, and I will always be with you." Or, he may say something as simple as, "I am just crazy about you. Don't let anyone tell you any different."

Whatever he says, it will often brings tears of joy to the recipient because whatever Jesus tells them is so personal, so on-point, so healing, that they feel this incredible emotional release from all the years they have been holding that ugly lie inside. They are so relieved to finally know the truth, and to feel the darkness go.

It's not the event itself that's the long-term problem; it's our emotional response to the event, and the lie that is attached to it that damages our soul. Lies such as, "You are the cause of your rape. You are no good. You can't trust anyone, including God. You will always fail." Those deeply buried lies cripple your soul, and hinder your success in life.

On the other hand, the truth makes us free. So the more we can get rid of these lies in our inner heart, these strongholds of the devil, the freer we are to receive heavenly health and provision. And the more we will experience God's peace on a deep level.

And the coolest thing is whenever we need inner healing—the Counselor is always in.

Dr. Wade showed us the way, and eventually I got to where I could attain a certain level of inner healing alone, just me and the Lord. But even today, I still avail myself to a godly counselor; there are still times I need someone objective to help me push through the tall weeds.

These lie-based strongholds kept me from receiving the fullness of God's healing, I would get healed, and two months later it was back with a vengeance. There were strongholds that had lodged in my subconscious years ago that needed to be rooted out. There is no time with God, not as we experience it. He is omnipresent,

Appendix 2

which means, He's everywhere throughout all time at once. And since God inhabits the past, the present, and the future simultaneously, He has no problem healing anything that happened to me at any time in my life. Way cool!

The ancient word for God is, *ehyeh asher ehyeh*, I AM THAT I AM, which means "He Who IS," or "He Who has no beginning and no end." God IS the only Self-Existing One, everything that was made comes from Him. (Hebrews 11:3) He spoke and it was done, He commanded and it stood fast. (Psalm 39:9).

Therefore God can take us back to a traumatic event, and reveal the lie that was planted in our heart, and heal it. Remember, He was actually with you when the event took place. Then, through His son Jesus, He will speak truth to you, and heal that place of hurt, filling the 'room (in your heart) that is swept and garnished' with his light and truth. (Luke 11:25) God will never leave that place empty, or seven demons more wicked than the first will try to re-enter. (Luke 11:26)

In Psalm 51:6 David did some inner healing when he asked for God to reveal truth to him in his *inward* parts: and in his *hidden* part (subconscious), to make him *know* wisdom. This entailed two things, revealing to David his own lie-based thinking, and then giving David the truth to replace it. Jesus said the truth shall make you free, and he was right. That's why David asked God to:

Create in me a clean heart, O God; and renew a right spirit [attitude] within me... Restore unto me the joy of thy salvation; and uphold me with thy free spirit. Psalm 51:10,12.

When you get this gunk out of your heart, it is amazing how light you feel physically and mentally. You can tell that something major has shifted, for the better. Thankfully, God gave us all the

Appendix 2

tools we need to receive full restoration in our soul/heart. Isaiah 53 further elaborates on Jesus' ministry.

*Surely he hath borne our **griefs**, and carried our **sorrows**: yet we did esteem him stricken, smitten of God, and afflicted. But he was wounded for **our** transgressions; he was bruised for our iniquities: the chastisement of our peace was upon him; and **with his stripes we are healed**. Isaiah 53:4,5.*

Jesus bore our sin and sickness, but he also took our grief, and our sorrows, the inner pains of life. Calvary covered both physical and emotional healing. The greatest healing I have ever experienced in my life is inner healing, emotional healing, because it affects every other area of my life, including my health.

We need this to live fully restored lives, and not just keep putting a Band-Aid over the same old wounds. Job asked this insightful question, "Who hath put wisdom in the inward parts? or who hath given understanding to the heart?" Job 38:36. The answer is, the Lord.

The Lord is the giver of all truth, wisdom and healing. It's one thing for me to tell someone that Jesus loves them, but it's a whole different experience when Jesus himself tells them he loves them. It changes a person in the most profound way.

*My sheep **hear my voice**, and I **know** them, and they follow me: John 10:27.*

Should it really come as any shock that Jesus still talks to us today? No. We are the body of Christ, and he is the head. My head communicates with my body all the time.

Religion has told us this just can't be, while the Lord himself is saying, why not?

Appendix 2

And he said, The things which are impossible with men are possible with God. Luke 18:27.

Amazingly we have this hotline to heaven, and the line is never busy. Papa says, "Call unto me, and I will answer thee, and shew thee great and mighty things, which thou knowest not." Jeremiah 33:3. What a glorious invitation!

Do not think it strange that Jesus still talks to us today. In fact, we should be shocked when he does NOT talk to us!

We need to hear from heaven to have victory here on earth. The Lord is our constant companion and helper.

For the weapons of our warfare are not carnal, but mighty through God to the pulling down of strong holds; 2 Corinthians 10:4.

Through the supernatural experience of *inner* healing, the Lord can pull down these strongholds in our heart. No psychiatrist and no amount of reasoning in the world can get rid of them like He who knows our hearts. Only the Spirit of the living God working through His son Jesus, the Wonderful Counselor, can heal us from the inside-out.

The Truth makes you free. When your experience genuine inner healing you can tell that something major has changed for the better. You will feel elated, you can sense the weight lifted off your heart; you will effervesce with joy, like that clear shining after rain.

People say that you can't *feel* God. How wrong they are.

When God does his mighty work in you, you will feel lighter, you will feel His joy and you will feel elated. Everyone agrees that you *can* feel fear, anxiety, and worry. These feelings make you jittery, weigh you down and tie your stomach up in knots. Why wouldn't you feel the godly side of emotions just as profoundly when His heavenly peace enters your heart and mind?

The Lord wants to restore our souls, and deliver us from evil. Do you know how He makes that deliverance happen? Any way he wants to! I don't know how inner healing works, I just know that it works, and that's good enough for me. I don't have a clue how my laptop works, but when I press certain keys I get the desired results. That's all I care about.

I sought the LORD, and he heard me, and delivered me from all my fears. Psalm 34:4.

I may not be all the way there, but my train has certainly left the station; and I'm a lot closer to who I want to be than I used to be.

I'm not going to sit here and tell you that I am never fearful. Let's get real. Stuff happens. But no matter what life throws at me, it is short-lived. Now I know how to stay on top of my fear, I push pause, and take my concerns to the Lord. I enquire of the Lord, I ask Him to give me His peace and comfort, and to show me how to deal with it. And He does.

Like the old hymn says, "What a wonderful change in my life has been wrought, since Jesus came into my heart." These words sum up my experience with inner healing.

In a nutshell, inner healing is an exchange.

The counselee exchanges God's truth for the devil's lies, His peace for their pain. It is a time of enlightenment, forgiveness, and restoration: a time of inner transformation. There is a saying, "Let Go and Let God." That pretty much sums up inner healing; they let go of the pain of their past, and let God heal their wounded heart.

Appendix 2

When it comes to living a peaceful life, I don't look at how far I have to go, but how far I have come. That encourages me and fills me with joy and hope. Then, when and where I do have fear, I take it to the Lord and we deal with it—together.

God wants to live at the center of your consciousness all the time; He wants to be the anchor of your soul. Your mind was designed to hold God's thoughts, but it will still wander from Him. The question is how far will you allow it to wander? When your thoughts drift away from God for too long that's when even seasoned Christians get ensnared in the web of Satan's endless suggestions. So the key to abundant living is to stay close to Him all day, by keeping God in the center of your thoughts as much as possible.

This habit will bring joy and peace and faith to your thought patterns, and make your day better in every way. I like to say, "Today is a good day to have a good day!" But I know I can't accomplish that without God in the center of my thoughts and activities. Life is a "do-it-together" trip, you and God.

That is why I teach and share God's word, because it works.

What God did in my heart that afternoon by the lake at Berry College was just the beginning of my Jesus journey. And countless times since then he has proven himself faithful to me. In return I have done my best to be faithful to him. What a deal.

Romans 2:4 says that it is the goodness of God that leads us to repentance, a change of heart, a new way of thinking. God is so incredibly good. He would never think of harming a hair on your head. He is your protector and healer—in a word—He's your loving Father.

Appendix 2

Inner healing can help you embrace that truth, in the depths of your heart. That's when you will really start to see signs, miracles and wonders in your own life.

And you, too, will be on the road to more abundant living.

Appendix 3

How to Get Help

You were created for freedom, not captivity.

You were made to be loved, by the Author of love Himself. You were created to have godly dignity and self-worth. God did this, not because He had to, but because He wanted to. God is the most loving Father in the universe, in every sense of the word.

Unfortunately, we have all been in some very unloving situations that have scarred our souls. That hurt can be mended and your soul can be restored. God is sovereign, and He wants your complete deliverance. He wants you to be as happy and whole as Adam and Eve were before the fall.

Now, you have a choice to make. You have searched for truth and found a good bit of it by reading this book. Now you can reach a little deeper for the inner healing that is your birthright.

There are many wonderfully skilled and trained deliverance ministers that can help you in your journey. I suggest that you pray for God's wisdom and guidance when you begin your search for a good counselor or healing ministry. And, believe God, your deliverance is out there, waiting. I have included a resource page that can help you in your journey.

The Spirit of the Lord is upon me, because he hath anointed me to preach the gospel to the poor; he hath sent me to heal the brokenhearted, to preach deliverance to the captives, and recovering of sight to the blind, to set at liberty them that are bruised, to preach the acceptable year of the Lord. Luke 4:18,19.

NOW is the acceptable year...
Today is the day for your deliverance.

Additional Resources

Books:

Virkler, Mark. *How to Hear God's Voice.*

Leaf, Caroline. *Who Switched Off My Brain?*

Douglas and Gregg. *Inner Healing: A Handbook for Helping Yourself and Others.*

Hammond, Frank. *Pigs in the Parlor.*

Resources:

Light of Christ Ministries
Audio Class: Angels and Demons
http://locm.org/angels-demons/
Contact us at: locm@rexbonum.com

Time to Fly Foundation
For those who need their self-worth and dignity restored:
http://timetofly.org

Elijah House
For inner healing/counseling:
https://www.elijahhouse.org

AA
And its affiliates for addictive behavior:
http://www.aa.org

Acknowledgements

First and foremost, my heartfelt thanks to God, who loves me and pulled me from the muck and mire of my past through the work of His dear Son. They cleaned me up, and put my feet on solid ground. Without them, I would still be a lost soul.

I am grateful for the love and support of my Light of Christ family; for their prayers, encouragement, and support through this long process of my first book.

To Dr. Henry J. Wade, the gentle healer who opened my eyes and showed me a better way to counsel. Along with Rev. Ken Sudduth, who helped me get to the next level with inner healing.

To my editor, Helen Thompson, who saved my bacon when I thought this project would never make it to print. She's the best editor on the planet, and is another healer who shares the love of her therapy dog for the purpose of helping others.

Special thanks to my niece, Alice Dunn, whose long frank talks about recovery, and insights about growing up in our family, helped me synthesize much of what went into this book. Her honesty and input were invaluable throughout this process.

And to my husband, Chris, who can finally stop saying, "Peg, you've got to write a book." (Although he's already after me to write the next one.) His own life long work, mentoring juveniles and prison outreach, has inspired me on so many levels. Chris has the genuine heart of a healer, less talk—more action. All love to you, my dear partner and friend on this incredible journey called Life.

Made in the USA
Middletown, DE
25 June 2018